Books by **HOLLIS ALPERT**

FELLINI *A Life*

FELLINI *A Life*

by HOLLIS ALPERT

Atheneum   NEW YORK   *1986*

Simon & Schuster
1230 Avenue of the Americas
New York, NY 10020

Simon & Schuster and colophon are registered trademarks of Simon & Schuster, Inc.

Designed by Cathryn S. Aison

Manufactured in the United States of America

10 9 8 7 6 5 4 3 2 1

Library of Congress Cataloging-In-Publication Data
Alpert, Hollis-----
        Fellini, a life.
        Bibliography: p.
        Includes index.
        1. Fellini, Federico.   2. Moving-picture producers
and directors-Italy-Biography.   I. Title.
PN1998.A3F315 1986   791.43'0233'0924   [B]   86-47667
ISBN 0-7432-1309-2

For Joan

ACKNOWLEDGMENTS

IN the very early days of my film-reviewing stint, I happened across *The White Sheik*, made by a director whose name was unfamiliar to me. If I had been paying more attention to the credits prior to my taking on critical duties, I would have seen the name attached (as a writer) to such distinguished films as *Rome, Open City*, and *Paisan*. *The White Sheik* made little impact on the American box office, but soon enough there was *La Strada*: Federico Fellini had arrived for American audiences, and for much of the rest of the world.

I was able to see *La Dolce Vita* before its American release, and then saw it again, and again. It convinced me that a new dimension had been brought not only to the Italian film, but to the art of the cinema. After *8½* arrived, I had no doubt that Fellini was an artist—not only a film artist—of major caliber, and it was then that the notion of someday tracing his life and career occurred to me.

For me the job of reviewing films was not always pleasant. Being somewhat emotional, I tended to take films seriously, whether they were good or bad. "You ought to save your sense of indignation for something more worthwhile," a friend once counseled. But when certain films came along that gave me a sense of illumination, of communication, of a shared concern for humankind, the job became more than worthwhile to me, if only because I felt that I was contributing something by helping to spread the good news. Fellini's films were, of course, prominent among them.

I have been fortunate to meet Fellini several times, and a few years ago I mentioned that I was doing a book on him, a biography. He looked at me with surprise. "But there has been so much written already," he said. I told him that yes, I had gone through much of the material, but it had not been put together in any orderly biographical shape or form, and that the preponderance, in any case, seemed more concerned with theories about the meaning of his films. As the book developed, he did not cooperate actively, but was always helpful, answering queries, correcting some supposed facts, supplying information when asked.

While in the midst of my work I received from him a small book, just published in Rome by Gius. Laterza & Spa, titled *Fellini: Intervista sul cinema.* Fellini felt that this book—a lengthy interview with him by Giovanni Grazzini—contained more accurate biographical information than any other source. I was free, he told me, to make use of it. Indeed, this interview, translated with the able assistance of Susan Rosenstreich, was helpful in filling several puzzling gaps in Fellini's life story.

When Fellini was not available, his secretary, Fiammetta Profili, was, and so was Mario Longardi, his long-time public relations aide, a man of infinite courtesy and knowledge. I thank them. But I also owe thanks to more helpful people than could possibly be mentioned in the course of a "Thank you" speech at the annual Academy Awards. I list them below, in no special order.

Tullio Pinelli, Gianfranco Corsini, Massimo Mida, Bernardino Zapponi, Alberto Lattuada, Eileen Hughes, Gore Vidal, Sandra Milo, Paul Mazursky; Serge Sevilloni and other staff members at RAI in Rome, Dr. Suzanne Wagner, George Wagner, Maria Pia Fusco, Lino Micciche, Robert Lawrence, Martin Poll, Lillian Gerard, Jan and Robert Lowell, Norma West, Roland Flamini, the late Richard Basehart, Daniel Talbot, Anthony Quinn, Heidi Stock, Simianetta Toraldi, Wilton Wynn, Logan Bentley (the last three of the Time-Life Bureau in Rome).

Then there is Beatrice Corsini, in Rome, who helped arrange interviews, translated, acted as all-around assistant, and gave me palpitations as she raced her little Fiat through the city's traffic. Susan Rosenstreich ably translated the mounds of material that I gathered at the Cineteca Nazionale of the Centro Sperimentale di Cinematografia in Rome, and from the excellent files at the Italian Cultural Institute in New York City. A surprisingly rich source were the files kept by Logan Bentley, the Rome correspondent for *People* magazine. She granted me complete use of them, as well as her office facilities.

I would be remiss if I did not mention two book-length bibliographies, one compiled by Barbara Anne Price and Theodore Price; the other by John C. Stubbs. Such compilations make the writer's and researcher's task infinitely smoother. Through their listings of books and periodicals, and brief descriptions of the information these publications contained, I was able to select and track down what seemed to me most applicable. Much of this I located at the following institutions: The Theatre Collection of the New York Public Library at Lincoln Center, and also at the main branch; the Library of the Academy of Motion Picture Arts and Sciences; the library of the American Film Institute; and the National Film Archives of The British Film Institute. Professor G. William Jones of Southern Methodist University kindly made available to me, for re-seeing, his collection of Fellini films from the valuable film archive he maintains.

Friends and colleagues provided aid, too, with their support and encouragement, among them Jack X Fields, Arthur Knight, Janet and Douglas Kaften, Charlotte Chandler, my agent Mitch Douglas, my editors Tom Stewart and Judy Kern, and my former associate on *American Film* magazine, Antonio Chemasi. He granted me permission to include excerpts from his illuminating article on Fellini's *Casanova*, as did *American Film*, in which it appeared.

What was apparent to me throughout the writing of this book was the immense respect for Fellini held by almost all I contacted for information about him, their admiration (not always uncritical) for the body of his work, their fascination with his personality. With Fellini it is all but impossible to separate the work and the personality, and there was no way to avoid the intertwining of the two. His films, he has said, are like love affairs. Much of this book, then, is the story of those affairs.

ILLUSTRATIONS

FELLINI *A Life*

I

THE evening of February 5, 1960, was cold and windy in Milan, but this deterred none of the several hundred fashionably dressed guests of Angelo Rizzoli, the host for the world première of *La Dolce Vita*. It was Rizzoli's financing that had made possible one of the costliest of all Italian films, and, as it turned out, the longest. Federico Fellini, the director, had already made news during the preparation of the film by quarreling with the original producer, Dino De Laurentiis, and then going through several more before Rizzoli came along. Even while the film was in the making, stars announced for some of the roles either cancelled their appearances or were cancelled by Fellini. On one occasion, to find an actress he wanted he made an appeal on television and radio, and when that didn't work he advertised in newspapers.

The audience was intrigued, too, by advance word of the subject matter of the film. It was said by those who had seen an earlier private screening that it dealt with some of the more gossipy goings-on of Rome's fashionable Via Veneto set, and that some notorious scandals of the past were recreated. But some in the audience had heard, too, that *La Dolce Vita* was a masterpiece, declared as such by critics prior to its release. A special showing had been held for the distinguished members of an international literary conference in Rome. Some in that audience, which included two Nobel Prize winners, declared it to be one of the greatest films they had ever seen, if not the greatest.

Yet, in the theater in Milan, many were unprepared for what they saw. Ostensibly the story of a thirty-five-year-old journalist whose work puts him in the midst of Roman high life, it was also a nearly three-hour, unremitting display of amorality and hedonism—the sweet life gone sour and rancid. Those who saw truth and powerful film-making in the series of vivid episodes broke out in applause, but they were soon outnumbered by the majority, who took the film as an assault on their own moral integrity, and a bitter attack on the new freedom and prosperity of their country. There were murmurs of dismay, then shouts of disapproval, and barrages of hisses. Toward the end, an orgiastic party at a seaside villa invoked cries of *basta!*

Fellini, seated with his wife Giulietta Masina, was shaken by the response. The film had occupied his mind, thoughts, and energy for two years, allowing him few hours of sleep at night. As he and Guilietta made their way to the lobby, they were met by a sea of hate-filled faces. A bejeweled, mink-coated elderly woman shook a fist at him and shouted, "You are putting Italy into the hands of the Bolsheviks!" A dinner-jacketed man with a florette in his buttonhole came up to Fellini and spat in his face. In effect, Fellini later realized, he had been challenged to a duel.

This was only a prelude. When the film was released widely in Italy it caused a near civil war that was fought in the media, the pulpits, in public debates, in parliament, and sometimes with fists in theater lobbies. More than once, the police had to be called to control angry members of the audience.

Before the film's general release, church authorities had apparently given it their approval. Father Angelo Arpa, a Jesuit friend of Fellini's, had reviewed *Le Dolce Vita* favorably in the Catholic *Il Quotidiano*; he saw the sinful behavior in it as illustrated with moral values. But he was soon squelched by the more authoritative *L'Osservatore Romano* that, with Vatican approval, blasted the film as disgusting, obscene, indecent, and sacrilegious. *Il Quotidiano* then reversed itself and declared that the film should be retitled "The Disgusting Life." A priest advertised a mass that would offer "expiation and atonement" for the sins committed by the many people who saw the film.

During the furor in the political arena, a shocked Christian Democrat deputy asked, "What would Mazzini and Cavour have said if they had seen *La Dolce Vita*?" In a newspaper, an editorialist warned, "If Italy is to become communist, this film will rank high in the place of honor of any revolutionary awakening."

The Italian parliament took up the matter. During an angry debate, several deputies proposed a measure that would prevent the continued circulation of the film, even suggesting an outright ban. Meanwhile, the Catholic Cinematographic Center listed it as a forbidden work, unsafe for all to see.

Elio Vittorini, a prominent writer, joined the fray on the other side, scolding "Catholics who understand nothing, who do not recognize their own children. . . . These Catholics speak only as fascists and not as Catholics."

The novelist Alberto Moravia chaired a public debate on the questions raised by *La Dolce Vita*, but made his own position perfectly clear by declaring it the greatest motion picture ever made in Italy. The poet and film-maker Pier Paolo Pasolini saw in it a truly Catholic spirit, and a Jesuit priest spoke for its "subtle merits of constructive criticism."

Fellini was moved finally to make a public statement, that read, in part: "We are making a national case out of *La Dolce Vita*. We Italians are always ready to tear each other apart. We are creating a morbid psychosis that gives viewers an unhealthy sense of curiosity. Let's quit this. As for myself, I only wanted to tell about something that concerns me."

Unhealthy curiosity or not, Italians joined the long lines at theaters showing the film. It was their arguments during and after that made the police presence necessary. To avoid waiting for hours at the large city cinemas, many drove fifty and more miles to smaller towns where the queues were shorter. The fuss over the film, which engaged Italians for most of that year, benefitted Rizzoli and his financial partners at the box office to a truly dizzying degree. Distributors from abroad clamored for it, and complicated deals were made that at times hampered its exhibition in later years.

One of those to benefit the least financially was Fellini, who had long given up his share of the profits in order to make his film the way he wanted.

Italian film-making had reached a prestigious plateau by the time *La Dolce Vita* came along. Fellini was already one of Italy's most highly regarded directors for such films as *La Strada* and *The Nights of Cabiria*. He was one of a group of post–World War II directors that included Vittorio De Sica, Roberto Rossellini, Michelangelo Antonioni, and Luchino Visconti, who, if they did not always dominate their country's box offices, were dominant at international film festivals and award ceremonies. In a larger sense, it was they who brought to the attention of the outside world Italy's postwar problems and its efforts at recovery.

Hardly fifteen years earlier there had been no Italian film industry to speak of. The country had entered the war late, had been defeated early, and was occupied by both Allied and German forces. Battles and bombings had devastated cities and towns, uprooting millions. The nation's miseries increased when prisoners of war, forced laborers, and displaced persons returned. A black market flourished. All endeavors, including film-making, were for a time under the control of Allied commissions. Studios such as Cinecittà were used to house the returnees.

With the deliverance of aid from international agencies, Italian spirits began to rise, and a long-deferred surge of creative and artistic energy was unleashed. Rome had sustained relatively little war damage after being declared an "open city" by the Germans and the Allies, and soon regained its beauty. Tourism not only revived, it flourished as never before, helped by the strong growth in air travel. The dormant film industry came to life, and suddenly was able to look around with clear eyes and capture what it saw. Providentially, in Hollywood, a new film process called Cinema-Scope was born, and one of the first films to utilize its enlarged panoramic screen was *Three Coins in the Fountain*, with a story that provided a romantic tour of Rome. The views and vistas it provided of fountains, monuments, gardens, and villas encouraged even more airline bookings to the city.

The postwar growth of Italian film-making was further aided by American-backed productions that took advantage of blocked currencies, cheap labor, and the undeniably picturesque locations. American film unions called this "runaway production," but it was partly caused by the expansion in screen size and the need to compete with television by providing eye-filling dramas and spectacles beyond the capabilities of the small home screen. There were tax advantages for Americans who worked abroad for eighteen months or more, and many in the film industry transferred their addresses to Rome, where what was known as coproduction abounded. Well-salaried work was available in small epics like *Hercules* and large ones like *Ben Hur*, with dozens in between. By the mid-1950s Rome was being called "Hollywood on the Tiber."

Toward the end of the 1950s, jet travel shrank time and distance and Rome became a stop on the international circuit of the newly named "jet set," whose members included ersatz and genuine royalty, sons of Caribbean dictators, best-selling pop novelists, and movie people—stars, producers, directors, and their omnipresent agents and publicists. Their favorite place to meet, to see and be seen, was on the Via Veneto.

It was not much more than a hilly quarter-mile stretch, beginning at a corner occupied by the Hotel Excelsior and ending before reaching Porta Pinciana, the gateway to the gardens of the Villa Borghese. This portion of the avenue was lined with cafés and shops, and stands that sold newspapers, magazines, books, postal cards, and maps of the city. Noted cafés such as Doney's, Rosatti's, and the Strega had formerly attracted a literary and artistic clientele, who moved elsewhere when the international crowd moved in.

"Inevitably," wrote Paul Hofmann, a Rome correspondent for the *New York Times*, "the Via Veneto cast had its chorus of hangers-on—dazzled provincials, social climbers, adventurers, bored aristocrats and rich people, pretty girls on the make, would-be movie stars from the boondocks, and the paparazzi, unaware at the time that such was to be their generic name."

It was this milieu that Fellini apotheosized in *La Dolce Vita*. As though he had plucked representative samples from reality, his characters included a journalist overly bemused by the people and events he covered; a quintessential blonde movie queen; an aristocratic, bored, and perverse young woman; an intellectual writer whose seemingly fulfilled existence proves to be a sham; a castle full of odd and aimless nobility; and as sort of a counterpart, two cunning children fooling their gullible elders with a story about seeing the Virgin Mary. And there were more: the journalist's lecherous father, a nightclub dancer, whores, homosexuals, actors and agents and poets and industrialists. They lived high, most of them, sped about in fast cars, and seemed to care only about finding ways to enjoy themselves and relieve their boredom. The film's denizens startled Italians, because they seemed so recognizable, if not in real life, then as typical of the time.

Italian films of the postwar period were admired for their gritty realism and honesty. Why, then, the outraged reaction to *La Dolce Vita*? Largely because it was taken as an indictment that was social, moral, or political, depending on a person's ideological orientation. Italians were said to have produced a postwar economic miracle. *La Dolce Vita* seemed to imply that the miracle had been reduced to a shoddy pursuit of materialistic goals and pleasures.

When the film went into international release, it was with much less fuss and scandal. Its commercial success—larger than any previous Italian film export—was aided by its accompanying aura of sensationalism. It became *the* film to see, to talk about—and to write about. Long essays in intellectual journals interpreted the film in often contradictory ways. Fellini was interviewed in Paris, in London, in New York. Everywhere he went he attempted to explain his film, but he did not always explain it the same way. On one occasion he said he had made a semidocumentary by taking society's temperature and finding it feverish. Another time he said it was not the real Rome he had shown, but an interior city of his mind. He had had no intention, he said, of criticizing, or denouncing or satirizing anyone or anything. Nor had he meant the title to be ironic; only that life, in spite of everything, kept its undeniable sweetness. But, he also said, how could he explain himself to the lady who came out of her Mercedes, grabbed his tie, and yelled, "You should tie a rock around your neck and throw yourself into the sea!"?

How Fellini came to create so astonishing a work will be considered later. It might be helpful, meanwhile, to look at Fellini in relation to the creative forces at work in his country, and to other prime movers of the cinema in particular.

Until his *La Dolce Vita*, Fellini was thought of as a member of the group of Italian film-makers who subscribed to a theoretical concept called "neorealism." Although only a fraction of the films Italians made during the post–World War II period were identified as such, it was the neorealist films, with their artistry and profoundly human qualities, that so impressed and moved audiences in many other countries.

Neorealism has defied precise definition; it was more as though you "knew a neorealist film when you saw one." If there was a flagship film that helped give it a visual definition, it was Roberto Rossellini's *Roma, città aperta* (*Rome, Open City*), which came along just after the war and which listed Fellini among the director's collaborators.

Ideas differed about what neorealism was, but this only deepened discussion of the theory and the movement it engendered. Identifiable signposts were found in the films: an emphasis on ordinary people and ordinary life; a clear-eyed, even stark portrayal of contemporary social conditions; actual locations in preference to studio filming; acting so unstudied it seemed that people were playing themselves—which was often the case; an ideological slant, more often than not, that made a case for social and political change. Understandably, Marxists gave the movement their adherence.

Neorealism served as a line of demarcation between prewar and postwar Italian films; the change involved techniques as well as subject matter and ideology. Yet the term had come into being before the end of fascism in Italy, a country that had contributed much to the film industry from its beginnings.

In fact, at about the time (1896) when the first public projection of a motion picture was given in New York, a film was screened for a paying audience in Italy. Ten years later a production company, Cines, was formed. Already there was a movement called *verismo* (realism), allied to naturalism on the stage, but which had to do more with recreating the colorful national history.

Typical of the movement was the almost three-hour-long *Cabiria* (1913), made just before the outbreak of World War I. Its techniques (including the revolutionary use of a dolly) were so advanced, its success so large, that movies everywhere were influenced by it. Two other early Italian spectacles, *The Last Days of Pompeii* (1912) and *Quo Vadis* (1912), won substantial international audiences and the enthusiastic praise of the French sculptor Auguste Rodin. The impressive success of these large-scale works encouraged D. W. Griffith and Cecil B. DeMille to take the same spectacular direction.

When European film-making all but shut down during World War I, the American industry seized the advantage and kept it well into the postwar decade. The Italian industry had to contend not only with the importation of American films but, after 1922, with a fascist form of government. Then, Hollywood came to Rome in 1923 to make *Ben Hur*, starring Ramon Navarro and Francis X. Bushman, and took over much of the available studio space while grandly distributing largess to the labor force. The native industry fell into the doldrums.

Early in the 1930s, Mussolini's government decided to come to the rescue. A central film organization and a special fund were created to spur production. In 1934, the arts festival held in Venice was expanded to include film, and the film festival was born. The next year a training school, the Centro Sperimentale di Cinematografia, was opened to breed new cinema artists. A huge new studio was commissioned, and in 1937 Mussolini himself inaugurated the complex known as Cinecittà.

During the first years of sound, Italian films showed the influences of Hollywood. There were musicals with silly plots (and

Neapolitan love themes), boudoir comedies and romances—the latter giving rise to what was called "the white telephone film," because much of the action centered around a white telephone in a lady's frilly bedroom.

When, in the mid-1930s, Mussolini embarked on his African adventures, generosity toward film-making took another tack. To encourage themes and subjects of a patriotic nature, subsidies were awarded to eighteen approved film companies. Mussolini's son, Vittorio, took over the direction of Cinecittà.

But unlike in Nazi Germany, outright propaganda was seldom in evidence, other than in a negative sense, which is to say that democratic ideas, notions of individual freedom and civil liberties, were conspicuously absent from films. Talented people were still allowed to work and develop their skills. Documentary techniques became popular and, by the time World War II began, the era of the white telephone was over.

The revolt against artificiality in subject and technique was also occurring in literature and the stage, and the general movement bore the name of "the neorealist revival." This naturalistic trend spread even to the propaganda films made during the early years of the war, which were a kind of training ground for directors who emerged at war's end.

Fellini was influenced by *Rome, Open City* almost from the moment he began working in films. By the time that he made *La Dolce Vita*, however, his style, his material, his qualities were so unique that simply to term him a neorealist was almost beside the point. It can almost be said that *La Dolce Vita*, in its baroque way, signaled the end of neorealism.

Seen in today's context, *La Dolce Vita* is not so overpowering, and certainly is hardly shocking. Today's youthful film student might wonder why the critic Andrew Sarris wrote, "it could be argued that in terms of social impact it is the most important film ever made." Sarris himself might wonder about it. The effect of a film invariably changes with time, and particularly so when a film reflects its time to the extent *La Dolce Vita* does.

When the film opened in Italy in 1960, France was ending its bitter war with Algeria, Princess Margaret of England became engaged to Anthony Armstrong Jones, and Marlene Dietrich was being escorted around by the Italian actor Raf Vallone. The United States was in the midst of a presidential race between Richard Nixon and John F. Kennedy, and Marilyn Monroe (Mrs. Arthur Miller) was rumored to be having an affair with Yves Montand. An earthquake destroyed the Moroccan city Agadir, causing thousands of casualties, and Hollywood was rocked by a marijuana scandal.

No one expected to be drafted to fight in a faraway land called Vietnam; the Beatles had not yet invented themselves; a Volkswagen cost $1,500; a gallon of gas about thirty cents. A luxury apartment on New York's fashionable East Side went for $300 or so. Savings banks paid 3 or 4 percent interest, and people under thirty still respected people over thirty. There were, of course, murders and scandals, and on the beaches of St. Tropez there was a section where people bathed in the nude, a reaction against the old-fashioned bikini.

"Into this boiling lava," an Italian critic wrote in recalling the era, "Federico Fellini plunged his artist's hands."

La Dolce Vita still fascinates, but now the thermometer Fellini held up to society appears to read normal. Without the context of the time in which it was made, it is the people in the film who emerge strongly, and who seem to be viewed with surprising warmth. They appear neither very sinful nor evil, merely fallible and confused. There are glints of satire to be seen and, without question, sheer cinematic brilliance.

In 1982 Paul Hofmann wrote of Via Veneto, the street that Fellini glamorized and, for non-Italians, created. It had become tawdry, he said, "lined with travel bureaus, airline offices, a hamburger eatery, stores selling overpriced shoes and apparel, a double procession of neon signs, and café terraces with South Sea decor." Romans stayed away from it after dark, he said.

My own visit late in 1984 belied the last statement. True enough, there were the tourists (of which I was one), and perhaps the mafiosi, pimps, and plainclothes policemen, but it also seemed to me that a good many Romans had rediscovered their favorite

street and were promenading again, and sitting at the cafés, even
at night, proving perhaps that it is perilous to attempt to fix a time
and place.

Fellini had just turned forty the night of the Italian première of *La Dolce Vita*. "No other director," declared the *New York
Times*, "can at this moment quite measure up to his stature." With
his growing fame, Fellini threatened to supplant Alfred Hitchcock
as the public's symbol of a film director. Familiar to millions were
the piercing gaze of Fellini's black eyes, the floppy black hat, the
large frame, the operatic gestures. In physical stature, he is large
but not imposing. Not exactly given to humility, he will sometimes
seem surprised by the amount of interest taken in him. After Fellini became famous, an Italian critic asked him to describe his early
years and the effects of those years on his film career. "Until I was
seventeen," he said, "nothing happened to me." The critic could not
help being skeptical, since, like others, he had assumed the material
of Fellini's films came from the director's experiences. Fellini said,
too, that he had a poor memory, especially for exact details.

Through the years, however, his remembrance of things
past has expanded, and in one way or another—through his own
writings and what he has told others—he has provided a great deal
of autobiography.

His biographers have had their problems, though. It seems
true that Fellini has had little use for precise dates and locations.
To further complicate things, his recollections have had a way of
changing, perhaps out of boredom at having to tell the same story
in the same way over and over again. Some of his childhood experiences have taken on a mythic quality. Other stories he has told
about himself have failed to be substantiated, causing reporters to
say they never happened. He is not happy about this, and less so
when malicious gossip or a falsehood appears about him in the
press. His wife, Giulietta, has declared him flat out to be a liar. If
so, he is a delightful and harmless one, whose tales are told in a
spirit of fun.

In Rome, there are those who still regard him as less Roman

than a provincial. It is true he did not arrive in the great city until he was eighteen, but though he grew up in the region known as Romagna, he feels himself a Roman in soul and heart. It is for this reason that nothing said about *La Dolce Vita* nettled him more than when Roberto Rossellini remarked, "It is the film of a provincial." Probably only born and bred Romans knew precisely what he meant.

II

RIMINI, where Fellini was born on January 20, 1920, is a town on the Adriatic coast about 100 miles south of Venice. Then populated by less than 50,000 inhabitants, it has swelled to more than three times that number, and is crowded and livelier during the warm months, when it is a popular seaside resort.

For tourists Rimini has some history, but not enough to make it an obligatory stop on charter-bus itineraries. It does go back well into the time of the Roman emperors, when its name was Ariminium, and a few artifacts of the period remain, the most important being the arch and the bridge that bear the name of the emperor Augustus. Another storied name associated with the town is Malatesta, the medieval family that literally owned it for two centuries. Family members built the fine Renaissance structure known as the Malatesta Temple (*ca.* 1450) and also as the Church of San Francesco.

During World War II, Rimini, an important rail and road hub, was so extensively bombed that the largest part of the town was destroyed and had to be rebuilt. The early Romans can be said to be responsible for this; they made Rimini the starting point for the venerable Via Emilia. The monuments have been repaired, however, and Rimini thrives to the degree that hotels and houses extend along its beaches for many miles.

Fellini's father's family were mostly respectable farming and tradespeople of Romagna, the region to which Rimini belongs.

Urbano Fellini was born in the nearby village of Gambettola in 1894. When he was eighteen he went to Belgium to find work, and at the start of World War I was conscripted by the Germans and forced to work in the mines. Upon his return to Italy toward the end of the war, he went first to Rome, where he found employment in the Pantanella pasta factory. There he also met young Ida Barbiani. "There has always been some secrecy in the family about how he happened to marry her," said Fellini, "because it appears he kidnapped her."

He described her as coming from "a very Catholic and bourgeois family. When he asked to marry her he was refused. Then, strangely, she decided to elope with him. Her family never forgave my father for running off with her. They were quite rich—and it was my mother's brother who inherited all the money; it came from a chain of dairy shops." Only at Christmas time would the brother send packages of presents. Fellini knew about and was fascinated by this rich uncle, but it wasn't until he was ten that he finally met the famous relative who sent the presents.

Ida Fellini recalled that it was love at first sight between herself and Urbano, and that her family did everything possible to keep them from marrying. Being stubborn, she agreed to elope with him, and the wedding took place in July 1918. The couple left Rome to live with Urbano's parents in Gambettola, but moved to Rimini soon after.

It is because of his mother that Fellini likes to think he is at least half a genuine Roman. A cousin on her side whose hobby is genealogy traced the Barbiani name as far back as 1400 and discovered one such in the court of Pope Martin V. This forebear was involved in a trial for poisoning—the victim unknown—and was incarcerated for thirty years. According to Fellini, this is his most noteworthy ancestor.

On the Romagnola side he doesn't feel himself to be typical of "the conventional belief that all Romagnolas are extroverts, that they are sensual, generous, gregarious, good talkers, good eaters, blasphemers who consider themselves atheists, given to bad language, but who send their daughters to church because someone in the family has to have some kind of relationship with the eternal father." If some of the labels seem to fit him, one that doesn't is political ability. "In that," he said, "I'm more of an Eskimo."

Ida remembers the night Federico was born: "It had to be with the aid of forceps because he was in the wrong position. It was some evening—thunder, lightning, wind, high seas, heavy rains. My husband ran to get the doctor, because I was moaning with pain. Just as a clap of thunder shook the house, I gave birth to Federico. The first thing I noticed was his hair, thick and dark. He was a pretty baby. I don't know how much he weighed, because I had no scale."

Urbano Fellini had by this time established himself as a salesman representing a wholesale firm that dealt in confectionaries and preserves; later he added coffee with another company. He was soon able to provide well for his family, but because of his need to travel he was away from the house much of the time. He has been described as a reliable man, thoroughly middle class, not really the man of the world he liked to assume he was. (In *La Dolce Vita* Fellini took pains to portray accurately the mentality of a character based on his father.)

Federico was followed a year and a half later by a brother, Riccardo, and, in another five years, by a sister, Maddalena. Discipline in the family was provided mostly by Ida, a handsome, humorous woman with a wide smile and a touch of mischief in her black eyes. She was also intensely religious, and determined that her children would receive proper religious educations.

Thus, Fellini was sent to a kindergarten run by the large-coifed Sisters of St. Vincent, who also maintained a primary school. The memories of his early years, Fellini once said, consisted of a kind of vibration, but now and then out of the vibrating vagueness would arise a distinct image. One such had to do with a Sister in the school who was fond of him and who would hug him frequently. She was young, and smelled of rancid soap. Fellini regards the experience as giving him his first sexual feeling. The Sister would stroke his back while holding him close, and the odors that emanated from her—potato skins, stale broth, the starch of her habit—

remained with him to the extent that for a long time after, he said, the smell of potato skins made him weak.

Not all the Sisters were so nice to him. One who wore glasses like Harold Lloyd's admonished him while he was holding a candle in an outdoor procession: "Don't let the candle go out because Jesus won't like it."

A strong wind was blowing, and he was overwhelmed with the responsibility of keeping the candle lit. He wondered what Jesus might do to him if it blew out. The procession of children began to move amid a crowd of monks, priests, and nuns. "Suddenly," said Fellini, "sprang a melancholy and monotonous chant. All of it frightened me. I broke out sobbing." Such early religious memories would have their later effects.

One winter Sunday, when Federico was seven, Urbano took his family out for a ride in the family landau. The children were bundled up against the cold. The carriage turned up Via Fumagelli, a wide road, and Urbano pointed out a house to Federico, saying, "You were born there."

By then they were living in a rented house on the Corso, Rimini's main street, and soon after they moved again, to a house in the town's center near the train station. This house had a back garden which ended at the wall of a large building with letters on the wall: POLI . . . [AR]AMA RIMINESE. Federico was playing in the garden one morning when he heard a strange rumbling noise. The wall of the building was slowly rising to reveal the interior of a theater. Awed, he approached and saw gilded balconies and what seemed to be half a locomotive suspended on ropes. This was his first glimpse of the inside of a theater.

It was at about the same time that he discovered movies. He was taken to the local cinema, the Fulgor, by Urbano who, because it was so crowded, had to hold Federico on his lap. It was hot, and someone kept spraying an antiseptic that irritated Federico's throat. "In that slightly opiate atmosphere," he recalled, "I remember the yellowish images on the screen of a throng of people in hell, of priests in a large room with wooden benches, of churches."

When he moved on to his primary schooling at age seven, he showed an aptitude for drawing. This pleased his mother, who enjoyed doing some sketching of her own, but it made little impression on his father, who was already seeing his son as an eventual candidate for the bar. At home Federico spent hours drawing with pencils and crayons on any blank surface he could find.

The Pierino Circus came to Rimini that year (1927), and Federico was taken by his father to an afternoon performance. "There was an explosion of trumpets," he remembered, "lights, applause, drum rolls, the loud jokes of the clowns; their shuffling, clowning antics, their hilarious ragamuffin irrationality, made it seem to me somehow that I was expected, that they recognized and were waiting for me. I went back to the circus as often as I could, getting there early for the rehearsals and staying through the shows. Once, my family and teachers sought me everywhere until midnight, and never realized I was only a few paces away."

Soon after, in school, a teacher made him an example with a public reprimand. Pointing him out with a cane, the teacher said, "We have in our class a clown." The reprimand worked in reverse. "I almost passed out with joy," Fellini recalled.

It must be said that the above is the most reasonably accurate account of the birth of Fellini's life-long love affair with the circus. Through the years he has told other tales. In one of these he said he had stayed away from school to go to the circus grounds and watch the workmen at their tasks. A man gave him a sponge and pail and told him to wash down a zebra. It happened that the circus was packing up and about to move on, and he went along with it, staying, according to varying versions, a month, a week, a few days.

The early circus adventure became part of Fellini's mythology, and he has good-humoredly admitted that he exaggerated. When Ida Fellini became aware of the story, she labeled it as ridiculous. "My boy behaving like that at the age of seven—running away with the gypsies? He couldn't have been out of the house for half a day without our knowing it." So much for the circus story.

One Christmas, the boxes of presents from the mysterious uncle in Rome included a magnificent marionette theater for Federico. Soon after, Ida received word that her brother had suffered a stroke and was now paralyzed and unable to speak. Even though she was still formally ostracized by her family, Ida was urged by her sister-in-law to pay her brother a visit. Federico was ten when the whole family took the train to Rome to pay its respects to the fabulous uncle. It was his first train trip, his first sight of the great city. Ida's brother lived in a large, richly furnished home on the outskirts. Federico was surprised by the sight of his mother kneeling before his immobile uncle and kissing his pale hand.

Following two years at the school run by the Sisters of St. Vincent, Federico was sent to another ecclesiastical school in Fano, a small town on the nearby coast several miles south of Rimini. This was a boarding school, founded by the Carissimi fathers, dull, provincial, and squalid, as he described it. "We ate badly and were severely punished by the fathers." Should he fail an examination, he was made an example for the others by being trotted around to all the classrooms, his exam paper, with a large zero drawn on it, pinned to his chest.

While at that unpleasant school, he apparently absorbed enough religious fervor to flirt briefly with the notion of becoming a priest. But soon enough his fervor declined. During confession he would kneel to recite his misdemeanors, but the moment he began with "Father, I have . . ." a skinny hand would dart from the monk's brown robe and land, unerringly, a slap on his face. This bewildered him, for he hadn't managed to say what he had done wrong. Then, when he did, the priest would doze off.

Federico seized one such opportunity to invent some dreadful sins, including setting fire to his house and causing hundreds to perish, and axing a priest to death. At the finish he raised his voice and confessed that he had kicked a friend during recess. He was told to say 100 "Hail Mary's," and then came another slap. He became adept at jumping out of reach, and avoided confession if at all possible.

During his three-year residence at Fano, "the revelation of woman," as he put it, came to him. Federico, then aged ten, and some schoolmates were at play on the beach when they encountered a plump, unkempt woman who, they knew, traded her favors for sardines brought back by the local fishermen. The boys pooled their funds for the opportunity to see her lift her skirts, and Federico was elected to hand over the money. Agreeably, the huge woman lifted her skirts to reveal a fullness of flesh. Saraghina (for "the sardine girl") is the name Fellini has given her, and she has persisted in his memory as his first image of sexuality.

The lure of the opposite sex also figured in a prank the older boys played on their teachers. The students were being given a slide lecture on St. Francis of Assisi. One of the boys had obtained a slide of a naked girl and managed to slip it in among the others. Suddenly, in the darkened room, the full back view of the girl appeared on the screen, shocking Federico, and undoubtedly the good Fathers.

Summers were a relief as well as a vacation from the oppressive school at Fano. He spent many of those months at his grandmother's house and farm in the village of Gambettola, the ancestral home of the Fellinis. Federico admired and loved his strong-willed grandmother, was friendly with the farm people, and intrigued by the itinerant workers, gypsies many of them, who migrated there during the warm season.

Before going to the school at Fano his favorite childhood companion had been Titta Benzi, a boy his own age. When, at thirteen, he entered the lycée in Rimini, he was able to renew that friendship. Titta was more serious about his studies than Federico (and would eventually become a lawyer) but he was fun-loving enough to join in the pranks of a group of boys, of which Federico was often the ringleader.

The countryside was dominant in Rimini during the winter months. There were cattle markets to which sheep, goats, and oxen were driven through the winding streets, accompanied by the loud shouting of farmhands. Then would come the flowering of spring, and after, what seemed to Federico an explosion into summer, the season most eagerly awaited by him and his adolescent companions. The town's population would swell with the influx of tourists and vacationers from the north. Rimini was a favorite resort among the Germans, Swedes, and Norwegians, and many of the women who came were wonderful to look at. In comparison with the "fat, dark-haired Riminese women who walked the streets with downcast eyes as though guilty about something," these fascinating creatures from the north were "tall women, their blonde hair whipping in the wind, with golden thighs and bellies, swimming in the morning in the still icy sea."

One summer day, Federico wandered to the beach hoping to observe some of these blonde goddesses who would spread lotions on their bodies, then lie on the sand for hours, gleaming in the sunlight. He found a vantage point behind a wrecked boat from which he could stare unobserved, or so he thought. Suddenly one of the blonde women leaped up, came rushing at him, picked him up in her strong arms, and carried him back with her to her amused friends. Mortified, he fled as soon as he could, followed by their laughter.

Summers, too, were when his beloved circus came. So did provincial vaudeville troupes and, on clear nights, the sky over the beaches was filled with bursts of fireworks.

Fellini was born only two years before Mussolini came to power and brought fascism to Italy. But for him, growing up in a fascist society meant few hardships. There was a secret in the family to which Federico wasn't privy. It had something to do with his father, who had gotten into trouble with the fascist authorities (he had been beaten during an interrogation, Federico later learned), but if the conversation at home veered toward the subject when Federico was present, mother and father would exchange glances and talk about something else. He was aware, however, of the black-shirted louts who hung around the local bars, and felt an instinctive dislike for them. It was confusing for him to see these same brutes singing their heads off in church.

Mussolini was a popular figure, especially among the country people and small-town folk. "Mussolini's technique," Luigi Barzini wrote in *The Italians*, "was obviously not meant for men of taste and culture. But he gave the appearance of raising a third-rate country into a first-rate power. He became a conqueror, of Ethiopia."

Fellini, like all students, joined a fascist youth group and wore the required uniform. But early on, a spirit of skepticism and rebellion manifested itself. He somehow always managed to lack some necessary item of the uniform: he would forget the fez, or wear brown shoes instead of black.

The war with Ethiopia began during his first year in high school, and he and Titta used the patriotic fervor to their advantage. Whenever a victory in the field was announced, classes would be dismissed for the remainder of the day. Federico, Titta, and their collaborators made sure that no victory, no matter how minor, went unnoticed. As soon as they saw a bulletin in the newspaper, or heard it on the radio, they went to the principal, saying, "Please give us the flag. Our glorious troops have conquered . . ." Raising the flag, they would march from classroom to classroom, and one by one classes would be dismissed. If several days passed without a victory to announce, they would invent one. The place names they gave to the supposed fields of battle were sometimes bawdy anagrams.

As mischievous as he was, Fellini was not attracted to outdoor sports. The closest he got to them was chasing balls for the tennis players at the Grand Hotel, Rimini's finest. But it remained a mystery to him how two grown men in white shirts and trousers could have fun racing around after a ball for hour after hour.

At school he claimed he learned very little. He was poor at mathematics, passable at grammar, and good at drawing and sketching. His favorite subject was art history.

"I learned, though," Fellini said, "to develop the ability to observe the silence of passing time, to recognize far-off sounds, rather like an imprisoned person who can tell the sound of the bell of the Duomo from that of San Augustino. I have a pleasant memory of entire mornings and afternoons spent doing absolutely nothing."

"Look," Titta Benzi remembered, "there's no point pretending that Fellini was thrilled with high school, even though he had an eight in Latin, a nine in Greek. He didn't know a word, and technically he deserved a zero. But perhaps through some premonitory sense his teachers realized he was a mature person, special, and they promoted him."

On the other hand, Fellini's sister Maddalena claimed he was a brilliant student. "For years Olivieri, the headmaster, read his themes to the class, he was so perfect."

It was at school, Fellini admits, that he developed a taste for humor and caricature, "a way of looking at people ironically, and with compassion—the latter because of our teachers yelling at us, their eyes flashing behind glasses as they insulted us, even in our essay notebooks: 'You should be in jail, not in school.'"

At the same time, the students were not exactly easy on their teachers, and there were unfortunate girls in the class who lived in terror of Fellini and his friends.

His "gang" numbered fourteen juvenile terrorists. They hooted at and made sarcastic remarks to laborers. In the early morning hours they woke up monks at a monastery by shooting water from a hose at their cells. And they tormented the ardent young couples who sought privacy behind the boats on the beach. A favorite diversion was for a few of them to strip naked, then stroll up and ask for the time.

Love came to Federico when he was fifteen. His family had moved again, this time to a house owned by Titta's father. Opposite theirs was a house occupied by a family from the south, the Sorianis. Of three Soriani sisters one, Bianchina, a petite, dark-haired fourteen year old, caught his eye.

When he first glimpsed Bianchina, she was wearing her fascist youth uniform. Then he saw her through the window of her home, "a pink and doll-like little fairy," as he described her. He wrote her a message (backward) on the window, asking her to meet him at the Augustine Arch. Sure enough, she came, and he presented her with a bouquet of flowers. They went walking outside the town to the countryside while he made up marvelous stories to which she listened in wonder.

Fellini has told a story of their taking a train for Bologna, his plan being to find work to support her in the city; for sustenance, he brought along a bag of sandwiches. But they found themselves on the wrong train, bound for Ravenna. Bianchina, tearful, said she didn't want to go to Ravenna, and besides, his money had all but run out. He had only enough left to get them back to Rimini.

A more mature Bianchina was consulted about the accuracy of Fellini's account of their romance. Never had they taken a train anywhere, she said derisively. True, they had taken some walks together, and a few bicycle rides, she on the crossbar, Federico pedaling. He had given her a little ring, and they talked of becoming engaged. But the idyll ended when she moved with her family to Milan. It was some years before he saw her again.

Bianchina gives us a glimpse of Fellini at sixteen: He was, she said, reserved but headstrong, "with a love for elegance. In summer he dressed in white, or wore a close-fitting dark jacket over white trousers." He did tell her stories. He was a dreamer; he told her he wanted to do wonderful things for her, like taking her off to America, where he would buy her 100 beautiful dresses. They never went dancing, nor did he take her to the movies. She liked to go to the beach, but when he came to see her there he didn't bring a bathing suit. He was self-conscious about his skinny build.

Fellini saw a picture of himself at that age wearing a red and blue bathing suit that came to his knees and, indeed, he was skinny. "I'm smiling in the picture," he said, "looking up at the sky, posing like an innocent calf, my hair soaked in brilliantine and stuck on my forehead. Who knows what someone offered me to have myself photographed in that way? I know I liked to appear to be mysterious, indecipherable. I enjoyed being vague, feeling victimized, and not understood."

In *My Rimini*, an essay accompanying a book of photographs he published in 1967, Fellini evokes the town he knew as he edged toward adulthood. His imagination was particularly touched by the Grand Hotel, an ornate luxury establishment built at the turn of the century. It was grand indeed. Besides its tennis courts, it had an expanse of well-kept gardens shaded by tall palms. Its clientele was made up of prosperous Milanese and equally well-off visitors from the chillier reaches of Germany and Sweden. Royalty had stayed there.

The youthful Fellini explored the hotel's boundaries, where gleaming Bugattis, Delahayes, and Mercedes were parked. In the evening darkness, the hotel, for him, became "Istanbul, Baghdad, Hollywood." Creeping as close to the tall windows as they could, Fellini and his friends, caught glimpses of women in bare-backed dresses dancing with men in white dinner jackets. The music, mostly popular American tunes, was carried to them on the breeze.

Early one Sunday morning, determined to see the interior, he made a solitary foray into this pleasure palace of the Adriatic. "I ran up the steps with my head down, crossed the terrace, dazzling with light, and went in. At first I saw nothing, because it was dim inside. There was the cool, scented smell of wax polish, as in a cathedral on Sunday morning. I saw sofas as big as boats, armchairs bigger than beds, the red band of carpet curving up the marble staircase toward the gleam of colored glass suspended miraculously in midair, the biggest lamp in the world." He had little time to enjoy the vision. From behind a high desk rose a black-suited concierge, who held out his arm stiffly in the direction of the entrance. Federico retreated meekly.

Access to Raoul's bar on the Corso presented no such problem. The bar was a gathering place for the town's sports buffs, would-be artists, and other nonconformist types. It was at Raoul's that Fellini became drunk for one of only two occasions that he could recall. He, with Titta and others, was to meet a slightly older friend at the bar. When the friend arrived he wore a hat that only a grown man would wear, signaling his having reached maturity. During the ensuing celebration, Fellini passed out.

Tall and skinny, he was noticing women. There was one (he has named her Gradisca) who was often seen strolling past another of the town hangouts, the Café Commercio, instantly attracting the attention of the males inside. The fine clothes she wore displayed a full figure. Once, Fellini happened to notice her sitting in the local cinema. He chose a seat near her, then moved furtively closer to her, seat by seat, until he was sitting next to her. She smoked a cigarette while watching the movie. He, meanwhile, stealthily slipped a hand beneath her dress and along her plump thigh. "She didn't interfere," he wrote in *My Rimini*, "just went on looking at the screen, magnificent, silent." But when he tried moving his hand for further exploration, she slowly turned her head toward him and asked: "What are you looking for?" The adventure ended abruptly, as he hastily withdrew.

Can we be certain the above incident occurred? Fellini's memories are often intertwined with his imaginings, as is often the way with creative people. For them, memory can expand through a process of association. Or change, as one memory merges into another. Fellini, who will claim again and again that he has a poor memory, actually has a rich storehouse of memories, but with resonances that don't always fit with sober fact.

In 1973 a reporter from Rome located Gradisca, who was still living in Rimini. As portrayed by Fellini, she was a hairdresser. In real life she had been a seamstress.

In her salad days, she asserted proudly, she'd had flocks of young men eager for her favors. But she had little to do with them. "I wasn't beautiful, but I was striking, with nice legs, and I was very well dressed." She had long ago settled into a comfortable marriage.

"One of the reasons for my reputation," she told the reporter, "was that I sewed, and I could always have the latest styles in clothes. Of course everyone looked at me, and I liked to be looked at." She came from a strict family, and to be able to get out of the house she would pretend she needed to buy needles and thread.

"Sometimes I'd plan to meet someone on the rotunda of the Grand Hotel." Was Fellini one of those she met there? "Of all the boys who wanted to make time with me, how would I be able to remember which one was Fellini? Of course, he would know *me*. In Rimini I was an institution. Moreover, his uncle had a store just a few steps from my father's store, so who knows how many times he would have seen me pass by? But I do remember something specific. I remember a skinny boy who stopped me once, and asked me if he could take a picture of me. I let him. He asked when he could see me to give me a copy of the picture. I said, let's not make plans. But later, this young fellow, in the ballroom of the Grand Hotel, asked me to dance, and he gave me the picture. I think that was Federico, but I wouldn't put my hand in the fire to prove it."

Fellini's talent for caricature enabled him to attend the Fulgor Cinema free of charge. With Demos Bonini, an older friend who lived next door, he fashioned caricatures of film stars from the posters that accompanied the showings. As Bonini remembered it, "We were there from dawn to dark, seeing one film called *Red Shadows* twenty-two times." Fellini pompously signed himself "Fellas" on the sketches, which were displayed in the theater's windows.

The pair decided to open an art business, using a shed for their place of work and business, which they called Febo. Fellini did the drawing, and Bonini the coloring. They charged five lire for a collection of sketches.

Bonini said that Fellini, at sixteen, already felt suffocated by his family, and that his release was working with pencils and brushes. "One day I tried sending a few of Federico's illustrations to the editor, Nerbini (of *420*, a humorous paper published in Florence), who wrote back with a check and an offer of work. I teased him: 'Here's your passport.' " Fellini's mother never fully forgave Bonini for his indicating that pathway to her son.

Mario Montanari, one of Fellini's group of pranksters, said that "growing up was a big bother to Fellini, like measles or chicken pox. But from time to time he hinted at some rather exotic profession, out of the way, journalism. Just think of it! In Rimini!" After Titta, Mario, and Federico discovered the English thriller writer Edgar Wallace, they decided to become a band of robbers. Among the exploits they pulled off was stealing some dried cod from tubs outside a shop. They stole a chicken from a local colonel. They heisted a bird cage and some sacks of flour. Titta, being on the large side, was sometimes the butt of Fellini's pranks. Once, riding together in the town's little trolley, Fellini slid two cream puffs on a seat just as Titta sat down. "Grosso," Federico giggled, "you've sprung a leak."

While in high school together Titta, Mario, and Federico were already planning to attend the law school of the University of Bologna. "Instead," Titta remembered, "Federico began to change after his final exam at high school. He isolated himself from everyone, became thoughtful. You could see he was mulling over some problem. He wasn't the same Federico who was full of fun, discoveries, creations. He was unhappy because his family didn't understand him."

The rift came about because his father was insisting he become a lawyer, while his mother wanted him to be a doctor. Before leaving high school, he made a train trip to Florence to visit the offices of *420*, and there he met the paper's principal illustrator, Giove Toppi. Fellini was vastly impressed by Toppi's workplace, a large room that seemed like a palace to him. It had curtains, rugs, statues of nude women and ancient heroes, and in the back of the room a large couch with pillows. Best of all was the large drawing board on which Toppi worked. Toppi was kind to the boy, and encouraged him to return when he was finished with school.

During September and October of 1936, Fellini went to stay with a friend of his father in Bologna, where he attended an accelerated program that would allow him to finish high school in half a year and facilitate attendance at the law school of the University of Bologna. Cesarina, now a restaurateur in Rome who had a restaurant in Bologna at the time, met Fellini as a student. She remembered him well, because he was unable to pay his bill and ran out. She went after him and told him he was to eat there whether he had money or not. Lonely in Bologna, and already set against becoming a lawyer, he returned to Rimini and finished high school there.

In the latter half of 1937 Fellini finally acted on his resolve to become a journalist and went to Florence, where he was hired by *420* for a job he has described as "halfway between doorman and editorial secretary. I stuck stamps on envelopes." The paper ceased publication long ago, but those with memories of it describe its humor as anything but delicate. Fellini was paid a meager salary, which he was able to supplement through the occasional sale of a drawing.

While he was with the paper, the importation of American comic strips was banned by Mussolini in retaliation for some sanctions imposed by the United States. The strips were wildly popular among students in Italy, and Nerbini, who then ran a weekly that published the strips, circumvented the ban by using local artists to keep the strips going. Toppi, commissioned to continue *Flash Gordon*, asked Fellini to help him. He not only drew the strips, Fellini claimed, but invented a new series of adventures for Flash. Fellini was well ahead of his time, for in one of the strips he had the hero become amorously entangled with the high priestess of the planet Phoebus, who then rocketed him off to a sinister planet inhabited by hawkmen. But how much truth there is in this is hard to say, because he stayed in Florence for only four or five months. One journalist, Oreste del Buono, investigated the story, and judged it another of Fellini's imaginary memories. "It might be," Fellini admitted recently.

Rome was already exerting its pull, but to get there he needed some help from his family. "After long, drawn out negotiations with his parents," Mario Montanari recalled, "which concluded with one of those ecumenical compromises which are Federico's specialties, he got his way. He could go to Rome, but must give his word that he would enroll in law school at the university there, and live with his aunt."

While in Rimini with his family before leaving for Rome, Fellini made a trip to Milan with his friends Titta and Mario. The Fair of Champions was in progress, but Fellini's main preoccupation was finding the love of his adolescence, Bianchina. He'd had other girlfriends by then, he later confirmed, but he still held sentimental feelings for Bianchina. There was a reunion, which was to be repeated several times in the years following. But Bianchina eventually married someone else, and in her later years became a writer for magazines. On the return trip to Rimini, Titta remembered, "he kept torturing himself, saying over and over, 'I'm going back to Milan. It's better that I go back . . .' " But his resolve to make his life in Rome was stronger.

In his more youthful years Fellini would tell fanciful stories about his coming to Rome. In one such, he had fallen in love and gone off with a large blonde. This tale was recounted in several biographical sketches, and even led to speculation that the woman was a prostitute. More recently, Fellini wrote me a letter acknowledging that the story was false.

In fact, he was followed to Rome by his mother, with his small sister in tow; this to make certain that he got himself properly settled. Mario Montanari remembered going with him to the train station in January of 1938. "Federico, Titta and I had our pictures taken in a garden nearby. We were a little dazed. We couldn't believe what was happening. Federico, who wanted to leave, was actually leaving. We were very sad."

In Rome, his aunt (the wife of his mother's brother) put him up briefly, and then found lodgings for him at a pension in a respectable section of the city. His mother left only after she felt assured that he was properly installed, and that he had, indeed, registered for law courses at the University of Rome.

III

FELLINI went to Rome in search of a journalistic career and also, as he was to say later about one of his film characters, "in search of himself." He did not remain long at the pension, which was far from what he regarded as the heart of Rome. He remembers, however, his next-door neighbor there, a working man of nearly forty. This fellow, attempting to remain young, went regularly to a hairdresser, slept with a piece of raw meat, held by rubber bands, on each cheek, and spent all of Sunday in bed. Fellini would notice him leave his room on Mondays, then suddenly open the door again and stick his head back inside. The youth asked him why he did that. "He was finding out," said the man, "if there was an odor of aging in the room."

Fellini had no such problem. Once the obligatory visit of his mother to his lodgings was over and she had pronounced them respectable, he moved to a district near the train station "haunted by poverty-stricken provincials, prostitutes, and Chinese necktie hawkers." Being near the station made him feel less homesick; there was always the daily train to Rimini.

He described himself as "tall and thin," adding, "I wore white canvas shoes, and wandered about the sleazy pizza bars and neon restaurants, trying not to let the holes in my trousers show. My shirt was always dirty and my hair long. I was very pale and romantic."

True to his word, he enrolled at the University of Rome, but there is no record of his ever having attended a class. Ostensibly, though, he remained on the rolls as a student.

While still at the lycée in Rimini, Fellini had become enamored of the humorous biweekly, *Marc' Aurelio*, which was difficult to obtain in Rimini because of the objections of the high priest, who found it immoral and sacrilegious. Fellini got his copies at train stations. On one occasion, looking for it a few miles south, in Riccione, he recognized a contributor to *Marc' Aurelio* taking the sun at the beach. He was a writer and editor named De Torres, whose caricature had appeared in the journal. Fellini hung around him all day, on the chance he could speak to him. Finally De Torres asked Fellini to fetch him a basket of fruit. Fellini told him about his drawings and his journalistic ambitions. The next day he found De Torres again at the beach and showed him some drawings. The man was kind and said, if he came to Rome, to look him up at the *Marc' Aurelio* offices at 68 Via Regina Elena.

When he went to the *Marc' Aurelio* offices to look up De Torres, Fellini was told he seldom came there but could be found at the offices of a daily paper, *Il Piccolo*—which Fellini had subscribed to while in Rimini. The *Piccolo* offices were in a rapidly decaying small palazzo in one of the city's more squalid districts, and the corridors smelled of minestrone.

Fellini's ideas about newspaper offices and the journalistic profession had come from the American movies he saw at the Fulgor Cinema. Reporters and editors wore their hats on the backs of their heads; they worked in vast city rooms and made phone calls constantly to remote parts of the world. When he located De Torres, the editor was in a small room furnished with a desk, a chair, and a typewriter. "Come back later," Fellini was told. When he returned, the room was full of people. Fellini recognized one of them, Vitaliano Brancati, a well-known novelist who had written a chronicle of a visit he had paid to Mussolini that was required reading at Fellini's lycée.

Fellini kept going back until De Torres finally decided to let him try writing something. "Let's see what you can do," he said. He pointed to the Remington on his desk. It was raining outside, and he said, "I'll give you a title: 'Welcome, Rain.' No more than four lines, and a little sketch." De Torres went out the door, leaving Fellini at the typewriter. It took him forty minutes to write the piece and draw a sketch. When De Torres did not return, Fellini wandered into another room, where he found someone who looked like an editor. "It's ready," he told him.

"What's ready?"

" 'Welcome, Rain.' "

The man shrugged, accepted the paper, and that was the last Fellini saw of it, until many months later, when snow came to Rome, and the piece appeared under the title, "Welcome, Snow."

He didn't stay around *Il Piccolo* for long. He had to scrabble at odd jobs to pay his rent and buy enough pasta to fill his stomach. When he didn't have the rent money, he moved out and found another room. He made a friend of the almost equally impecunious illustrator, Rinaldo Geleng, and they banded together to visit restaurants and cafés, where they drew sketches of the patrons. Fellini would do the outlining and Geleng the coloring. Their subjects usually weren't overly impressed with the results, but the more kindly ones treated them to a meal.

They then tried decorating shop windows. The method they used was to draw figures of curvaceous women on the window and write messages about sales and price reductions. If business was good, they split up, each to do a window alone. When Fellini tackled the window of a shoe shop at the lower end of Via Veneto, he followed Geleng's practice of using oil paints, even though he was unfamiliar with them. Soon he was making a mess of the window. Onlookers gathered to watch him at work, while he sweated in embarrassment. A pretty girl gave him smiles of sympathy, but the owner was less than pleased. Fellini offered to clean the window with turpentine, but ran away when he saw the red-faced visage of the shop owner, followed by the laughter of the onlookers.

Fellini has recounted this story more than once, most interestingly in an unproduced screenplay called *Moraldo in the City*, clearly based on his early experiences in Rome. The pretty girl plays a much larger part in the screenplay, in which she is given the name

Andreina. When the two meet again by chance in the story, a love affair develops between them, and she represents for him a choice between a free and easy bohemian-style life, and a more prosaic and orderly existence.

In his first year or two in Rome, Fellini certainly showed a preference for the former. One friend he made was something of a swindler. He told the gullible Fellini that he knew how to obtain diamonds at a less than wholesale price and, if Fellini would do the selling, he would split the profits with him. Fellini took the bait and traveled to the recently built Cinecittà studios, where a friend of his was working. He tried to sell one of the jewels, mounted in a ring, to a well-known actor. The actor examined the stone, and then ground it beneath his heel. So much for diamond selling.

He kept on, writing humorous sketches and doing illustrations, sending them to *Il Piccolo,* his beloved *Marc' Aurelio,* and other publications with little or no success, and he worked briefly as a crime reporter for *Il Popolo di Roma.* Fellini had discovered the novels of Georges Simenon and, asked to cover the suicide of a girl who had drunk poison, he overdid his reportage by talking to everyone remotely concerned. He interviewed the girl's mother, her friends, the concierge of her building, her lover, and built a story of despair and thwarted love. The editor cut the story to a few lines and changed the suicide to accidental death. (Suicide was not an approved subject in the Rome of the time.) When he was given the task of reporting the local court news he found it so dull that he quit reporting altogether.

Soon enough, however, he was given a staff job as the editorial secretary at *Marc' Aurelio* and was taken more or less in hand by the paper's editorial director, Vito De Bellis. One of Fellini's tasks was twice a week (the publication schedule) to take the copy to the printer where, late at night, it went through the presses. While they waited for the completed proofs, De Bellis often took Fellini to dinner and instructed him in table manners. He was to sit with his knees pressed neatly together, open his mouth only when there was no food in it, chew with his mouth closed, and never look at what was on the plate. After the meal, De Bellis would drive Fellini back to the typographers.

"I was blissful," Fellini recalled.

To keep the proofs from smudging, he bought a pair of chamois driving gloves. He read proofs until four in the morning, sitting in the huge and noisy press room.

It wasn't long before *Marc' Aurelio* was accepting some of his pieces and caricatures, and he also found more work on a new magazine about the film world, *Cinemagazzino*. He interviewed personalities and contributed a column in which he answered letters from readers. As his work found more acceptance at *Marc' Aurelio* he became a contributing staff member there, a position that carried with it considerable prestige, for the periodical was regarded as the best of its kind in Italy and was left relatively unscathed by the Fascist minister of culture. *Marc' Aurelio* is still remembered as one of the few journalistic bright spots in the overall Fascist grayness.

Fellini's screenplay (written with Tullio Pinelli), *Moraldo in the City*, provides a lively and only barely fictionalized account of what happened to him during his first year or so in Rome, and reveals the considerable amount of discouragement he endured. "I can tell you," he wrote Professor John C. Stubbs, who translated the screenplay into English, "that it draws on my memories of my first year in Rome. The episodes, the characters, the situations were more or less as I experienced them at the time."

The story involves not only Moraldo, who we can assume is the counterpart of the eighteen- and nineteen-year-old Federico, but two friends in need and comfort, Lange and Gattone. Lange, Fellini has said, was based on his illustrator friend Rinaldo Geleng, and Gattone on a poet and writer of children's stories whose actual name was Garrone.

In the screenplay, Moraldo's adventures in Rome begin three months after he has left his home town and "his gang of friends there." He has been getting along on the small amount of money he brought with him and another sum sent him by his mother. He is already thinking of returning home, because the swimming season has begun and his friends are probably already at the beach. He meets the raffish and alcoholic Gattone while waiting for word on an article he has submitted. Again, rejection.

Gattone suggests they have supper together, and at the trattoria they meet Lange, another new friend for Moraldo. Among the three of them they haven't enough money to pay for their meals. Lange does a comic drawing to mollify the restaurant manager, but they're thrown out anyway.

By this time, Moraldo is somewhat used to living by his wits, though not in as hardened a manner as Gattone, who hasn't paid his hotel bill, and whose belongings have been seized. Moraldo, too, has room trouble. He owes a month's rent, and the landlady has taken his door key. He gets in by calling up to a man inside who comes down and lets him in—along with Gattone. The landlady discovers them, but she is rather taken with Moraldo.

He manages to avoid her not very coy advances, but soon enough becomes entangled with a mature and well-off woman, Signora Contini, who is publishing a new literary magazine. Fellini has identified the woman's real-life counterpart as Signora Lenticci, presumably deceased, but also as a composite of a few older women who, he said, looked after him during his early years in Rome. In the screenplay she is described as a beautiful woman in her mid-thirties, "with a proud nose and the eyes of a person accustomed to giving orders and to having them carried out."

Although the reception room of Signora Lenticci's office is filled with copies of her magazine, *Life and Letters*, only one issue has so far appeared. Even so, the quarters are luxurious. Moraldo can't sell her his manuscript or get a job with the magazine, but the Signora likes his looks, invites him for a drink, and asks him to telephone her.

Soon enough, another romantic possibility turns up for Moraldo. To earn money, he has joined forces with Lange to paint pictures and advertising slogans on store windows, and the screenplay recounts the story Fellini has told of his window-painting adventures.

A beautiful, well-groomed girl is watching, with others, his bungling job on the window. "What strikes Moraldo is that the girl is not laughing with the others." She tells him that a little turpentine

will help the situation. A while later he thanks her for not laughing
at him, but is too shy to carry the acquaintance further. When by
chance they do meet again, he learns that her name is Andreina, and
eventually a budding romance will turn serious. But there is also the
"buxom cashier of a café he frequents." When he asks her out for a
Sunday afternoon, she is dressed in a white outfit, "her hair piled
high and tinted black," her nails lacquered under net gloves—not
exactly the right costume for the entertainment he is offering, a
movie. She feels Moraldo isn't up to her standards, and walks off.

Moraldo decides it's time for him to telephone Signora Contini and, when she answers, he tells her he must talk to her. She invites him over.

"What must you tell me that is so urgent?" she asks him.
But soon enough she understands the boy's need, his discouragement and loneliness. "Get a grip on yourself," she advises him.

Desire comes to Moraldo as Signora Contini sits down and
crosses her "long and shapely legs. Her dressing gown reaches only
to the top of her knees." (She has been about to go out for the evening.) Moraldo's "look becomes slightly hard and insistent." Signora Contini notices and touches the edge of her dressing gown
lightly with her hand. "What are your plans for the evening?" she
asks.

So, after some conversation concerning replacing a fuse that
has burned out, the Signora cancels her date and, sitting on her bed,
murmurs, "Little boy."

Moraldo may have trouble getting his work accepted, but in
this situation he is as adept as any Latin lover. "In an instant Moraldo is beside her. He embraces her, and she puts up a faint struggle, arching her breasts and flaring her nostrils dramatically. 'No,
no. Are you mad?' she says," all the while searching for the lamp
switch.

Signora Contini accepts not only his advances but also one
of his articles. However, it is not to be paid for until the issue appears. Having been thrown out of his room, along with the tag-along
poet Gattone, he is in dire need of funds. Gattone solves the problem
for a day or two by taking a room for them at the luxurious Savoy

Hotel. They will figure out how to pay for it later. But both he and Lange feel that Signora Contini is the solution.

She is surprisingly agreeable when he tells her his need for money. Not only does she give him twenty thousand lire; she suggests he use the spare room in her place. There isn't much else for him to do but agree. He does odd jobs for Signora Contini in exchange for his room and board, but his major efforts are reserved for the bedroom.

But then he discovers that the lady has found another young writer friend who looks as robust as a lifeguard. And by now he realizes that in her eyes, the eyes of her friends, and the household help, he has become a gigolo, a servant who has to ask for pocket money. Angry at himself, he turns in his key to her apartment.

Through a friend, Ricci, Moraldo soon moves into another circle of friends, "people with worn-out shoes, with fingers black from nicotine, and with dirty collars on their shirts. They are people always on the move, always with their ears pricked up, full of winks, fast nods of comprehension, and continual calls made from telephone booths." They're hoping always for that one big break. Ricci puts Moraldo into business with him selling memo books put out by a charity organization, but he doesn't do well at it.

Again discouraged and hungry, he enters a small restaurant, and there is the girl who had smiled at him, and is smiling at him again. A little bolder this time, he learns that Andreina clerks in a store, and off they go to a movie. Soon he is seeing her almost every night, and she becomes his lover. But she is hardly enchanted with his bawdy friend, Gattone. At the same time, Moraldo begins to be aware of her "middle-class mentality." Sure enough, Andreina makes the assumption that they are engaged and that it is time for him to come to dinner and meet her parents.

Once there, "Immediately Moraldo finds an instinctive sense of comfort that, through a thousand small details, recalls the home of his parents—the same unmistakable air of middle-class orderliness and prosperity."

Moraldo, for the moment in pursuit of a more bourgeois way of life, finally finds a job, but the petty, bureaucratic nature of it quickly disenchants him. He quits, informs Andreina, and tells her he can't adapt to that kind of life, and though he loves her, cannot marry her. So ends that phase, with Moraldo returning to his friends, Lange and Gattone, and the always resourceful Ricci.

The Moraldo of the screenplay is a sensitive youth striving to find the proper place for himself in the bustling life of the city. Moraldo is sympathetic, but not idealized; indeed he has a harder time of it than did Fellini, whose charm was manifest very early on. Even though the screenplay was never filmed, it cast a long shadow over much of Fellini's future work.

Only recently did he talk about the relationship with the real life prototype of Andreina. "She was a sweet, sensitive girl," he said, "but her intentions were far more serious than mine." In the introduction to his translation of the screenplay, Stubbs, citing a colleague of Fellini's, refers to the real life "Andreina" as the daughter of a guard at the Museum of Valle Giulia. For Moraldo, if not for Fellini, the affair is a watershed experience. Like others he encounters in the city, Andreina represents a distinct direction that he might or might not take. *Moraldo in the City*, then, is a kind of portrait of the artist as a youth. Andreina would lead him on the path toward a solid, middle-class existence. But, good soul that she is, she loses him. It is the budding artist in Moraldo that defeats her.

Writing regularly for *Marc' Aurelio*, Fellini did several series of sketches. One, "Third Year in the Lycée," was based on his own student escapades and those of his friends. Other feature columns to which he contributed were called "City Lights," and "Will You Listen to Me?" His own caricatures accompanied the pieces. The pay was good for the time: six hundred lire a month. It's unfortunate that none of this material survives; Fellini kept none of it and has no idea to where to find such prewar ephemera.

Quite significant in the evolution of his career was the short-lived work he did for *Cinemagazzino*. With another writer he surveyed and interviewed the most prominent people of the entertainment scene. In this way, he met Anna Magnani and the comic actor Toto. But most important of all was an interview he did with Italy's most popular variety performer, Aldo Fabrizi.

Fellini had begun frequenting the Castellino Bar in the Piazza Venezia, a popular hangout for artists and performers. There he ran into Fabrizi again. Fellini was now living near Piazza San Giovanni, in the southern part of the city and, as it turned out, so was Fabrizi. They would walk home together late at night, with Fellini listening with fascination to the tales Fabrizi told him of his adventures touring in the provinces with his variety company.

Fabrizi specialized in humorous monologues, and since Fellini was already being noticed for his comic pieces in *Marc' Aurelio*, Fabrizi suggested he write some material for the monologues. Fellini complied willingly, and received some fees in return. Working together helped cement their relationship. Fabrizi was fond of good food, and he introduced Fellini to some of his favorite restaurants. He was an excellent cook, too, and Fellini was a frequent guest at his home. In fact, so fond did the entertainer become of Fellini that when Fabrizi's wife gave birth to a son, he asked Fellini to become the boy's godfather. Fellini had no way of knowing it at the time, but fate was arranging things nicely.

Once launched on his writing career, Fellini moved fast. He discovered a market in radio for his comic sketches and, with two other staff members of *Marc' Aurelio*, formed a combine that furnished material to stations in need of brief time fillers. As explained by Fellini, "We were a little office for comic pieces." This work led him and his partners to films. Together they furnished gags and comic episodes for the comedies of Erminio Macario. Fellini was not yet twenty when he received his first screen credit, for his contributions to Macario's *Lo vedi come sei?"* (*Do You Know What You Look Like?*).

Fellini was expanding his literary horizons as well. One of his cowriters on *Marc' Aurelio* gave him a translation of Franz Kafka's *Metamorphosis*, and Fellini was affected by it "emotionally and profoundly. I was struck by his mysteriousness, his way of confronting daily happenings which suddenly became magical." The works of such American writers as William Faulkner and John Steinbeck struck him as "realistic, sensual, adventuresome, palpitating—a sensation of liberty, of landscapes without horizons."

His relationship with Fabrizi proved valuable once again when the actor, who was making films, employed Fellini to rework some scripts. He soon progressed to collaborating on stories and screenplays for other movies. On one film, *Documento Z-3*, there were no less than eight writers. Alfredo Guarini, the director and producer, held meetings in his beautifully furnished home. As Fellini remembered it, "We did nothing but drink whiskey, eat ice cream, and smoke up terribly." He was already in the midst of a group, including the Marxist writer and theorist Cesare Zavattini, and the novelist Vitaliano Brancati, that would later have a significant effect on Italian films.

Financially, too, it was a pleasant time: "That magic moment of waiting from the time you signed a contract for a script and that just as marvelous moment of the check about to be signed. It was hard to stay calm, to pretend indifference, while your producer was picking up his checkbook, the check already made out in your name." One of the screenwriters Fellini worked with could hardly contain himself. His eyes would gleam, and he would keep the check stretched out in both hands, as though folding it might lessen its value.

Between his work for *Marc' Aurelio* and his film stints at Cinecittà, Fellini's circle of professional acquaintances widened. At the *Marc' Aurelio* offices, while working late on copy for columns, he would hear De Bellis discussing political matters with others in the publishing world—Leo Longanesi, for one, and a clever writer named Ennio Flaiano. But politics were beyond him, and while enjoying the talk, often humorous, he made no contribution to it.

At Cinecittà, there was ferment. New and younger directors were beginning to break away from insipid romances and pale Hollywood imitations. If Fellini did not belong to the first-rank group, which included Alberto Lattuada, Renato Castellani, Luchino Visconti, and Roberto Rossellini, he at least knew who they were and what they were doing. It was French film that was exerting the most influence on the maverick Italian film-makers, and Fellini was among those who admired the work of René Clair, Marcel Carné, Julien Duvivier, and Marcel Pagnol. It was a busy time for film-makers. During a three-year period Fellini made contributions to eleven films. "They weren't much," he admitted, "but they foreshadowed neorealism, with small scenes and social sketches depicted in good-humored fashion. I think I went beyond the paraphernalia of white telephones and mawkish situations of that era."

When Hitler began his march through Poland in September 1939, Fellini, busily attempting to make a career in Rome, felt himself, if anything, to be a neutral in the war that resulted. He had remained relatively immune to the Fascist glorification of war, of heroism, of sacrifice for the motherland and, in any case, Mussolini had declared his country a nonbelligerent. It did not occur to Fellini that Italy, though not strictly neutral, would actually enter World War II on the side of the Germans. But he knew that it was important for him to stay out of the army, and to that end he kept afloat the fiction that he was a student at the university. The majority of Italians were not pro-German, and it came as a profound shock to Fellini when on June 10, 1940, he heard the stentorious voice of Mussolini on the radio in the porter's room at *Marc' Aurelio* calling "People of Italy, to arms . . ."

Worried, shaken, he wandered into the streets, which were all but empty because most of the inhabitants were glued to their radios. "In the whole of Via Veneto," Fellini remembered, "there wasn't a soul to be seen. Then a man came riding down on a bicycle toward Piazza Barberini without touching the pedals. He raised a hand from the handlebars in greeting and shouted: 'Hey, war's been declared!' "

The twenty-year-old Fellini failed to respond with patriotic fervor to the call to arms. With no politics other than, perhaps, the vaguest socialistic leanings, he was not anti-fascist as much as non-fascist. His instinct toward caricature was, if anything, sharpened by the bombast and pretension of the regime. By his own admission, he did everything he could think of not to be called up. Through the help of friends, he obtained a medical certificate stating that he had a heart murmur. Once, when due for a physical examination, he arranged to stay in a clinic, swathed in bandages.

De Bellis, the editor of *Marc' Aurelio*, was viewed favorably by the Minister of Popular Culture, and the paper continued on its humorous course with the proviso, from on high, that it devote itself more often to current matters in line with officially decreed policy. This, of course, meant supporting the war effort, both Italian and German. In fact, the paper was for a time printed in a bilingual edition for German consumption.

"The press," according to Fellini, "suffering from the regime's oppression, became hollow, false, empty. In our office, the goings-on approached madness."

One day, the entire editorial staff was lined up for inspection, as though on parade, by the Fascist Party secretary. As the functionary went along the line, each editor and writer in turn clicked his heels and stated his position. The secretary paused in front of Fellini, and gave him a long, disapproving look. "Allow me," he said, "to give you some advice. Get your hair cut."

As his own contribution to the general morale, Fellini began a new feature, a series of letters written by a girl to her fiancé at the front. He signed the first letter with the name of his early love, Bianchina. De Bellis, when he read the letter in the paper, was furious. The girl, he said, was a whiner about what was occurring on the home front, and was thus only demoralizing the brave soldiers in the field. "No more of these columns and letters," was his decree to Fellini.

There were more repercussions. A copy of the issue with the letter reached the Ministry of Popular Culture, and Fellini was ordered to appear before its chief. The building which housed the ministry had a wide marble staircase. A sign at the foot of the staircase ordered: MOUNT STAIRS TWO AT A TIME. The chief of the Fascist militia had ordained this measure for public buildings to demonstrate that Italians were bursting with energy and vitality. At intervals on the staircase, armed guards stood at attention.

Fellini, already rebellious over what had happened to his letter and the abandonment of the series (although some of his colleagues had defended him) took further offense at the sign. Instead of mounting the steps two at a time, he took four halting paces to mount each step. The guards probably thought him a semiparalytic, for they only looked at him with surprise.

The minister asked Fellini to explain his motives in composing the letter which, he said, the ministry regarded as sentimental and detrimental to the war effort. Fellini gave him some reasons having to do with the human condition, in wartime and in peace. Unimpressed, the minister asked: "Young man, just what is your military status?" Fellini said that since childhood he had suffered from heart palpitations and murmurs. The minister made a notation in a notebook and dismissed him.

It became clearer than ever to Fellini that his beloved *Marc' Aurelio* was being increasingly dominated by that same Ministry of Popular Culture, that its writers and editors had become the tools of the government. "Very soon we had to reveal to the Italian public that Churchill was a schizophrenic, that English women were nymphomaniacs, their offspring degenerates, and their husbands alcoholics." Disheartened, he handed in his resignation. He was not giving up his only source of income, however, for there was still the occasional movie job, and his radio writing.

Fellini, during the early war years (1940–1942), stayed out of the army by means of the "sick leaves" granted to him each time he presented his medical certificate. But early in 1943 he was ordered to report once more for examination (the notation made by the Minister of Popular Culture may, he suspected, have been instrumental in this). He went to the military hospital to have his disability certificate renewed. Each time, in the past, friends on the staff had helped him, but this time he saw only one familiar face, and he was given a shrug of resignation. The reason became clear when Fellini saw that German officers were observing the examination procedures. After a cursory going-over, Fellini was declared fit for military service and handed three documents. One notified him that he was hereby inducted into the army, a second indicated his regiment, and a third ordered him to report immediately to its headquarters in Puglia. He also learned that the regiment was to embark for Greece.

Fellini was in an unreasoning rage when he left the hospital. While an astonished sentry looked on, he tore the army documents into shreds and raced away. When reason returned to him, it was with a vision of his being shot as a deserter. He consulted with friends about what he should do. One, appalled by Fellini's action, rushed him by car to the town of Forlì, near Rimini, where some Party people handled the situation by sending him to Bologna for a new physical examination.

Fellini was still determined to be rejected on medical grounds. He went to the military hospital an hour early, and spent the time running up and down four flights of stairs as fast as he could. When his name was called out, he sprinted to the examination room, sweating, weak in the knees, his heart pounding. Hoping that in this condition his heart would reveal a murmur or a valve leak, he faced the inquisitors sitting behind a green baize-covered table. And at precisely that moment the shriek of air-raid sirens was heard over Bologna.

Almost at once, two hundred Flying Fortresses began dumping their bomb loads. The hospital was hit, badly damaged, and the examination team disappeared in the wreckage. Fellini, luckily, emerged from the debris with only minor scratches. Somehow, he found himself out on the street and running—running through ruins. "Suddenly I was alone in the open country on a road lined with farms. I could hear the crescendo of exploding bombs behind me. People were screaming. Church bells were tolling. Airplanes were droning in. The heavy odor of death was in the air. . . . A lifetime is not enough to forget it."

He received no more draft notices after that experience, which brought home to him the full nature of war, its horrors and murderousness. Apparently, his military records had been destroyed in the bombing. He returned to Rome, where he continued writing for radio. While still at *Marc' Aurelio* he had written several sketches around two young marrieds he named Cico and Pallina. He then used the sketches and the characters as the basis for a radio series sponsored by a perfume company. Cast for the role of Pallina was a young actress who was then still studying at the University of Rome and acting in an experimental theater.

Federico and Giulietta have given differing versions of their meeting. Fellini's is that he had not met the young woman playing Pallina on radio but came across a picture of her in *Radiocorriere*, a weekly devoted to news of radio and its personalities. So struck

was he by the remarkable embodiment of his Pallina that he decided to telephone her and invite her to lunch.

Giulietta agrees about the telephone call and the lunch, but
she claims that there had already been talk about making Cico and
Pallina into a film, and that Fellini was concerned about the casting. "He called me on the phone and asked for my photograph in
order to decide whether they could use me in the film. A few days
later we met and discussed plans for the film."

Another time, she said: "He telephoned me one day, and
he said, 'My name is Fellini and I am fed up with life, but before I
die I would like to see what my heroine looks like.' I thought he
might be joking, but I couldn't risk having a corpse on my conscience."

The meeting between the twenty-three-year-old Federico
and twenty-two-year-old Giulietta took place in June of 1943. She
was born in San Giorgio di Piano, near Bologna, into a family of
teachers and musicians. Her father, before becoming a teacher when
he moved the family to Rome, had been first violinist at the Teatro
alla Scala. Giulietta's early ambition was to become a musician, too,
but at her family's urging she went to the University of Rome to
prepare for a degree in classical studies. At the University she
joined an experimental theater group, the Teatro Ateneo, and was
outstanding enough to win critical attention and scholarships. In
one play, *Angelica,* she co-starred with a fellow student, Marcello
Mastroianni. Because of her studies, she was unable to accept an
offer to join a professional theater company but, with other student
actors, auditioned for a new radio serial. To her surprise, she landed
the lead role of the heroine, Pallina. When Fellini telephoned, she
was living with her aunt, who cautioned her about accepting a blind
date; but lunch seemed safe enough to Giulietta.

Fellini chose one of Rome's most fashionable restaurants,
but he struck Giulietta as shabbily dressed for such a fine establishment. His suit needed pressing and mending, his shoes were in need
of repair, and his hair was long overdue at the barber's. She wondered about his ability to pay for the meal, but Fellini wasn't dis-
mayed by the prices and insisted she order the more expensive and
exotic items on the menu. She chose with an eye to economy, just in

case, yet when the bill came Fellini revealed a fairly fat wallet. "If he has so much money," she found herself wondering, "why won't he buy himself a new suit?"

She was charmed by him, however, and their romance blossomed while Rome rocked under an Allied bombing that left a thousand dead. It was a convulsive time for Italy. Its troops were dispersed in Russia, Greece, southern France, and Sicily. Two hundred thousand of its soldiers had been captured in the African campaign. Then in August came the American and British invasion of Sicily, and the subjugation of that strategic island. Invasion of the mainland was imminent. The defeats led to the collapse of Mussolini's regime, and a new government formed to negotiate with the Allies for peace. When invasions came at the boot of Italy and at Salerno, the Germans quickly occupied Rome and its airfields, and in a matter of weeks the ally became the enemy for the majority of Italians. A loose coalition of communists, socialists, Christian democrats, and unaligned anti-Fascists fought not only against the Germans, but against their own still partially Fascist government. Some, communists mainly, joined with the British forces in the fierce fighting up the peninsula. It was not so much a resistance, as in France, but a movement toward liberation—from the Germans and the past.

It was in this unsettling atmosphere that Federico and Giulietta, only a few months after their first meeting, decided to marry. "It took awhile," the properly brought up Giulietta said, "for my mother and father to digest this American-style engagement." They exacted a promise from her to continue her studies toward her degree. The marriage was solemnized on October 30, 1943, in Giulietta's aunt's apartment, next door to which lived a monsignor who made an impromptu chapel out of one of the rooms. Times being what they were, a honeymoon was out of the question, and so was a place of their own in which to live. Giulietta's obliging aunt made room for the newlyweds in her apartment on the Via Lutezia.

It was indeed the worst of times. For Federico there was nothing to do but wait for the Allies to battle their way into the city. Nor was it wise for him to visit his usual haunts, for the occupying Germans, aided by Fascist accomplices (Mussolini had been "rescued" and had set up a puppet government in the northern half of Italy), were rounding up men for work in labor camps and factories in Germany. Giulietta continued her studies at the university and kept house for Federico in their cramped quarters. Hardly a week had gone by when their idyll was almost shattered.

Fellini, crossing the Piazza di Spagna, saw some women nearby giving him sympathetic looks, and only then realized that he had walked into a trap. Members of the Fascist Brigate Nere (Black Brigades) were rounding up the men in the piazza and herding them into trucks manned and guarded by German soldiers. Fellini felt the muzzle of a machine gun in his back and was prodded toward one of the trucks and made to climb in. The truck began moving off, and Fellini knew that he was headed for forced labor.

"I thought I'd had it," he said, when recounting the experience, "and what I did was more through instinct than reason." About to make a sharp turn, the truck slowed, and at the corner Fellini saw two German officers in conversation. He shouted at them, "Fritz, my dearest Fritz!" and leaped out of the truck. The soldiers in the convoy looked up with puzzlement as Fellini held out his hand to one of the officers and embraced him, still saying loudly, "Dearest Fritz."

The annoyed Germans pushed him aside. Fellini heard the truck's gears grinding as it moved on, and immediately dashed into the Via Margutta, a street not much wider than an alley. Then, ready for collapse, his heart thumping, he went into a pharmacy, for the moment safe from captivity. Years later, merely remembering the incident gave him the shivers.

He seldom ventured from the apartment on Via Lutezia after that. This fallow period lasted several months and was not without its rewards. His newly found domesticity was a kind of return to bourgeois orderliness. He has said again and again, "I do not know what would have happened to me if I had not found Giulietta." While waiting and hoping for the Germans to be driven from Rome, they also awaited the birth of their child.

* * *

The Americans arrived first, entering the city on June 5, 1944, and welcomed riotously by the populace as liberators. Two months later Giulietta gave birth to a boy whom the Fellinis named Federico, but, tragically, the child died within a few weeks. The sadness of the bereaved couple was intensified by the city's circumstances—hunger and deprivation everywhere, a vicious black market, vital services all but nonexistent, soldiers and displaced persons wandering the streets. Film work didn't exist. Cinecittà had taken some bombs and, in any case, it was being used to house displaced persons and returning prisoners of war.

Fellini and some friends found a means of supporting themselves by opening a shop they called the Funny Face on the crowded Via Nazionale. One of the associates in the enterprise was a famous prewar director, Mario Camerini; another an intellectual who later became a director, Vittorio De Seta. With soldiers of several nationalities passing through Rome, the shop provided a service of sorts. Fellini drew caricatures. Blown-up photographs of such places as the Trevi Fountain and the Colosseum were used as backdrops for soldiers to pose against while having their pictures taken. Voice recordings were made to be sent home to the soldiers' families— unfortunately they could be played only once before becoming unintelligible. Pretty girls were employed to help sales. The shop became so successful that a second was opened, and a financial administrator was needed to keep track of receipts.

"It was a kind of casino," Fellini said. "It had an atmosphere not unlike western movies, something halfway between a saloon and a waiting room." Across the street was an American military police station, and frequently the shop boy was told to run there for reinforcements to quell the fights that broke out between drunken soldiers, or to subdue pawing of the female assistants. Its siren howling, a jeep would make a U-turn, and some beefy MPs would enter the shop and start slugging whoever seemed in need of quieting while Fellini and his associates dove under tables until peace returned.

Fellini claims that in terms of buying power he earned more money from the shop than he has before or since. The receipts were augmented by the generosity of the soldiers, who not only tipped

lavishly, but would add cans of rations (corned beef, beef, and vege-
tables) that were luxuries at the time, and also cans of beer and,
most valuable, American cigarettes. "If we had even been able to
get hold of those cigarettes before the war," Fellini said, "everyone
would have understood we could never have won."

Late in 1944, Fellini was in the Funny Face shop at work on
a caricature of an oriental-looking soldier, when in came a man he
recognized. "He had the thin, drawn face of an immigrant and was
wearing a small gray cap and a short overcoat. He appeared to be
someone who thought a great deal." Fellini wondered if perhaps he
were there in hopes of becoming associated with the shop. "He signaled with his hand that he wanted to talk to me." Fellini continued
to work on the drawing while Roberto Rossellini waited patiently
for him to finish.

IV

DURING the German occupation of Rome, a priest, Don Morosini, was caught and shot by the S.S. for aiding the underground.
This shocking incident became the subject of a short film Rossellini
was planning to make, and he wanted Fellini to help him persuade
Aldo Fabrizi to play the role of the martyred priest. It was fairly
common knowledge that Fellini and Fabrizi were good friends.

While Rossellini waited, the subject of Fellini's drawing
raised his voice in loud protest. Fellini had thoughtlessly given the
caricature a yellowish wash, and the outraged soldier took this as
a racial slur. Rossellini attempted to smooth things over, but the
soldier stalked out unmollified.

Rossellini than asked Fellini if he could spare a few moments of his time. They stepped into the back of the shop, and
Rosellini explained his problem. A certain countess was willing to
put up the financing for his film, to be called *The Story of Don
Morosini,* but she was insisting on none other than Aldo Fabrizi for
the role of the priest. Would Fellini intercede with the actor? Unfortunately, the budget for the film was limited; the fee for Fabrizi
would be small, but the subject had importance for this time of
transition.

Fellini knew Rossellini by reputation. Then thirty-eight, he
was the son of the owner of a cinema in Rome, and he had entered
the film profession by working in a dubbing studio. During the
Mussolini period all films from abroad had to be dubbed into Ital-

ian—an effective means of censorship. Prior to the war, Rossellini had made a few short, poetic films that had brought him some recognition. No one less than Mussolini's film-enthusiast son, Vittorio, had chosen him as a collaborator on a film about the Abyssinian war. When Italy entered World War II, Rossellini co-directed or directed several films with patriotic themes. For one of these he employed the intellectual and talented Michelangelo Antonioni as a script writer.

These wartime films, though fictionalized, were made in near-documentary style. The locations were actual, and more often than not the actors were nonprofessionals. With Italy's defeat and German occupation, film-making had come to a halt. Rossellini was a Christian Democrat favorable to the coalition that had banded together to rid the country of fascism. Indeed, during the German occupation of the city, he gave shelter to a communist writer, Sergio Amidei, who was being sought by the authorities. It was Amidei who had suggested to Rossellini the idea for a film about the priest who had given his life for the underground. The Germans were still in Rome when Amidei began writing the script; Rossellini, meanwhile, went out with a camera hidden in a truck and made shots that he hoped would be useful when the time came to shoot the film. Film-making was still under wraps when he went to see Fellini, but Rossellini had a permit from the American military authorities to film what he had told them would be a "documentary" about a brave priest.

The countess, Rossellini went on, would be willing to put up the money for a second short film if Fabrizi could be obtained; Fellini, since he had written for films, could perhaps work with Amidei on that. Fellini agreed to meet with the countess, who turned out to be a woman of majestic size and indeterminate age. When she learned that Fellini drew caricatures she suggested that the second film be a comic one, done in animation.

Fellini, willingly enough, conveyed the offer to Fabrizi, whose response was negative. He complained it would be a comedown for him to do a short film; also, as a comedian, he would confuse audiences in such a somber role. In any case, the money offered was an insult to an actor of his stature. It would take at least five times the amount to get him to reconsider, and the film would have to be of feature length.

Rossellini then took the countess's suggestion of two short films and came up with another proposal: two short films that would go together well enough to constitute, in effect, a feature, the second to be based on the youthful gangs that roamed the Italian capital during the war years.

At Rossellini's request, Fellini went to work with Amidei on the second of the two scripts. One evening, as the three collaborators discussed this story, Amidei suggested that they combine the two stories into one. Rossellini said "Of course!" and immediately put Aimidei and Fellini to work on a new script that would portray Rome under the heavy boots of Nazis and Fascists. The new title was ironic: *Rome, Open City*.

The writing was done mainly in the kitchen of the apartment Federico and Giulietta shared with her aunt. Fuel was short that winter, as was most everything else, and the only warm room was the kitchen. The outline took only an evening, and the new script was hammered out in approximately two weeks.

Rossellini soon learned that the full-length script required more money than the countess could provide, even with Fabrizi's participation. Desperately scrounging for more financing, he took to denuding his apartment. "I sold my bed," he recalled later, "an antique chest of drawers, and a mirrored wardrobe." He went to the black market for film stock; what existed was of poor quality. Rented equipment was augmented by sympathetic American film buffs from the Army's Signal Corps in Rome.

Fabrizi demanded one million lire for his services (about five thousand dollars at the then-current exchange rate), while Fellini's entire pay came to about fifty dollars. He has insisted that he made only minor contributions to *Open City*. "I limited myself to a few ideas for the theme," he said. However, the credits for the finished film list him as co-screenwriter with Amidei and Rossellini.

But Fellini was hardly being modest, for the film's power and vision, and its technique, came from Rossellini, whose work during the war had trained him in documentary realism. He was courageous in reflecting the starkness of the period covered by the film—the year following the German declaration of Rome as an open city to save it from further Allied bombing.

The story focused on the worker partisans and the priest (renamed Don Pietro because another film about Don Morosini was being planned) engaged in a struggle against the Nazi and Fascist repression. Major characters included an underground leader named Manfredi; a diabolic Gestapo officer, Major Bergman; and Pina, a working-class woman engaged to Manfredi's close friend. Pina would be played by Rossellini's then companion, Anna Magnani.

In one of the more shocking scenes, Magnani is cut down by a Nazi machine gun while racing after her captured fiancé, who is about to be taken off to a labor camp. In the story, too, is the betrayal that leads to the death by firing squad of Don Pietro. If Magnani as Pina is given a marvelous cinematic death, Fabrizi as the priest is given some memorable last words: "Oh, it's not hard to die well. It's hard to live well."

Peter Bondanella, a noted chronicler of Italian cinema, called Rossellini's film "a crucial watershed in the evolution of the seventh art." In it a "profoundly tragicomic vision of life," was expressed as a fictional narrative that at times seemed close to newsreel reality. Comic moments were juxtaposed with melodrama and tragedy. The overall texture was that of a documentary.

Living with the film turned out to be a crucial watershed for Fellini, too. "Rossellini was the man," he said years later, "whose example and personality first inspired me to realize that the cinema was the means of expression best suited to my nature. It was in this sense that he gave me something fundamental. It was meeting him that guided me on to one path rather than another."

Some of the film's incidents had real-life antecedents, and whenever possible Rossellini used the same settings. The film was shot silent, of necessity, for there was not enough money to record sound simultaneously. Actors dubbed their own voices during the editing. When an early cut of the film was screened for distributors in the reawakened industry, the reception was disappointing. Italians were not used to seeing ordinary people in lifelike roles and recognizable locales. Rossellini decided to strengthen the film with some retakes, and he shot these in a former gambling saloon on a street that also housed a bordello. What follows has been told by Fellini and others, and if their versions differ slightly, it must still be regarded as one of the most significant events in the history of moviedom.

An American soldier, so it has been said, came out of the bordello and, while making his way along the street, tripped over a tangle of cables that led into a building. The cables were feeding the camera and lights inside. Fellini was there on the street at the moment, and as he described it, the soldier who fell was half drunk. Fellini helped him to his feet, and the soldier then stared at the cables and, curious about them, followed them inside, where he found Rossellini at the camera. He asked about the film that was being made, declared himself a producer, and requested a viewing. Perhaps the soldier did not come out of a bordello, or was not half drunk, but it is true that he was there and that he introduced himself as Rod (for Rodney) E. Geiger. Rossellini accepted him at face value, screened the film for him, and Geiger was so taken with it that he grandly said he would arrange for its American distribution.

"He lied," Fellini said, when he gave his account of the incident. "He wasn't a producer. He was in advertising, but his lies sparked off the flame of fortune for Italian films."

Rodney Geiger should be followed a bit further because of his effect on Fellini's destiny. It is to be remembered, though, that in 1945 (when Geiger stumbled over the cables) there were few distributors of foreign-language films in the United States. One of these was the small firm Mayer-Burstyn. Arthur Mayer was more the showman of the two, while Joseph Burstyn had a deep and abiding love for the "classics" they imported and distributed, mostly to the so-called "art houses." It was to this firm that Geiger went with the print of *Rome, Open City* entrusted to him by Rossellini.

Both Burstyn and Mayer are deceased, but Lillian Gerard, who became an assistant in their office, remembers Burstyn's telling her: "This soldier came in carrying a duffel bag with some cans of film." Arthur Mayer was in Germany overseeing the films suitable for the Germans to view, so Burstyn had to make the decision on his own. But he knew he was seeing something good and unique, even though the print on the poor film stock was grainy, and making new prints from the negative would not help much. He agreed to contract for the film, and cabled Mayer to look up Rossellini in Rome.

While this was happening, Fellini kept at his work in the Funny Face shops, which had begun to hit the doldrums. The first wave of American soldiers was leaving Rome, and the new breed that came in to aid the Italian postwar recovery effort were not the kind who liked to send caricatures of themselves and voice recordings home. "We made a sport," Fellini said, "of catching flies and staining them with aniline."

When *Rome, Open City* opened at the World Theater, just off Broadway, it was, in the words of a reviewer for *Variety*, "a critical smash," and soon enough a box-office one as well. To help it along, Mayer and Burstyn advertised it with a misquotation from *Life* that read: "Sexier than Hollywood ever dared to be." With the quote went a still from the movie showing two young women embracing, and another of a partisan being flogged. It played for more than a year at that theater alone, and the film's success in the United States was repeated in Europe. Even in Italy, after a poor start, it became something of a box-office success. Rossellini, according to Arthur Mayer, "always claimed that he lost money on it, although it should have earned him a fortune as it proved a terrific moneymaker for distributors and exhibitors all over the world." The total cost of the film, eighteen thousand dollars, should have been recouped easily.

Rodney Geiger, jubilant over what he had wrought, wired Rossellini to go forward on another film; he would do the financing himself. Did he want American stars for his next picture? Geiger would get them for him. Rossellini had already asked Fellini and Amidei to work with him on an episodic new film that would focus on the activities of American soldiers and Italian partisans in Italy during the war. Since Americans would be needed in the cast, they naively cabled back to Geiger a list of star names that included Gregory Peck and Lana Turner. Geiger cabled that he was boarding a ship for Naples and that he was bringing with him money and several important stars.

Robert Lawrence, a young American officer with ambitions to become a producer, volunteered to drive Rossellini and Fellini to Naples to meet the arriving ship. He knew Geiger, and though aware that he had no producing experience, did not regard him as dimly as Fellini later did. "His father," Lawrence (now a producer himself) said, "was a prominent New York acting coach. It's true that he was exuberant and prone to exaggerate, but he had a certain brilliance, and he did, after all, immediately recognize the quality of *Open City*." Lawrence was there when Geiger, a small man, trooped down the gangway with his "four American stars," none of them recognizable to any audience anywhere. Fellini claimed they were amateurs. In any case, they appeared in the film. More important, Geiger brought with him a quantity of fresh American film stock.

On *Paisà* (*Paisan*), as the new film was called, Fellini, in addition to working on the script, was employed as a full-time assistant to Rossellini. In form, the film would be a kind of journal that would recount recent history with emphasis on the meeting of two disparate cultures—Italian and American—and the struggle of each to comprehend the other. The title came from the American G.I.s who addressed local people with "Hey, Paisan." The word *paesano* is Italian for countryman, neighbor, or friend.

Once shooting began, the project became ever more ambitious, requiring financing greater than any film in Italy at the time. "Rossellini's business methods," Arthur Mayer wrote, "are, to put it mildly, somewhat confused." Eventually several financial participants were involved. Geiger set up his own company, which he called Foreign Film Productions, into which money funneled. "That whole part of it," Lawrence said, "was byzantine in its complexity, but Rossellini's name and success with *Open City* brought in investors." Somehow, in all this, American rights to *Paisan* were sold to both Mayer-Burstyn and a leading competitor, Ilya Lopert.

Several names have been associated with the scriptwriting, but it was Fellini who received the major screen credit. Ideas for episodes also came from Amidei, Klaus Mann, a son of Thomas Mann's, and a young American writer, Alfred Hayes.

Also employed as an assistant to Rossellini was a young critic and documentary maker, Massimo Mida. "Go at once," he was told, "and meet with Fellini." "It was a time of great hope," Mida recalled. "All of us had a heady feeling of excitement. We saw the distressed conditions, but bad as they were, we had faith that they would improve and change." Several communists worked on the film because, having been partisans, they best knew the stories the film covered, particularly the battle for Florence.

Rossellini described Fellini at the time of *Paisan* as "tall, thin, with enormous eyes and black hair." Mida agreed, but added, "thin as he was he gave the impression of being large."

Another who became well acquainted with Fellini during the making of *Paisan* was Gianfranco Corsini, a scholarly man, communist in his politics, who had fought with the partisans in the battle for Florence. Fellini found him while researching material on the battle. In the "Florence" episode, an American nurse who works in a hospital attempts to find her Italian lover, and learns he has been wounded in the savage street fighting between the Nazis and the partisans. Corsini not only provided details of the battle, but took part in the film's action, some of it directed by Fellini himself. (Corsini later became a noted professor, a specialist in American studies, and has enjoyed a wide acquaintance among American intellectuals. When he visited the United States during the early 1970s he became known as President Richard Nixon's "favorite communist.")

"We had many conversations, Fellini and I," Corsini remembered. "Giulietta was with him in Florence, and was very much the housewife, cooking meals and looking after Federico. Some of the things I was able to tell him about the time and the battle made their way into the screenplay. . . ."

As though in deference to the man he called "Maestro," Fellini has tended to downplay his work with Rossellini. However, when credits were listed for the finished film, he shared the screenplay credit with Rossellini while others who worked on the script were listed as having suggested ideas. Since Fellini was constantly with Rossellini during the six months of location work on the film, he helped shape the final script (though never really final until actually shot).

Mida has it that so many were involved with the six episodes that 30 percent of the narrative content could be attributed to Rossellini, 30 percent to Fellini, and the remainder to almost everyone else involved.

"Everyone liked Fellini," Mida said. "Not only did he have an attractive personality, we were all impressed with his quick mind." Less impressed was Corsini, who suspected that Fellini had an anti-intellectual bias, "no culture to speak of, and very little education."

Rossellini, too, provided an assessment of the Fellini of the mid-1940s: "He is both yielding and stubborn. He dreams and then comes awake all of a sudden, revealing his ability to materialize his dreams, to act. He is both imprecise and precise at the same time." When they worked together, he said, there was much talk and exchanging of ideas, like batting a ball back and forth. Mida said that the talk would lead to a point at which Fellini would roughly work out an idea on paper, after which Rossellini would further adapt the material to his actors.

Rossellini explained his method of work: "I began by establishing myself with my cameraman in the middle of the district where such-and-such an episode of my film was to be shot. The rubberneckers then gathered around us and I chose my actors from among the crowd." The script was regarded as incomplete until arrival on location, after which adaptation was made to the circumstances and the selected actors. Even dialogue and intonation were determined by the nonprofessional performers. *"Paisan,"* according to Rossellini, "is a film without actors in the accepted sense of the term."

Fellini modestly has said, "I may have given Rossellini a hint to turn in a certain direction, or directed his attention to some particular situation, but nothing more. For instance, when he was directing an episode at Majori (near Amalfi) I discovered a little monastery of Franciscan friars and, since as a young boy I had been sent to a boarding school run by friars, I entered it full of

curiosity, and actually discovered a charming place, very much resembling a picture. There were five or six friars, very poor, extremely simple. One evening I took Rossellini to dine with me there,
and I suggested the possibility of filming an episode.

"At first the idea was to have a meeting between American
chaplains and Italian friars; between an active belief, as that of military priests should be, and this kind of faith, so meditative, a life of
prayers only, as it was lived in medieval monasteries that can be
found here and there in Italy. The idea was there, but not yet the
episode, which I wrote in that same monastery."

The episode, when filmed, had three American army chaplains arriving at such a monastery in a just-liberated area, bringing
with them a supply of food. The monks, half-starved, look forward
happily to a festive evening meal but, to their dismay, they learn
that only one of the chaplains is Catholic—the others being a Prot-
estant and a Jew. At mealtime, the chaplains find only three places
laid out. The monks are praying for the two souls not yet converted
to the true faith. The Catholic chaplain is unable to change their
minds, but he tells them that they have given him a lesson in "humility, simplicity, and pure faith."

Of the six episodes, this one drew the most mixed reactions.
To a British critic, it had "a purity and beauty of which the film, at
this stage, is badly in need." In the United States, the distinguished
critic Robert Warshow complained that the Americans were made
to look like simpletons, "with the monks superior in their hum-
bleness." Peter Bondanella was able to pinpoint the flaw in the
reactions of Warshow, and other non-Italians. "The irony was completely intentional," he wrote. "Are the monks providing a lesson in
pure faith or, rather, one of religious intolerance and bigotry? Most
non-Italian viewers will undoubtedly overlook Rossellini's characteristic belief that true religious feeling cannot be explained by the
rules of logic."

The experience of *Paisan,* of working so closely with the
man he regarded as a master, was a revelation to Fellini. "For me,"
he said, "it was the first clear discovery that it was possible to make
a movie with the same direct complicity and rapport with which a
writer writes or a painter paints." Previously, when he had been

called onto a set to rewrite some dialogue, all the activity there, the artificiality of the sets, the megaphones used to move actors around like an army on maneuvers, had struck him as false and pretentious. But with *Paisan*, working with an enormous crowd in Naples, the film-making seemed "part of the city, part of the reality we were moving around in. It was extraordinary to see Rossellini there yelling through his megaphone while armored vehicles were moving behind us, thousands of Neapolitans screaming from their windows, selling wares, and crying out to each other. If the movies were like this, if you could do it in this completely relaxed way, if it could be experienced as a continuous happening between life and its representation, then it seemed to me this could be even more my kind of thing than writing or drawing."

While in Naples, he came upon Rossellini in a small dark room, at work with a moviola. "He was pale, he was tearing his hair out, staring at the first cut on the little screen. The images were shadowy; I could hear only the bobbin turning. But I was transfixed. What I saw seemed to me to have a mystery, grace, and simplicity that only rarely has the cinema recaptured."

With *Paisan* Fellini discovered his own country. He knew the little medieval towns in the vicinity of Rimini, knew Rome, had spent short amounts of time in Florence and Bologna, but traveling with the company, almost like a circus troupe, he saw Italy quite literally from toe to top. Once an episode was finished, the film troupe moved on to seek a new location. "Only the dialects changed in each region we moved to. And not only was it a moving discovery of my own land and people, but with it came the realization that the cinema allows you this double game of telling a story, and while telling it, living it yourself as an adventure, and with extraordinary people in each realm. One is spectator and actor at the same time."

He encountered "a whole new race of people, who seemed to be drawing from the very hopelessness of their situation." He saw ruined cities, and in the midst of disaster and loss "a wild spirit of reconstruction." Traveling in this way, seeing a country no longer in the grip of a regime "which had literally blindfolded us, taking in this mass of new impressions, so extraordinarily rich in suggestive power, was like filling my lungs with oxygen."

V

WHILE *Paisan* was having its première in Venice, and from there going on to a broad international success, Fellini, in the latter half of 1946, was busy working as a screenwriter for Lux Film, a large producing organization. He was one of several who fashioned the script for a film directed by Alberto Lattuada—*Il delitto di Giovanni Episcopo* (*The Crime of Giovanni Episcopo,* released in the U.S. as *Flesh Will Surrender*)—about which Fellini claims to remember nothing. Lattuada, who had already made his reputation in the prewar cinema, was busily developing projects, taking advantage of the resurgence in the industry. Also working on screenplays for him was a playwright by the name of Tullio Pinelli.

Both Pinelli and Fellini happened to pause at the same Rome newspaper kiosk to examine a paper spread out on a rack. Pinelli was the shorter of the two, and Fellini peered over his head. When Pinelli turned, Fellini said, "You are Pinelli; I am Fellini." Each had heard of the other; they had seen each other in passing but had never formally met.

The two began walking together, chatting animatedly about their mutual interest, the screenplays they were at work on for Lattuada. Fellini had been assigned the script for *Senza pietà* (*Without Pity*), while Pinelli was on *Il bandito* (*The Bandit*). Pinelli was Fellini's elder by twelve years, but the two might have been spiritual brothers, so quickly did they take to each other. "Almost at once,"

Pinelli recalled, "we began thinking about some screenplay subject we could do together."

The fertile Fellini proposed one immediately. As Pinelli remembered it, "the story had to do with an unemployed workman who woke up one morning and discovered he could fly. First he flew to the ceiling, then he opened his window and flew out over Rome. I'm not sure what happened next." That subject remained undeveloped, but soon Pinelli telephoned Fellini and suggested that the two work together on the screenplay for *The Bandit*. Fellini agreed, with the proviso that Pinelli work with him on *Without Pity*.

The collaboration developed into a virtual scriptwriting factory. "From morning till night it was like going to the office," Fellini said. "Mornings I went to Pinelli's house, and we wrote the most important scenes. In the afternoon he came to our apartment [that of Giulietta's aunt]. Evenings each would go to his own place for more work."

"From the moment we met," Pinelli said, "I regarded Fellini as a genius. Even though he was only twenty-six, already, in whatever gathering he was part of, he would become the center of attention. He has always had this ability to capture people. He had charm and a charismatic quality that made one feel somehow that he was important. That impressed me very much because, you see, I am exactly the opposite."

Pinelli had certainly at the time accomplished more than Fellini. He was the scion of a noble Piedmontese family, and at first opted for the law. He studied at the University of Turin, and practiced law in that city for ten years, but he was more attracted by the theater. He wrote comedies for the marionette theater of Turin, then he and his brother built their own theater, where he wrote and presented plays. After a few years of this, his plays reached Rome, where one was honored by the Italian Academy. When war came he entered the army, took his training as a machine gunner, and served at the front in southern France.

Lattuada, the director with the perspicacity to hire both Pinelli and Fellini, already in 1946 had a reputation for style and intellectuality. A Milanese, he had been a critic and writer for magazines before turning to filmwriting in 1940 and then to directing. In common with some other directors of that period, his films were stylish and literate, and were often adapted from well-known novels. Italian film historians labeled this genre "calligraphy," because of its emphasis on style rather than social content. After the war, however, Lattuada joined the growing group of directors devoted to the treatment of social subjects. And, coincidentally, he began by attempting to do the story of Don Morosini, but because of *Open City*, Lattuada abandoned his effort.

"I became fond of Fellini," Lattuada remembered. "I was convinced he had fantastic talent. He was very amusing, and at Lux Studios, where we worked, he was known to be developing more and more each day." Screenwriting paid relatively little then (even now the work in Italy pays far less than in the United States), and it was common to hire two or three or more writers on the same work. Fellini and Giulietta, Lattuada said, "had very little reserves of money." When *Without Pity* went into production, Fellini served as assistant director to Lattuada. "And," said Lattuada, "I gave Giulietta her first chance to work in films by providing her with a small but very good role."

Lattuada, among other Italians, was still under the influence of the great French director Marcel Carné, and he directed *Without Pity*, an interracial melodrama, in a moodily poetic style. The film takes place mainly in the port of Leghorn where the black market flourished and attracted both Italian criminal elements and American soldiers, whose supply port it was. The two main members of the cast are an American black and an Italian prostitute. Their tragic love affair leads to their death after several gun battles and car chases reminiscent of American gangster films. The mixture, nevertheless, promoted the message of human brotherhood, which was becoming one of the signposts of neorealist cinema. When the film was shown at Venice, it was greeted warmly, and so was Giulietta Masina, who was awarded a Silver Ribbon for her minor role.

In addition to their work for Lattuada, the two busy writers, Fellini and Pinelli, worked with several other writers on a Pietro Germi film, *In nome della legge* (*In the Name of the Law*), after which they rejoined Rossellini, who had just completed a movie based on Jean Cocteau's one-act play, *The Human Voice*, starring

Anna Magnani. Now Rossellini was looking for another vehicle for Magnani, so the two films could be joined and exhibited together. Amidei had already been enlisted in the search.

Rossellini, Fellini recalled, was "reading a pile of books, consulting other friends and writers, artists and vagabonds. Occasionally he would turn utterly pale and proclaim dramatically, 'I must begin shooting in five days.' And he would stare at us in hatred."

All four met one afternoon in Amidei's apartment. Pinelli took a volume of Pirandello stories from a shelf and leafed through them, while Amidei paced around the room. One or the other would make a suggestion, but Rossellini only shook his head in dismissal of the notion.

"It was half past three," Fellini said. "Suddenly I saw very clearly the two main characters of a story, and I perceived, though obscurely, the theatrical device. But I am a shy person [!]. I didn't have the courage to propose what, in the space of a second, had already taken form as a story. I gave a silly, embarrassed laugh. I said I remembered, from a long time ago, a story that had seemed very beautiful to me. In the face of the skeptical silence from the others, I mumbled confusedly that it was about a mystical madwoman . . . who met a vagrant one day, and who took him to be St. Joseph. . . ."

Interest was piqued at once. Whose story was it? they wanted to know. Fellini said he couldn't remember. Where, then, had he read it? In a newspaper, a magazine, perhaps an anthology? Maybe, Fellini lied, he had come across the story in a French newspaper, or it might have been a translation from another language. Amidei guessed that Fellini was hedging for some reason, and pressed him to reveal the source. Fellini finally gave in and admitted it was a story that had just come to him. Rossellini went quickly to the telephone, called Magnani, and told her a story had been found. It took Fellini and Pinelli only a few days to outline *Il miracolo* (*The Miracle*), and Rossellini scheduled its production.

The source of the story, as Fellini tells it, came from the time when he spent summers at his grandmother's farm in Gambettola. The small village was surrounded by a woody area in which gypsies camped during the summer. Toward the end of the season a man named Gaetanaccio would visit the gypsies to geld their pigs. One of the gypsies, a simple-minded young woman, conceived a passion for the wanderer, much to the alarm of the other gypsy women, who regarded the forbidding-looking man as a manifestation of the devil. When the young woman gave birth to a boy, the women of the camp claimed the child was the son of Satan. Both that story, which he heard about, and the man, Gaetanaccio, remained in Fellini's memory bank. In his version of the story, Fellini changed the man (in the deluded woman's mind) to St. Joseph, so that the woman imagines she is having an immaculate conception. Ready to give birth, she attempts to reach a little mountaintop sanctuary. After her struggle to get there, she finds the chapel closed, with only the door to the bell tower open.

Here is how Fellini and Pinelli, in their outline, described the final moments: "The big bell now begins to sway, moved by an exultant and desperate force. It swings back and forth, again and again, and more violently, until a deep, sonorous, solemn note falls upon the valley. . . . And other notes of the bell follow the first . . . more and more urgent, joyous, triumphant, announcing to the world that the child of the miracle, the new savior is born."

The simple-minded woman was to be played, of course, by Anna Magnani, but for the "St. Joseph" character Rossellini searched no further than Fellini himself. After some persuasion, he agreed to play the part, but balked when he was asked to dye his black hair blond. Eventually, he was cajoled into a beauty parlor.

The two films were released together in Italy and France, as *L'amore,* but the first part of the bill, *The Human Voice,* was not shown in the United States. Mayer and Burstyn released *The Miracle* in combination with a short French film under the title of *Ways of Love.* According to Arthur Mayer, *The Human Voice* couldn't be shown in the United States because of Rossellini's free-wheeling business methods. Either he or his agents had made a half dozen conflicting deals for its distribution.

A censorship furor attended the showing of *The Miracle* at Manhattan's prestigious Paris Cinema. It was at first passed by the then active New York State Board of Censors, but pressure by the city's Catholic Cardinal, and a condemned rating by the Catholic Legion of Decency, caused the New York State Board of Regents to overrule its censorship body and suppress the film. The main Catholic complaint was that the film was sacrilegious in content, although in Italy the religious authorities had taken the story as that of a simple woman's pious delusion. Burstyn courageously precipitated a legal battle that went all the way to the Supreme Court, which ruled in favor of the film's exhibition. As a result, film censorship in the United States was dealt a body blow from which it never recovered.

Along with his other chores, Fellini had served as Rossellini's assistant director on the film, and was again assistant director and screenwriter on Rossellini's *Francesco, giullare di dio* (*Flowers of St. Francis*). With Pinelli, he continued turning out screenplays for Pietro Germi and Lattuada. Inevitably, they took to developing ideas of their own as well as those assigned to them.

Pinelli described their mode of work. "First we would simply chat about a notion, using our imaginations. We each had a typewriter. He would do a scene, I would do one, and we would show our work to each other. . . . Fellini would, in outline form, do the first real writing of the story. And, after that, the two of us would go into the development of the screenplay." It was in this fashion that they wrote a screenplay called *Luci del varietà* (*Variety Lights*). It was Lattuada who provided the impetus when he told Fellini he would be interested in a story built around the Miss Italy competition.

The writers, however, took the story far beyond Lattuada's suggestion. Its only residue in the screenplay that emerged from their busy typewriters was in one of the characters—a young beauty-contest winner who becomes so infatuated with the idea of a stage career that she joins a troupe of third-rate traveling actors. Soon the girl is wooed and bedded by an aging comedian with a grandiose assessment of his talents. In the end, she dumps him in favor of a younger and slicker impresario. The movie gained richness from its portrait of a tawdry world in which actors trek by train from one country station to another, to perform in provincial music halls before indifferent audiences.

Fellini has claimed that his knowledge of this world and its

atmosphere came from his association with Aldo Fabrizi. Not long
after they met, he said, he accompanied Fabrizi and his troupe on
a tour of the southern provinces, during which Fellini was known as
the company's "poet." He painted scenery, so he said, helped to
costume the performers (some ladies among them claiming him as
their pet), and even took a turn on stage now and then. The name
of the revue was *Sparks of Love*. It was "an insultingly bad show,"
and it distressed Fellini "to witness the enjoyment of the poor audience in the pit." No less than six dancers in the troupe of eight, he
also said, fell in love with him and made his life so complicated that
he could hardly wait to get back to Rome and settle down to working for *Marc' Aurelio*.

In spite of the flamboyant nature of the above account, and
Fellini's age at the time (nineteen), most biographies of him have
taken it at face value. And Fellini continued to stick to the story in
spite of Fabrizi's denial that he ever took a company out on tour
with anything remotely resembling *Sparks of Love*. More than that,
Fabrizi said he had gone on tour only twice, in the years 1935
(when Fellini was fifteen) and 1945 (when Fellini was busy on
Open City and tending his Funny Face shops).

Angelo Solmi, in his account of Fellini's early career, theo-
rized that Fellini's knowledge of the "variety" tour life may have
come from his long talks with Fabrizi during their companionable
period. Fabrizi may well have told him tales of the tour he made in
1935. And Fellini has mentioned time and again his fondness for
those old variety shows, many of which he saw in his native Rimini,
and which he attended during his early years in Rome not only as
spectator but as a gag contributor to Fabrizi's humorous monologues.

Once *Variety Lights* was developed into script form, Lattuada made Fellini a venturesome proposal—that they produce the
film themselves, and thus break away from the confines of major
producing organizations such as Lux Film. They had a script, they
had a director (Lattuada), and they had a beauteous star in Carla
del Poggio, Lattuada's wife. Fellini's wife, Giulietta, would also
have a nice part in the film. For the musical score there was Lattuada's father, Felice, and, for production supervisor, Lattuada's sis-

ter, Bianca. As a further inducement for Fellini, Lattuada told him: "We will cosign the film as directors. In this way you will have your name on the screen as a director, and this will open the way to your becoming one. You will have your 'degree.' "

Once Fellini had agreed to the proposal, Lattuada brought in the major portion of the financing, and Fellini and Giulietta pooled their resources for the remainder. By Lattuada's account, it was "a small amount, because Federico and Giulietta were not very well off at the time."

Fellini and Pinelli, while polishing the screenplay, felt it needed strengthening, and they decided to bring in writer Ennio Flaiano for suggestions. Flaiano, then about forty, had been a theater and film critic, and went on to become a playwright and novelist. In 1945, he was appointed to the editorship of the weekly *Il Mondo,* but left soon after when his reputation grew as a screenwriter. Fellini had met him during his tenure at *Marc' Aurelio.*

Pinelli said, "Our meeting with Flaiano took place in a hotel where he was staying temporarily. He had a wife and family, but had fled from them. We discussed the script, and he agreed or disagreed about aspects of what we were doing, and made suggestions. Generally, he was more destructive than constructive, but this was a known characteristic of Flaiano. And, while he could be highly critical, he could also be clever to the point of brilliance. There were occasions, when we worked with him later on, that he could destroy a story with his criticism. But, even while arguing with us, he stimulated us."

So, with two directors, three screenwriters, two wives, a sister, and a father, the "family" production was mounted under the name of Capitolium Film, the company including all of the above as well as the noted cameraman, Otello Martelli, and other members of the crew and cast.

It has been a matter of continuing argument over the years as to the true authorship of *Variety Lights.* Was it primarily Fellini's film or Lattuada's? "My name as director came first," Lattuada said, in a conversation, "and Fellini's second. I set up all the shots and, although Fellini was with me at the editing, I was the one who did it."

Fellini, too, claimed principal authorship of the film. In an interview many years later, he told Charles Thomas Samuels, "For *Variety Lights* I wrote the original story, wrote the screenplay, and chose the actors. Moreover, the film recalls some worn-out routines I saw presented by a vaudeville troupe with Aldo Fabrizi. Lattuada and I formed a company with our wives, and everything was a cooperative venture. I can't remember exactly what I directed or he directed, but I regard the film as one of mine." (It should be noted that, in this interview, he had dropped his story of travels with the troupe.)

Massimo Mida, though not actively employed on the film, was close enough to the principals throughout its making to give a balanced judgment. Lattuada, he said, was responsible for all the technical aspects—camera angles and positioning, the lighting, and so forth, but, he added, "Fellini was always on the set, contributing ideas, working with actors, and he also made a less tangible contribution, that of the whole mood of the film, the way in which it revealed the nature of the milieu it covered."

Lattuada, in thinking back to the opportunity he gave Fellini in sharing the directorial credit, said: "I invented Fellini."

Mida, when told of this remark, replied, "If anyone invented Fellini, it was not Lattuada, it was Rossellini."

But aside from the argument over authorship, Lattuada remembered the making of the film as an enjoyable, even heady experience.

"For the first time we were free of production control. The people, the talents, actually making the film were also its owners. We were buoyed by the feeling that this method of production could have great importance for the future of the whole Italian film industry. If we were able to prove that the artists could surmount the system . . ."

But that dream soon faded.

"I lost all my money," Lattuada said. "My sister, who was also keeping track of the finances, kept warning me that we were using too much money and going over our budget. In our excitement, though, we kept on, but, by doing so, accumulated a lot of debt. Our dreams of autonomy went out the window."

Once the film was completed, they needed a distributor, and the one they found not only did a poor job, but soon went out of business. Lattuada and Fellini were held responsible for the accumulated debts, and further distribution of *Variety Lights* was hampered by legal injunctions and law suits. Lattuada and Fellini were still paying its bills well into the 1960s.

As for the film's reception, it was decidedly mixed among those who paid any attention. Left-wing critics were inclined toward regarding it favorably, but mainly because they approved of its method of financing. Giulietta Massina came out well in the part she played, an old comedian's neglected but still faithful girlfriend, Melina. Other critics carped at the film for what they took to be its stylistic imbalance. (But this was before Fellini became known as Fellini.)

Variety Lights found new life in 1964, when its legal and distribution problems were finally overcome and it was seen as "the first real Fellini film." The English critic, John Russell Taylor wrote: "There are scenes in the film that no one but Fellini could have conceived or invented."

The people in *Variety Lights*, while living in their tawdry world of one-night stands in dreary theaters, somehow manage to surmount failure and hang on to their illusions of ultimate triumph. Battered by the hard facts of their existence, they maintain a touching faith. The comedian, Checco Dalmonte (Peppino de Felippo) buries his sorrows and continues on to the next station stop. Peter Bondanella, commenting on the film, saw it as embodying "an important and innovative idea of character in cinema . . . the dramatic clash between social role (mask) and authentic personality (face). Moreover, Fellini and Lattuada have additionally gone behind the mask of the theater itself as a social institution and revealed the underside of this medium." What is also revealed in the film is a warmth, a love for the often pathetic and deluded characters. At the end, the comedian has recaptured his self-esteem, gotten Melina back, but no sooner does he see another pretty aspirant for theatrical glory then he tells her: "I have a variety company. You're very pretty . . ."

"I try to love everything in life," Fellini told Samuels in reference to the film's subject, "not only what we usually consider proper, honest, charming. I always like to show both sides of a thing. . . . The ideal and disillusioning sides of theater are two faces of a single truth. Both represent man."

VI

DURING the early postwar period, Michelangelo Antonioni, made a series of short documentary films, among them one that dealt with the *fotoromanzi* (photo romances) so wildly popular among the less literate elements of the Italian populace. They began as strips in newspapers, similar to comic strips except that photographs replaced the drawings. Dialogue was enclosed in balloons, as in cartoons. When published in book form, they sold millions of copies and the people who posed for the characters in the strips became stars of a sort. Antonioni's documentary was titled *L'amorosa menzogna* (*The Loving Lie*), and when shown at Venice in 1948 it won him a Silver Ribbon. He then thought of expanding the subject into a feature film and approached producer Carlo Ponti with the idea. Ponti was taken with it, and went to Fellini and Pinelli, who were to develop the subject into a story and screenplay, which Antonioni would direct as his first full-length film.

The title of the would-be film was *Lo sceicco bianco* (*The White Sheik*)—the hero of the photo-novel—but it lacked a story other than its basis, those female fans who identified romantically with the heroes of the strips.

"For weeks," Pinelli said, "we kept looking for ways to make a story out of it. We simply didn't know how to develop it. One day, the two of us sat in the Borghese Gardens, near the Casina della Rosa, talking about everything but the subject we were supposed to write, when I suddenly thought of a young couple who come to Rome and want to meet 'the White Sheik.' Fellini said immediately, 'Yes, and it all has to happen in one day.' A little later, out of nowhere, he added, 'she also wants to see the Pope.' "

This was enough to get them to work drafting the story, with additional ramifications, into script form, and giving it to both Ponti and Antonioni. Antonioni didn't like it. Ponti wasn't sure whether he liked it or not, and eventually he and Antonioni parted company over it. Ponti took the script to Lattuada who, still suffering from the financial ills caused by *Variety Lights,* decided against it. Fellini, by this time fond of the story, took it around to several producers in the hope, according to one source, that he would be able to direct it himself. This contradicts Fellini's own version, which has it that the script passed from Ponti to another producer and then to Luigi Rovere. "I didn't decide to become a director," he said. "It was the somewhat imprudent faith of Rovere that pushed me into it. He decided that I had to do the picture."

It would appear, though, that the first version is closer to the truth, since one of the obstacles Fellini had to overcome was his absolute insistence that a favorite actor of his, Alberto Sordi, be the one to play the White Sheik, even though Sordi was regarded by producers as unpopular with the movie-going public.

Sordi has said that he had known Fellini since 1940, when they met in a snack bar, and that "we were in the same class in school, and soldiers in Rome on leave together." Since Fellini almost never attended classes—although he did hang around the university a bit when Giulietta was acting there—and had never been a soldier, Sordi may have been confused. What impressed Fellini about him was his mimicking ability. On stage and screen he usually played swindlers and racketeers with a nasty flair. Producers couldn't see him in a role that would be attractive to the public.

Rovere, however, sold on Fellini, was willing to go along with Sordi in the role of a photo-novel hero (though ultimately a pathetic buffoon in "real life"), but balked when Fellini wanted Peppino De Filippo for the role of Ivan Cavalli, the husband of the young woman who idolizes her White Sheik. De Filippo had not advanced his career by playing Checco in the ill-fated *Variety Lights.*

Fellini went looking again and found his "husband" by chance when he happened to wander into a screening room at Cine-città. As he stopped to watch the cut of a film being shown, Fellini saw the man he was searching for: Leopoldo Trieste, not a professional actor but a well-known writer. Fellini was able to sell Trieste to Rovere, and he also cast a young actress, Brunella Bovo, as the wife, Wanda Cavalli. Fellini gave Giulietta the smallish part of an ingenuous prostitute he named Cabiria.

Rovere, wanting to take as few chances as possible with a relatively untried director, put Fellini together with Enzo Provenzale, a capable production supervisor who had often worked with the skilled and precise Pietro Germi. "Through an excess of affection," said Fellini, "Rovere would have wanted me to become another Germi at once. And I, in the meantime, couldn't sleep at night."

Ennio Flaiano, who had been called to consult on the script for *Variety Lights,* was brought in again to help with the final stages of the screenplay, and filming of *The White Sheik* began at the seacoast town of Fregene in October of 1951. The story involves a young provincial couple who come to Rome for their honeymoon, which is scheduled to include a visit with the bridegroom's relatives and an audience with the Pope. But hardly are they established in their hotel room when the newlywed Wanda slips off to try to meet her beloved Fernando Rivoli, who is the White Sheik of her favorite photo-novel. Almost before she realizes it, she is being transported to a beach at Fregene, where photographing of the strip is under way. It was here, well along in the story, that Fellini was to make his debut as a director.

Wanda by now has been taken by the "sheik" out to sea on a "pirate ship"—actually an old scow—and Fellini's first scenes were to be shot on the water. One of his favorite tales is of what happened on that day.

"One morning I found myself on a small boat which, having left the pier, was on its way to a motor fishing boat that was carrying the cast and crew of *The White Sheik.* They were waiting for me, the director, to start shooting. I had said good-by to Giulietta, just before dawn, with the same trepidation a schoolboy has when he is about to take his exams. I even went to church, attempting a prayer.

On the road to Ostia, one of my tires blew out. The troupe had already embarked. And down there, in the sea, I saw my destiny. I was about to shoot a very complicated scene between Alberto Sordi and Brunella Bovo. As I approached the fishing boat, I saw the faces of the workmen, the lights already on. I kept repeating to myself: 'What will I do now?' I didn't remember anything of the film. All I wanted was to escape. But as soon as I set foot on that fishing boat I was giving orders, commanding this one and that one, looking in the camera viewfinder—without knowing anything, without knowing what I wanted. In the few minutes between the pier and the boat I had become a demanding, self-conscious, capricious director with all the defects and all the good qualities that I had always envied in real directors."

There followed scenes in the studio and in Rome (Wanda, disillusioned with her sheik, and filled with guilt over her abandonment of her husband, tries to drown herself in the Tiber, except that the water is too shallow). Filming wound up on schedule in December 1951. The editing took until March, at which time Fellini, understandably keyed up, asked Rossellini to look at the cut. "During the projection," Rossellini commented, "I was in the grip of a thousand feelings because I saw on the screen Fellini as I had known him intimately for many years. I felt old and disturbed because he seemed so young."

Fellini hoped that his first sole-directed film would be shown at the Cannes Film Festival in May 1952. The procedure was for a selection committee, made up of film critics, to choose the four official entries.

One member of the selection committee was Angelo Solmi, who wrote: "I met Fellini for the first time and spoke to him. He was leaning against a radiator in a corner, half hidden, with his great head of ruffled black hair. As they took their places none of the members . . . guessed that this young man was destined to revolutionize the Italian cinema. Nothing particularly recommended Fellini to us. [*The White Sheik*] was one of many films to be viewed out of a sense of duty." Solmi confirmed that films such as Castellani's *Two Cents Worth of Hope*, Lattuada's *The Overcoat*, and Vittorio De Sica's *Umberto D* "were [already] destined for Cannes."

Following the critics' viewing of *The White Sheik* a verbal battle erupted over the film's merits. Some thought it showed originality and directorial promise. Others saw little of worth in it. The supporters of Fellini won out, however, and the film was selected as the fourth Italian entry at Cannes.

Fellini, six weeks later, was packing his bags for the trip to Cannes when he was told that the selection of his film had been cancelled and another put in its place. Swallowing his disappointment, he tried again—submitting the film to the selection board for the Venice festival, to be held in early September. This time, the Fellini supporters held fast, and *The White Sheik* was shown at Venice, where during an afternoon screening it generated laughter and applause. Fellini assumed his film was a success, but the reviews the next morning were unanimously harsh to the point of sadism. It seemed as though the critics had banded together to cut the film down. One wrote that Fellini had "not the slightest aptitude for cinema direction." When the jury voted its awards, there was not one for *The White Sheik*.

Sordi's unpopularity may have been a reason for the poor critical reception, although politics was the more likely reason, since the air was rife with arguments about what directions neorealism ought to be taking. *The White Sheik*, with its humor, its light-hearted satire, its skillful cross-cutting between the adventures of Wanda and those of her husband as he searches for her, was not in the prevailing mode. As time has gone by, what has become even clearer is that the critics simply missed the boat on this minor masterpiece. In the files of the Centro Sperimentale, Rome's film school and research repository, there are few reviews of *The White Sheik* to be found. Only one gives it serious and approving attention, and that one was written by the friendly Massimo Mida.

Pinelli still feels that Sordi's presence in the film (in spite of his fine performance) was what hurt it most. Beyond that, "The film," he said, "was badly distributed by a small company, and we held the producer to blame for this. In any case, nobody went to see it and, outside of the Venice coverage, almost no one reviewed it."

After dismal box-office results in Rome, Milan, and a few

other cities, the film was withdrawn. The distributor went into bank-
ruptcy, a plague of legal suits followed, and it was not until several
years later that rights to the film were reacquired and it was put into
limited circulation. "Perhaps," Fellini said mildly, "it was ahead of
its time. It's an ironic story, and Italians don't like irony—sarcasm
and buffoonery, but not irony."

Because seldom seen, *The White Sheik* has rarely been
treated by critics outside of Italy. Bosley Crowther in the *New
York Times* termed it "just a practice swing" for Fellini while, with
much hindsight, John Simon in 1971 called it "an early masterpiece."

Even after so dismal a failure, however, Fellini was not without support. There were those film critics who had thought his movie
worthy of presentation at Cannes and Venice, and there were producers who regarded him as talented. And, while Fellini may not
have been fully aware of it, he had brought together the beginnings
of an ensemble that included Tullio Pinelli and Ennio Flaiano; Otello
Martelli, the cameraman; his actress wife, Giulietta Masina; and a
new addition, composer Nino Rota.

During his screenwriting days for Lux Film, Fellini emerged
from the studio one day and saw a small man, wearing a hat, standing in the middle of the block. Fellini knew his face, knew the man
to be a musician, and stopped for a moment to chat. Was he waiting
for someone? Fellini asked. Yes, Nino Rota said, he was waiting for
a bus. No, Fellini assured him, the bus did not stop at this particular spot.

"Rota," said Fellini in recounting the incident, "is a man
well-known for his absent-mindedness, and he paid no attention to
my warning." Rota assured him that the bus would indeed come by
and stop right there. "The fact is," said Fellini, "that Rota was
gifted with visionary powers. The bus did come along and stopped
exactly where we were standing. I was so surprised that I got on the
bus and traveled part way with him. Some years later, when making
The White Sheik, I called on him for the music, and from that time
on I never thought of making a film without him." Rota, it may be

noted, was, when they met, already well-known as a serious composer as well as a writer of film scores.

Fellini, even after two setbacks—with *Variety Lights* and
The White Sheik—was not discouraged. If anything, the meanness
of the criticism acted as a goad and made him more aggressive. It
also left him with "a positive resentment," which he attributed to
his origins in Romagna where "the man who has been laughed at
goes arrogantly ahead." In any case, Fellini already had other ideas,
which he had communicated to Pinelli. Two years earlier, while filming location scenes for *Variety Lights*, he had driven into the countryside, and had noticed an odd pair of vagabonds camping in a
field. Fellini paused to watch as the woman stirred soup in a pot
over a fire, while the man stood apart from her, waiting for his supper. There was no exchange of words or gestures between them, and
Fellini was struck by their inability to communicate. Not long after
this, he and Giulietta took a brief vacation in the Italian Alps, and
they came across a similar gypsylike couple on a snow-covered road.
The woman was patiently helping the man push an overladen cart.

Coincidentally, Pinelli saw a similar couple while on a trip
north to his home country not far from Turin. He had noticed how
often one came across such pairs; some made poor livings putting
on performances or doing tricks at county fairs. When he met again
with Fellini, he said, "I have an idea."

"I also have an idea," Fellini said. "Who should speak
first?"

Astonishingly, they had independently come up with virtually identical notions. But also in their minds was a tale they had
considered writing and then abandoned, about a medieval knight
who would have adventures wandering throughout Italy and, in the
end, die alone and forsaken in the lonely countryside. They had
worked on the story long enough to do research in libraries on life
during the Middle Ages, and Fellini had already developed an almost mystical feeling about rural Italy from his work with Rossellini.

After he and Pinelli had done an updated treatment of the
story they titled *La Strada*, he took it to Luigi Rovere, his producer
of contract. Fellini was pleased when he saw Rovere wipe away tears
as he read the tale of a simpleminded peasant girl who is purchased

by an itinerant strong man named Zampanò. "You like it, then?" he said. The producer's mood changed instantly. "As a film this wouldn't make a lira. It's not cinema. It's more like literature. It should be written as a book, a novel."

Both Pinelli and Fellini had agreed that Giulietta should play the role of the timid girl, called Gelsomina. Rovere, however, ridiculed the notion that Giulietta, then thirty years old, could play the part. His advice to Fellini was to drop the project; there wasn't a producer anywhere who would be willing to finance it.

Fellini, now needing a sympathetic producer and also money to live on, found both in a Venetian, Lorenzo Pegoraro, who had liked *The White Sheik*. Pegoraro offered him an advance on the condition that Fellini sign a three-picture contract. Fellini first offered him the *La Strada* treatment, but the producer would not agree to Giulietta's playing Gelsomina. Fellini then turned to exploring other ideas with Pinelli and Flaiano. The three would meet and discuss concepts that might prove fruitful, and it was Pinelli who came up with a notion the other two liked: the pleasures and frustrations of growing up in a provincial town. "We found," said Pinelli, "that we had a host of stories to tell," and all three had a good time as they regaled each other with tales about their youth until, growing serious, they decided they had a viable film subject.

Pinelli's youthful experiences, because of his aristocratic heritage, differed from those of the other two, who had middle-class backgrounds. Flaiano had been raised in Pescara, in the Abruzzi region, and he had his own escapades to contribute. "Nevertheless the spirit of the script we wrote was Fellini's," Pinelli emphasized.

The story they developed concerned five young middle-class men who had grown up together in a town on the Adriatic coast. Fellini took the film's title from a memory of being called a *vitellone* by an elderly woman expressing disapproval of one of his pranks. In the regional dialect the word meant a veal, or calf, and was used to refer to callow youths. In explaining the fuller meaning of *I Vitelloni*, Fellini wrote: "They are the unemployed of the middle class, mothers' pets. They shine during the holiday season, and waiting for it takes up the rest of the year."

The five youthful characters range in age between nineteen

and the early twenties. A good-looking rake, Fausto, gets a girl-friend pregnant, and is forced by his father to marry her; worse, he must go to work in the family shop. Alberto, an immature day-dreamer, owes his support to his mother and sister. The intellectual Leopoldo thinks of himself as a budding dramatist, while Riccardo has unfulfilled ambitions to sing and act. Moraldo is the youngest of the group, the most sensitive, and the most appealing. The town, with its provincialism, its middle-class culture level, is too narrow for him. He is the only one of the group who leaves the town for an unknown future in Rome.

Pegoraro liked the story when it was given to him in outline form, and Fellini, with his collaborators, quickly turned out a finished script. To Pegoraro's dismay, however, Fellini insisted on once more using Alberto Sordi (as Alberto), and compounded the problem by casting Leopoldo Trieste (he of the failed *Variety Lights*) as Leopoldo.

"There is not a single big name in this film," Pegoraro complained. "You'll make another commercial disaster. Sordi makes people run away. Leopoldo Trieste is a nobody. Meet me half way— bring in a name."

"He really meant it," Fellini said later. "He wanted [Vittorio] De Sica. Pegoraro begged me to go and talk to him. He hit his head with his hands. I went looking for De Sica, who was making *Terminal Station* (*Indiscretion of an American Wife*)."

The part Pegoraro had in mind for De Sica was Natali, an aging ham actor who, while appearing to be interested in a playlet written by the intellectual Leopoldo, is actually out to seduce him.

Since De Sica was busy filming, an appointment was made for after midnight in a wagon-lit that sat on an unused track far from the waiting room of the station. Fellini, who obviously did not want to embarrass the great director and actor while he was alive, told a journalist, Giovanni Grazzini, about the encounter years later.

"De Sica signaled me to come in. I had never seen him up close before, and I have kept intact the soft and silvery fascination of his personality. He was extremely kind, kindliness being a profession, a philosophy, for him. In the darkness of the compartment, facing him, I told him tremulously about the part I wished to offer to him. A great dramatic actor, I said, who had once been famous, but was now forced to make compromises, who had come down to playing parts in a traveling variety company. . . ."

Fellini explained further that the actor comes to a town where there is a young man who dreams of entering the literary world, and who asks the actor if he may read to him from one of his plays.

"De Sica," said Fellini, "smiled understandingly, approvingly, and murmured something about young people. Encouraged, I went on with the story to the point where the old fellow reveals his true intentions to the innocent young man. De Sica continued smiling in his kindly way. But all of a sudden he understood, he peered at me, surprised and perplexed. . . . 'You mean he had something else in mind? Some other goal?' I nodded my head, embarrassed. He looked out the window. There was a silence. 'But,' he said, with a serious look at me, 'is he human?'

" 'Very,' I said.

" 'Because it is possible there is a great deal of humanity in such people.' "

"Oh, yes," Fellini agreed.

The meeting was interrupted by a crew member who came to tell De Sica that the lighting was ready for his scene. De Sica got up, adjusted his jacket, and offered Fellini his hand. "Good," he said, "that sounds like a nice character. I like it. Make an appointment with my lawyer to talk about it. But, I warn you, *human!*"

When it came to actually rewriting the part to conform with De Sica's image, Fellini found that it forced the story out of balance. "De Sica," he said, "was too nice, too fascinating, too distracting for the character. They might even have disapproved of Leopoldo when the actor tries to force him into an isolated place!" Ultimately, the part of Natali was given to Achille Majeroni.

The arguments about casting persisted, as plans for the production went forward. Among Fellini's casting choices was his own younger brother, Riccardo, who had ambitions of becoming an actor, and who was, said Fellini, naturally fitted to the role, being at the time something of a *vitellone* himself. Franco Interlenghi was given the part of Moraldo, and Franco Fabrizi was cast as Fausto.

A start date was set for early December 1952, even though Pegoraro was still attempting to pacify his financial backers—a group of Florentine businessmen and a French-based production company—all as concerned as he was about the unpromising nature of the cast.

So doubtful was Pegoraro, Pinelli said, that on the day filming was to begin, with the finances irrevocably committed, Pegoraro locked himself in a bathroom and refused to come out. By then, the company and crew were in Viterbo, a town near Rome with an atmosphere not unlike that of Rimini. Finally, Pegoraro came out of the bathroom and the first scenes were shot. Beach scenes took place at Ostia and interiors in a Florence studio, in deference to Pegoraro's financial associates.

Although Fellini went nowhere near Rimini for any of the scenes, the film continues to be identified with that town. Fellini denied that he had Rimini—neither the town nor its people—in mind for the story, in spite of the obvious resemblances between his own experiences and memories and many of the scenes in the film. Indeed, some observers wondered why Fellini did not shoot the film in Rimini. Friends in his home town have said that Fellini might have felt embarrassed at returning to Rimini as head of a film production. The friends he had grown up with were still there and living more provincial lives. On the other hand, shooting the film relatively close to Rome was far more convenient.

When the film was completed, Pegoraro and Fellini began to search for a distributor. "We went around," said Fellini, "begging for rentals like desperate men. I remember some terrifying screenings. Those present would, at the end of a showing, cast gloomy looks at me, and then shake hands mournfully with Pegoraro."

At one such screening, the head of a distribution firm entered the screening room bursting with energy, his face freshly bronzed from a sun lamp. In the small but comfortable room, the executive seated himself and put his feet up on the back of a seat, insisting generously that Fellini and Pegoraro follow suit. "The best position," he said, for viewing a film.

While the showing went on, the executive, with a telephone at his elbow, made brief calls. In the middle of the film, there was a knock at the door and two assistants entered bearing a large statue of a nude woman. "You're an artist," the executive said to Fellini, "what do you think of it?" After he came up with an answer, there was another knock, and a secretary came in with the mail.

Yet, at a certain moment, the film seemed to interest the distributor, for he suddenly turned to Fellini and asked him what kind of car Riccardo, Fellini's brother, was driving in the film. After being told the make, the distributor described its virtues. The film over, he took Pegoraro by the arm, led him out, and explained why he had decided not to distribute it.

Fellini, still without a distributor, submitted *I Vitelloni* to the selection committee for the Venice Festival, to be held at the end of the 1953 summer. The film was readily selected, and when shown it received an ovation from the audience. A Silver Lion was awarded for "its felicitous portrayal of society in the Italian provinces." The critical reaction was favorable, too, with those of the left firm in their support because of what they regarded as the film's adherence to neorealist principles.

There was, however, less faith in its audience-drawing power, and when a distributor finally agreed to take *I Vitelloni* on, the terms were for less than its cost of production. One liability, the distributor said, was the ambiguous title; another was the presence of Sordi. He suggested *Vagabonds!* as a better title, but Fellini refused to change it, and Pegoraro saved the day by offering to throw in two other films with more commercial appeal. But now the distributor insisted that Sordi's name be left out of the promotional material.

And more. The film's weakness, the distributor said, was its ending. Too dreary, nothing really happened at the end, except that a boy left his friends behind to go to Rome. "He actually asked for more scenes to be shot," Pinelli said. "This was his idea: toward the end of the story, an oil well would be discovered in the town. The young men would become rich, and the film would end with all of them going off to their work, singing happily. He told this to us in utter seriousness, and all Fellini and I could do was to stand there and laugh helplessly."

I Vitelloni, belying all doubts about its commercial appeal, was a success in Italy, and went on to distribution in other countries—the first time this had happened with a Fellini film. In France, particularly, the critics reacted with enthusiasm, seeing in the film a universe both visual and poetic. And they read into it much more: symbols having to do with the sea, costumes, the mask, and the naked face. "Fellini plays on a deserted piazza at nighttime," Geneviève Agel wrote. "It symbolizes solitude, the emptiness that follows communal joy, the bleak torpor that succeeds the swarming crowd; there are always papers lying around like so many reminders of what the day and life have left behind." Mme Agel, for a time, became Fellini's favorite critic.

Although others regarded it more simply as a satiric portrayal of small-town life mingling humor, drama, and social observation, the film ultimately came to take on a greater significance. In terms of style and technical competence, *I Vitelloni* was a leap forward from *The White Sheik*. Fellini was able to handle the often divergent adventures of the five major characters so that the stories blended smoothly into a whole. Not one of those characters resembles the others, yet they symbolically and literally hang well together as a group. To further tie them together, Fellini's voice is heard on the sound track with comments on what occurs.

If one segment impressed critics more than others, it was that of the masquerade ball at which Sordi, as Alberto, dressed and made up as a woman, dances clumsily with male partners, and with a huge empty papier-mâché head. Bondanella finds Fellini here exemplifying his concern with character as both "mask and face." The work becomes, in a sense, an unmasking operation. "The masks worn by the characters as they act in their socially defined roles are torn off to reveal something of the intimate personality beneath," Bondanella explains. As Sordi in *The White Sheik* is unmasked in this way, so he is again, more subtly, in *I Vitelloni*. "The female costume," says Bondanella, "underlines the effeminate qualities that set him apart from his strong and self-reliant sister. No other image in Fellini's works visualizes so clearly his interest in the clash of mask and face than the surrealistic dance between a man in drag and an empty mask." When the ball ends, the dance hall seems smaller and drearier to Alberto's dazed eyes, and he comes to a self-hating realization of his emptiness. Sordi, despite the worries of the producers and distributors, won high praise for his performance, and his career soared as a result.

It is with the early morning light when the young men wander to the sea, that Fellini seems to emphasize their sense of isolation and frustration. It is at the seashore that Leopoldo learns that the interest the old actor shows in his work is merely a cover for the sexual conquest he has in mind. Fellini turns the actor, Natali, into an almost sinister figure of sham and decay. It is quite understandable why he found it necessary to reject the gentle and gentlemanly De Sica for the role.

Few critics seemed aware, at the time, of the importance of Nino Rota's score. One exception was John Simon who, seeing the film in the United States three years after its release in Italy, regarded Rota's music as one "of the most brilliant features of the film." Of its two main themes, "the first is a soaring, romantic melody that can be made to express nostalgia, love, and the pathos of existence." The other is a kind of carefree march. "Slowed down," Simon wrote, "it becomes lugubrious; with eerie figurations in the woodwinds it turns sinister. The quicksilver changes in the music support the changing moods of the story."

Indeed, the collaboration between Fellini and Rota was now a close one. Fellini had no instrumental talents at all, but he knew how to whistle and sing, and he would come up with a semblance of the themes he wanted. Rota would build on these, and add others that came from his intuitive understanding of Fellini's musical needs.

While waiting for the release of *I Vitelloni*, Fellini occupied himself with another and less taxing project. Cesare Zavattini, a principal proponent of neorealist theory, asked him to join a group of people who were making a "cinema news magazine." In Zavattini's view, "the true function of the cinema is not to tell fables." Directors in search of reality, Zavattini believed, should be closer to reporters in their methods. For his "news magazine" he enlisted directors such as Lattuada, Antonioni, and Dino Risi, each of whom was to make an episode on the general theme of *L'amore in città* (*Love in the City*)—as the film was eventually titled. Viewers were told that the stories were being related by the actual participants in those events.

Fellini's experiment in pure realism was called *Un'agenzia matrimoniale* (*A Matrimonial Agency*) and, as might be expected, it dealt with an agency finding marriage partners for applicants. A journalist investigating such agencies poses as an intermediary for a would-be client who has a rather strange problem: he believes himself to be a werewolf. In discussing the man and his problem with a woman anxious for marriage, the newspaperman finds her quite willing not only to marry the fellow but to put up with the possibility of violence. Although appearing to be sympathetic to the woman's marital ambitions, the journalist's main satisfaction is that he has found himself a good story.

Fellini told Zavattini that there really was such a matrimonial agency in the building he lived in, and that he had come across exactly that story. Zavattini was pleased when Fellini showed him the first cut. "Now do you see," he said to Fellini, "how reality is even more fantastic than the most unbelievable fantasy?" Fellini, however, eventually admitted that he made up the story out of whole cloth. "I wanted to play a joke on Zavattini," he confessed, but he was also annoyed with those critics who sometimes accused him of betraying neorealism by inventing "a nonexistent world."

Although the quality of the individual segments was inconsistent, a good many critics took *Love in the City* seriously, and as a sign that cinema was moving in a direction that eventually came to be labeled *cinéma vérité*. When the film was shown at Venice, Fellini was complimented for his courage in putting such a real-life episode on the screen. The actors he used were film students, except for the journalist, who was portrayed by a professional actor. The film came out only a month after the release of *I Vitelloni*, and if notable for anything, it was for the contributions of two directors who, in less than a decade, were to become world famous—namely, Antonioni and Fellini.

VII

THE success of *I Vitelloni* made it possible for Fellini to reactivate the project he felt closest to—*La Strada*—even if it meant securing the financing himself. Pegoraro was more than willing to do another film with him, but not *La Strada*, so long as Giulietta was to play the part of Gelsomina. But why not continue the adventures of the "vitelloni"? Fellini took the suggestion seriously enough to write an extended treatment that would follow Moraldo, the youth who left his provincial town to pursue a career in Rome. This, written with Pinelli during the latter months of 1953, became *Moraldo in the City*, which was never filmed because, according to Pinelli: "He did not like the thought of following *I Vitelloni* with another film that would seem to be trading on the success of the earlier one. And he was stubborn, too, about making *La Strada*, which had now been hanging about for two years."

Fellini, in his headstrong way, moved ahead with his plans for *La Strada*, assuming that sooner or later backers would be found. His wife had a small part in a film being made at Cinecittà with Anthony Quinn and, one evening, he drove there to pick her up. Filming was still proceeding on the set and, as he sat beside Giulietta, he said to her: "That's the one. That's the face I had in mind for Zampanò."

When the scene was finished, Giulietta went over to Quinn and asked him to meet her husband. Fellini had neither seen nor heard of Quinn before—although he was already an established ac-

tor—and Quinn had no idea who Fellini was. He listened, half incredulous, while Fellini announced that in the movie he was about
to direct Quinn would play a starring role.

"Something about a strongman and a half-witted girl," he
later told a writer, Thomas Meehan. "I thought he was a little bit
crazy, and I told him I wasn't interested in the picture, but he kept
hounding me for days."

Fellini had been searching for a nonprofessional to play
Zampanò, who performed his feats of strength in village squares, at
country fairs, and circuses. He tested several such strongmen, but
none seemed right. Once fixed on Quinn, he kept after him while
still negotiating with producers for money.

When Carlo Ponti read the story he was captivated by it,
and almost at once signed a contract to produce it with Dino de Laurentiis as his partner. Ignoring Fellini's stated desire to cast Giulietta
as the girl, they proposed Silvana Mangano (a major star since her
earthy role in *Bitter Rice*), and Burt Lancaster as the brutish strongman. Fellini flatly refused. Anthony Quinn, all unknowing, became
a bone of contention, too; the producers felt he was wrong for the
part.

Quinn, still unsigned, received an invitation to have dinner
with Ingrid Bergman and Roberto Rossellini. After dinner they
screened *I Vitelloni*. "I was thunderstruck by it," Quinn said. "I
told them the film was a masterpiece, and that the same director was
the man who had been chasing me for weeks." Rossellini, naturally,
was able to fill Quinn in on just who Fellini was and the extent of his
talents. The next day, Quinn telephoned Fellini and told him he was
ready to do the picture.

"Fine," said Fellini, if Quinn's version is accurate, "we start
tomorrow."

We can gather, from a letter Fellini wrote to the critic Angelo Solmi, something of the time sequence. In the letter, dated
September 17, 1953, he stated: "Now *La Strada* has finally taken
shape. I shall begin it at the end of October, at some risk, because
the capital is small and uncertain. But I must begin, come what may."

In succeeding weeks Quinn came in, and Ponti and de Laurentiis became the producers, although, according to Quinn, with a

ridiculously low budget. Fellini at this point brought in Flaiano, who had this to say about his script contributions: "My job was to say derogatory things about the film for three months. I condemned a vagueness of atmosphere, certain affectations in the characters, and I insisted that the story, though very beautiful, should come down to earth and that the symbolism be integrated with the narrative."

Angelo Solmi read the first version of *La Strada* and found that while it contained most of the themes of the final script, it was more somber and legendary in character. And Gelsomina was closer to sheer madness than she is in the actual film. Flaiano's redoing of the script did indeed bring the story down to earth, but without lessening its poetic and at times mystical qualities. The first script had Gelsomina taking up a flute and making mysterious music with it. But in the film, she is taught to play it by a third important character, Il Matto (The Fool), a slightly mad, whimsical, and almost saintly high-wire performer.

For this character, Fellini approached Richard Basehart, an American actor then living in Rome with his wife, the actress Valentina Cortesa. Basehart had met Fellini through her, and accepted an invitation to have lunch with him. During the lunch, Fellini told the actor about his preparations for *La Strada*, and said there was a good part in the film for him, a character called Il Matto.

"What kind of part is it?" Basehart asked.

"He's a kind of clown."

"Me, for a clown? Why?"

Basehart had most recently starred in *Fourteen Hours*, which had had a great success in Italy.

"Because," said Fellini, "if you did what you did in *Fourteen Hours* you can do anything."

Basehart was quickly seduced into playing the role, the seduction being required because of the low salary Fellini was able to offer. But he, too, had seen *I Vitelloni*, and had thought it magnificent. In addition, he was immensely attracted to Fellini as a personality. "It was his zest for living," Basehart said, "and his humor."

Production on the film began in early December 1953 and, shortly after, had to be halted when Giulietta dislocated her ankle during a scene with Quinn. Then Quinn went into *Attila the Hun,* a De Laurentiis epic (which may have been the underlying reason behind his objection to Quinn for *La Strada*). When Giulietta was ready for work again, Quinn was already filming *Attila.* Fellini proposed that he work in *La Strada* in the morning, and the remainder of the day in *Attila.* "Impossible," Quinn said. But he was persuaded to do exactly that, and he found himself getting up at three thirty in the morning, driving from Rome to whatever location Fellini had chosen for the day, then getting into his costume, having himself made up, and being ready for shooting in time for the bleak early light that Fellini wanted. At ten thirty he would jump into his car and race back to the set of *Attila.*

"As soon as I started working for Fellini," Quinn told Thomas Meehan, "I realized he was far from crazy, that he was, in fact, the most talented, sensitive and perceptive director I'd ever worked for. He drove me mercilessly, making me do scene after scene over and over again until he got what he wanted. I learned more about film acting in three months with Fellini than I'd learned in all the movies I'd made before then."

Quinn gave an example of Fellini's rigorousness at an American Film Institute student seminar: "We had to select a box in which I carried cigarette butts. An assistant brought about one hundred boxes, but Fellini wasn't satisfied with any of them. As for me, any of the boxes would have been satisfactory to carry the butts in, but not Federico. He had a very specific idea. Finally after looking at some 500 boxes he selected one."

He was finicky, too, about costuming. Giulietta did not like the tramplike clothes he chose for her. "She likes to wear nice clothes, to dress like a lady," Fellini said. "I had to persuade her to wear the costume." And, as Quinn remembered it, Fellini helped her develop the embarrassed little smiles, the waiflike expressions that were to make her famous.

Giulietta complained: "You're so nice and sweet to the others in the cast. Why are you so hard on me?"

Later on, though, she had reason to be grateful.

Quinn had reason, too, for the performance Fellini got from him raised him to a new level as an actor. "Giulietta and I did a scene in a piazza," he said. "She was supposed to be flying and I, with a cork in my nose, was supposed to shoot her. We were surrounded by about 2,000 people who had come to see the scene— Fellini was using them, photographing everybody—and I was so thrilled, with 2,000 people watching me act that I really turned it on full juice. Everybody applauded when I finished the scene, and I thought I had done my job. I was in bed later when, long after midnight, the telephone rang, and it was Fellini. 'Tony,' he said, 'The scene you did today was all wrong. You see, you're supposed to be a bad, a terrible actor, but the people watching applauded you. They should have laughed at you. So in the morning we do it again.' "

Quinn remembered Fellini's facing monumental problems. Because of the skimpy budget, he had to improvise solutions. There was to be snow on the roads for one important scene, but a rescheduling meant the scene had to be shot with spring already arrived. Sacks of chalk were used to cover the road, and because there was not enough chalk, white sheets had to be borrowed from villagers as a bed for the chalk. The cameraman was due on another film, and he had to depart. Luckily, Fellini's favorite cameraman, Otello Martelli, was available.

Over the years a myth arose about Fellini's improvising from a loosely developed script. It is true that when he submitted a story to a producer it was usually in treatment form, which is to say it read more like a narrative than a script broken down into shots, set descriptions, dialogue, and camera movements. But Fellini's shooting scripts were unusually long and filled with notes that came from careful research. The *La Strada* script, Quinn said, was close to 600 pages, with every shot and every camera angle detailed. On the other hand, Fellini never hesitated to change, add, or substitute when seized with a new idea.

There were periods when Quinn was simply not available to work, and the ensuing delays strained the budget to the breaking point. Fellini's arrangement with the producers was that, if he ran over, he would be responsible for any excess, as well as losing any profit potential. Quinn became aware of Fellini's troubles, and went to ask De Laurentiis for the money that was needed to complete the film. As one account has it, Ponti and De Laurentiis took Fellini to a café and told him not to worry about any debts to them. "Let's pretend they were a joke. Buy us a coffee and we'll forget about them."

More recently, Quinn said: "There was more to it. There were two additional scenes that had to be shot for *Attila*. In exchange for the money to finish his film, Fellini had to direct those scenes." Scholars of the future may well have to search through *Attila* for the distinctive Fellini touch.

Richard Basehart, too, was stimulated by Fellini's working methods. "It was not so much what he told you," Basehart said, "but how he opened you up and gave you a sense of freedom." During off hours, Fellini could be an enjoyable companion. "He was always telling stories, not about his film projects, but notions that came from his imagination and curiosity. He was fascinated by ancient Rome, and had ideas about what it would have been like to live then. What it would have been like to be a gentleman of that time living in the country."

On Sundays, Basehart and Fellini often took long drives, looking for just the right place to eat. "He loved food," Basehart said, "and liked to find new and different kinds of places. He got that, I think, from his good friend Fabrizi, who was a great cook himself. We would enter a restaurant, and if Fellini saw too many people, or didn't care for the menu, off we would go looking for another. One Sunday we tried six restaurants before Fellini was willing to stay in one. There were times when the place would be no more than a simple farmhouse, but the food would turn out to be wonderful.

"One Sunday we drove all the way to Rimini. Fellini wanted to show his home town to me, because I had admired his *I Vitelloni* so much. Rimini, his memories of it, were embodied in that picture whether he was willing or not to admit it. We walked out on a pier— it was a misty, rather chilly day—and we looked back at the town through a twilight haze. Fellini said: 'Now, do you understand?' "

In the view of Angelo Solmi, Gelsomina "is an absolutely new figure in the history of the cinema and Italian culture. . . .

The peasant girl of *The Miracle* was only a crude, remote image of her. . . . Through a multitude of unfulfilled desires Gelsomina is a martyr to loneliness and to lack of love and charity. She is the complete expression of Fellinian ethics at their highest point."

Regard for *La Strada* has hardly lessened over the years. A very small minority find it a simple tale, with boring stretches, and some look upon it as a kind of adult fairy tale, but for most it is moving, often to the point of real tears.

Perhaps because its major characters are relatively uncomplicated, *La Strada* is on its surface deceptively simple. Gelsomina appears to be a peasant child-woman, "not quite right in the head," who is sold to the itinerant strongman Zampanò for 10,000 lire so she can help him in his act. Zampanò's previous assistant—also purchased—was Gelsomina's sister Rosa, who has died on the road. The "sale" of Gelsomina takes place near the seashore—the locale for both the beginning and end of the tale. Gelsomina is glimpsed wistfully regarding the sea before going off with Zampanò.

A short time later Gelsomina is roughly violated by Zampanò. Naive and innocent to the point of foolishness, she is also almost saintlike in her inchoate understanding of the sufferings of others, and in her undemanding loyalty. And she is a clown, too, deliciously and artlessly funny in her desire to please. In her ingenuous way she is attuned to nature; no sooner do she and Zampanò pause for a time in their travels than she plants tomato seeds.

The callous Zampanò picks up other women in her presence; when she won't steal for him he beats her. Yet she remains pathetically attached to him, her one anchor in her new world.

One of the film's strangest moments occurs when Gelsomina and Zampanò perform at a country wedding feast. After a time the two are invited to the farmhouse to have something to eat. Some children manage to get Gelsomina alone and they lead her through dim corridors to where an idiot boy is lying propped up in bed. She has only a moment to exchange an intense stare with the boy before a nun enters and chases her away.

The origin of the scene, Fellini said, was a recollection of the summers he had spent with his grandmother in Gambettola. On a

farm that he visited he discovered just such an idiot child, whose
peasant parents were ashamed and hid her from sight. The incident
made a great impression and stayed in his memory.

"I probably used it," he related, "to give Gelsomina an exact awareness of solitude. . . . Gelsomina, who ultimately is a creature who likes to be in the company of other people, and who wants
to take part in the singing and general gaiety, is led off by this host
of children . . . to see the sick boy. The apparition of this creature
who is so isolated, and a prey to delirium—and who thus has an extremely mysterious dimension—it seems to me that uniting him in
a close-up with Gelsomina, who comes right next to him and who
looks at him with curiosity, underlines with rather great suggestive
power Gelsomina's own solitude."

Because of her rough violation by Zampanò, the boy is, in
a way, an image of Gelsomina's exploitation and loneliness, and
their symbolic relationship is emphasized by Zampanò's taking up
with the farm woman who had offered them food. In the morning,
while Zampanò is still sleeping with his hostess, Gelsomina wanders
off and eventually encounters the tightrope performer, Il Matto, also
known as "the fool," who is with a traveling circus. Zampanò, with
Gelsomina, joins the same circus. Many have seen a "Christ symbolism" in the way Gelsomina looks upward at the "fool's" beatific face
as he balances above her, equipped with wings. Fellini hasn't always
taken kindly to certain interpretations of his films, but he did state,
in this case, that Il Matto represents Jesus.

And, if so, then by the end of the film he must be sacrificed,
the agent being Zampanò who, provoked by the mischievous "fool,"
viciously attacks and kills him. It is this final act of cruelty that
causes Gelsomina to retreat into herself and run away from Zampanò, who ultimately abandons her. Il Matto had taught her to play
a trumpet and, although she is gone, the little tune she plays, and
with which she is identified, persists, and many years later Zampanò
hears it. Someone is humming it: a woman, hanging sheets on a line.

"Where did you learn that tune?" he asks her.

"From a little creature my father found on the beach one
night," the woman answers. "She was always playing it on her trum-

pet. We took her in for a time, but she was always crying, and she never ate."

"What happened to her?" Zampanò wants to know.

"Oh, she died."

Zampanò's own decline, and his solitude, begin at this point, along with the realization, dim at first, that he loved and needed Gelsomina. The film, which began at the sea, ends there, with Zampanò stretched weeping on the sand.

The film, here sketched briefly, is laden with overtones that became more apparent with re-viewing. Some have cast doubt on Zampanò's seeming redemption; Gilbert Salachas, for one, felt that the man's sorrow was transitory. But Fellini said later on that *La Strada* was "the story of a man who discovers himself," and that though Gelsomina was his favorite of all the characters in his films, it was Zampanò he felt closest to.

On the evening of September 11, 1954, *La Strada* was shown at the Venice film festival. Fellini, having survived and surmounted all the vicissitudes of the film's production, was about ready to collapse from nervous exhaustion. The reception was reasonably warm, but not enthusiastic enough to hearten him. He sensed a division in the audience, signs that a critical battle was in the offing.

Dominique Delouche, a young French film-maker, was there that evening and "watched the film with mounting emotion, caused in part by the scandalous behavior of the audience, by its indifference, even its anger." She was convinced she had seen a masterpiece, and when she saw the Fellinis returning to their hotel she went to them and told them how strongly their film had affected her. "Fellini," she reported, "looked pale, and Giulietta was in tears." The encounter led to her becoming his apprentice and assistant—a relationship that lasted for five years.

La Strada was, however, rewarded with a Silver Lion; the major prize—the Golden Lion—went to Renato Castellani's more formal and quite beautiful *Romeo and Juliet*. Astonishing in retro-

spect is the fact that Giulietta Masina was awarded nothing at all
for her performance.

The Venice festival was turning more each year into a
political, ideological, and critical battleground, echoing the ferment
in the country generally. Films, thus, were not always judged strictly
on their artistic merits. Those who entered their films often needed
festival approval and awards for entry into the marketplace, and this
was particularly true for those films made with low budgets and
artistic aims.

Fellini found himself and his film in the middle of a battle
between conservative and church forces on the one hand, and the
ideological (Marxist) left on the other. Catholics saw *La Strada* as
a parable of Christian love, grace, and salvation, while leftist critics
deplored it as a departure from orthodox neorealism.

The most authoritative Marxist view was put forward by
Guido Aristarco, the editor of an influential film journal, *Cinema
Nuovo*, who accused Fellini of nothing less than bourgeois individ-
ualism. "He has gathered up and jealously preserved," Aristarco
wrote, "the subtlest poisons of the prewar literature. . . . He seeks
out his own emotions along the treacherous paths of suggestivism
and autobiographism, and mistakes agitation for an intense need
for poetic expression."

Fellini, finally, had enough of this sort of verbiage. He responded publicly with a *Letter to a Marxist Critic,* published in *Il
Contemporaneo*, and a credo of his own. The film, he wrote, "seeks
to realize the experience which is the most basic for opening up any
social prospect: the joint experience between man and man. . . .
Our trouble, as modern men, is loneliness, and this begins in the
very depth of our being. Only between man and man, I think, can
this solitude be broken, only through individual people can a kind
of message be passed, making them understand—almost discover—
the profound link between one person and the next.

"*La Strada* expresses something like this with the means
available to the cinema. Because it tries to show the supernatural
and personal communication between a man and a woman who
would seem by nature to be the least likely people to understand

each other, it has, I believe, been attacked by those who believe only in natural and political communication."

In this letter Fellini made clear his disassociation from neorealist doctrine as defined by the Marxist critics. "I do not believe in 'objectivity,' at least in the way you people believe in it, and cannot accept your ideas of neorealism which I feel do not fully capture, or really even impinge upon, the essence of the movement to which I have had the honor, since *Rome, Open City,* to belong."

The critical debate in which *La Strada* became a pawn extended beyond Italy's borders and became known as "the crisis of neorealism." Such critical hairsplitting was of little importance in the United States, where popular taste dictated success or failure. But in Italy the case was different. Critics helped develop audiences for the neorealist films, and they chose which films were represented at international festivals.

Peter Bondanella, in analyzing the films produced in Italy between 1945 and 1953, found that no more than 10 percent could be regarded as neorealist and that the majority of these were dismal box-office failures. By the time *La Strada* was shown, Hollywood films had flooded the Italian market, with little room for those serious works that adhered to the neorealist credo. Ironically, however, it was these same works that helped the Italian film industry as a whole. The luster they gained in international competition helped to open doors to the foreign market for the more ordinary and traditionally made films. It was here that *La Strada* played a key role.

First, the film became popular in its home country, aided immensely by Nino Rota's theme song that, when recorded, sold more than two million copies. In France, the critics rhapsodized over the film, and audiences flocked to the theaters. The same happened in country after country; Fellini and Masina were showered with awards and its producers with box-office gold. Fellini, of course, had given up his share in the film's financial returns.

La Strada provided audiences with a vision quite different from the kind of Italian suffering they had come to expect. Foreign interest in the Italian film, which had been on the wane, was revived. For Fellini it meant worldwide recognition, and for Giulietta international stardom. That familiar Italian suffering, Fellini remarked, "no longer existed, and one has to become a poet. One has to invent and have something to say."

He also said: "With *La Strada* I made at least thirty people in the world rich; small independent distributors who believed in the film. But I'm not envious. I gained nothing or hardly anything from a material point of view. But I was at peace with myself and my pride as an artist."

His material circumstances, however, were by now improved. He and Giulietta had moved from her aunt's apartment to a pleasant new one on Via Archimede in Rome's fashionable Parioli section. His happy producers bestowed on him a new automobile. "He brought it around one morning to my apartment house," Richard Basehart said, "to take me for a drive in his fine new car. I expected to see him in a Ferrari, or Mercedes. But when I looked out the window he was sitting in a Chevrolet convertible."

VIII

THE dazzling success of *La Strada* made international travelers of the Fellinis, who went from country to country to help launch the film. Giulietta received thousands of emotional letters from people touched to the core by her characterization of the little waif. And Fellini, as might have been expected in view of the film's commercial success, received offers to make others. "To make *Il Bidone?*" he asked, in an essay titled "The Bitter Life of Money." "No, to make *Gelsomina on a Bicycle*, or anything with Gelsomina in the title. They all wanted Gelsomina. I could have earned a fortune selling her name to doll manufacturers, to candy firms; even Disney wanted to make an animated cartoon about her. I could have lived on Gelsomina for twenty years."

Just as he had avoided continuing the adventures of the "vitelloni," he was similarly reluctant to follow *La Strada* with anything resembling a sequel. Instead, in the latter months of 1954 he worked with Pinelli on the story he called *Moraldo in the City*, as autobiographical as any he had told so far in his career. The story got as far as the narrative treatment, and then he abandoned it as a project for filming. Contrary to his usual practise of keeping his work-in-progress to himself and his collaborators, he allowed the treatment to be published in the Italian magazine, *Cinema*.

Professor John C. Stubbs, who translated the story into English in 1983, has suggested that Fellini may have felt hesitant about going ahead with a film that would have made him its main subject. "He may not have been ready to open his life to inspection in the way *Moraldo in the City* would have done. Furthermore, there is the problem that unflattering treatment of real people who served as models for characters might cause those people pain."

The latter reason overlooks the changes that inevitably would have been made in developing a shooting script; and Fellini knew enough to be careful about resemblances that were too close to real-life counterparts. Pinelli, who was there as coauthor, saw the matter in simpler terms. "Fellini was not happy about the idea of following a picture with a sequel. Even though *Moraldo* was a fresh story, in the sense that only one character from *I Vitelloni* was followed, he was aware that the link with that picture would be commercially exploited, and this for him would be an artistic comedown. So, for that time being, we abandoned it, fond of it as we were. We wrote nothing more than the outline and the treatment."

Since Fellini habitually mulled over ideas—aided and abetted by Pinelli and Flaiano—he soon had one that attracted him. While *La Strada* was in the making he had become curious about the various kinds of people who lived a nomadic way of life. While at dinner in a small town, he struck up a conversation with a man who traveled about selling shoddy woolen goods to simple people who assumed they were getting bargains. In drawing the man out, Fellini learned a good deal about how swindlers of various types preyed upon the unsuspecting. During his early days in Rome, he, himself, had been victimized by the swindler who had used him to sell phony diamonds. Now he came up with the idea for a tale of three swindlers who tour the provinces fleecing country folk out of their savings, and titled it *Il Bidone*. As John Russell Taylor says, "The Italian language is curiously well-equipped for defining the various grades and shades of roguery." In this case, *bidone* had entered the spoken language to mean the kind of swindle that victims don't complain about for fear of looking stupid.

Back in Rome, Fellini looked up "Lupaccio" (the wolf), the man who had foisted the "diamonds" on him, treated him to some meals, and got from him a thorough rundown of the tricks of his trade. As first drafted, *Il Bidone* was an adventure tale, whose rogue characters were not without humor or charm. And the landscape they would travel (those areas of Italy Fellini was continually discovering) would loom large in the story, on both the realistic and symbolic levels. The three swindlers were modern-day knights errant of a sort, gone totally wrong, but without the loss of their humanity. Added to the story was an abandoned wife who, with her children in tow, sold fake goods at village fairs.

After a script was drafted with the help of Pinelli and Flaiano, Fellini made the rounds of producers, speaking optimistically of using Humphrey Bogart to play the lead Augusto, who was based to some extent on his friend, the wolf. He thought he saw a facial resemblance between the two. Bogart, already ill with the cancer that would end his life, was unavailable, and Fellini looked around for a substitute, meanwhile turning down offers to make sequels to *La Strada* and *I Vitelloni* (the Moraldo story). Finally, the head of Titanus Film, Goffredo Lombardo, was willing to finance *Il Bidone* in return for a long-term contract with Fellini for future films.

When a production was assured, Fellini and Pinelli applied themselves to serious research on the lifestyles of swindlers. Those they encountered struck them as without human feeling. They were sinister individuals who traveled from city to city in dilapidated cars and hung around unsavory bars and seamy nightclubs. Fellini found the milieu he uncovered so distasteful that he was close to abandoning the project. However, he reworked the story with Pinelli, concentrating on Augusto, who would now be an aging rogue, weary of his profession, and eventually remorseful about the harm he had done. Echoes of Zampanò crept into the conception, and Fellini found himself, again, addressing themes of loneliness and spiritual barrenness.

But who to play Augusto? Fellini vaguely considered the fine French actor Pierre Fresnay, but while walking in Piazza Mazzini one evening he saw a large poster that had been half ripped away. "I saw on it half a face, and under it half a title and, under that, half the name of the actor." All these halves struck him as significant. "That half-face made me remember the sharp expression of a man in Rimini who was famous for having sold a part of the beach in front of the Grand Hotel to a German visitor."

The half a face belonged to Broderick Crawford, and the film being advertised was *All the King's Men,* which Fellini had not seen. Nor had he heard of Crawford. "He had the same dry, wolfish face as Lupaccio," said Fellini, "a face desperate with the knowledge he would end badly." Anthony Quinn's career having received a decided boost after *La Strada,* Crawford cabled his acceptance. Fellini ran a print of *All the King's Men* to learn something about him as a performer, and one thing he learned was that, good actor as he was, Crawford wasn't exactly a comedian.

Lombardo, the producer, also learned something about the actor, specifically stories about his drinking. He insisted on adding to Crawford's contract a long list of beverages that he was either allowed or not allowed to drink.

The roles of the other two swindlers in the story, Picasso and Roberto, were given to Richard Basehart, who was still resident in Rome, and Franco Fabrizi of the *I Vitelloni* cast. The character of the woman in the original story was changed to accommodate Giulietta; she became Picasso's reform-minded wife. Augusto was given a grown daughter (played by Lorella De Luca) who learns about her father's criminal side only when he is arrested for an earlier crime. The story became radically different from its earlier conception; it lost its humorous element, and the capers performed by the swindlers became mean, even despicable.

Early on, disguised convincingly as priests, the swindlers trick two old farm women out of their savings by claiming to know where a stash of jewels has been buried. For a major donation to their "church," the swindlers show the women the place where they had earlier buried the fake jewels. Later in the film, posing as government officials, they collect money from some impoverished slum-dwellers in return for phony and useless permits to move into new government housing.

While Augusto is after the big score that will enable him to retire, Picasso has an artistic side, loves children, has a feeling for nature, and eventually does try to please his wife by getting out of the trade. Even the woman-chasing Roberto settles down, but not

Augusto, who tries one last trick, again garbed as a priest. During the course of a swindle he has a talk, just as a priest might have, with a paralyzed girl whose sincerity finally awakens his dormant conscience. Lying to his companions that he has given back the money—and probably intending to—he is beaten up by them. During an escape attempt he falls, crippled, into an abandoned quarry where, while dying, he regrets his wasted life and calls upon God for help.

When Fellini was about ready to film the scene between Augusto and the paralyzed girl, he picked five likely candidates for the role and lined them up. There were times when he rounded up as many as twenty or thirty for the same part and made his choice only when it was imperative that the camera begin rolling. "The choice," he said, "is made a little mysteriously, in a superstitious manner, not rationally." The five girls were costumed for the scene and hopped about on their crutches while Fellini deliberated on which to use. Just as he was about to choose one, another of the girls hit a stone with her crutches and fell to the ground, crying. She was an American, Sue Ellen Blake. Much too tenderhearted to allow her tears to continue, Fellini awarded her the part.

His research into the lower depths of the swindler's way of life led him to film a New Year's Eve party where emptiness and loneliness lie behind forced gaiety. A girl at the party, Marisa (Irene Cefaro), claims she has the kind of perfect breasts that will help her in a beauty contest. The men accuse her of wearing "falsies," and leeringly look on while she proves her case. There were those who thought the scene more tasteless than proof of moral corruption, but for Fellini it was meant to show how men unable to love turned women into sex objects.

The film was hurried into production, the producer being eager to capitalize on the success of *La Strada*, now on a second and even more succesful go-round in theaters, and to make the deadline for entry in the Venice festival. Filming took place between the last week in May and the middle of July, with many of the scenes shot in Rome (where a good deal of the action had been shifted). When Augusto finally meets his agonizing end in the deserted quarry, that hastily shot scene was done at the Titanus studio. Editing proceeded rapidly, too, with whole scenes that didn't seem to work being dropped.

When the film went to Venice, the audience expected, because of the colloquial title, a crime story on the humorous side; what they got was a crime story of sorts, but a dark one, filled with anguish and meanness, and one that appeared to have Christian and philosophical depths. "With Augusto," states Peter Bondanella, "Fellini takes a petty crook and uses him, as he had Gelsomina, as a means of exploring the implications of human anguish, solitude, grace, and salvation." For him, Augusto becomes "a kind of existential hero, alienated from authentic meaning in life and feeling remorse for his crimes, yet driven to commit them by some strange compulsion. After a hellish voyage of self-negation, he comes to attain a Fellinian state of grace through suffering."

It is safe to say that few people in the audience on that evening of September 10, 1955, in Venice, saw the film in quite those terms. The Venice crowd was vastly more titillated by a newspaper report that Giulietta Masina had fallen madly in love with Richard Basehart and run off with him. Hundreds of journalists badgered Fellini about the false report. He threatened legal action, but newspapers were full of supposed revelations about Fellini's private life.

In the midst of these sensations the film, when shown, cast a pall over the audience. Toward its end, a violent storm broke out over the cinema palace on the Lido, and the crash of thunder outside added unwanted effects to the sound inside. A mild smattering of applause greeted the picture's finish, but the audience, for the most part, filed out in silence, leaving the Fellinis sitting alone with a palpable sense of failure.

Although *Il Bidone* was a financial disappointment, there were some among the critical cognoscenti who saw in the film a development in Fellini's style, a deepening exploration of his cinematic universe, and undeniably exquisite photography. The French critic Geneviève Agel not only admired the film, but went into a paroxysm of high-flown interpretation of the body of Fellini's work.

Another admirer, John Russell Taylor, viewed *Il Bidone*'s final sequence as a kind of calvary. "Has suffering shown Augusto to the way of God? We are at liberty to believe so, if we wish. Fellini offers us the perfect resolution of his films' earlier conflict between light and dark, the worlds of *I Vitelloni* and *La Strada*."

When the film reached New York, however, Bosley Crowther, in the *New York Times,* labeled it "a cheap crime picture," and added grudgingly, "but worth seeing."

Fellini, for a time, was puzzled over the film's lack of success. He came to the conclusion, finally, that it was the connotations of the title that had put audiences off and that the movie-going public simply didn't like a crime film which was not only unconventional in its telling but which also left the hero in a hell of his own making.

Fellini was still committed to Goffredo Lombardo of Titanus for his next film, and went in search of new ideas. A doctor by the name of Mario Tobino had written a book, *The Free Women of Magliano*, based on his experiences with patients in a mental hospital. Fellini went to the asylum and spent two weeks absorbing the atmosphere and learning about the doctor and his patients. His most vivid impression came from a girl suffering from Down's syndrome. When he entered the ward on which she was kept, the girl was in bed being fed spoonfuls of rice by a nurse. Fellini was told she had been deaf, mute, and blind since birth.

He outlined his projected film about the asylum for Lombardo, and in the presentation wrote about the girl: "How could she have sensed me? How did she catch my scent? She stopped eating and started to yelp, with joy, almost like a little dog's cry of welcome. My presence, my 'shadow,' my warmth, were able to communicate something to her. As soon as I started to leave she made all kinds of grimaces of despair. . . ." He added, "The book itself is rich with episodes that are as powerful, as tender, and as heart-rending as this one."

Lombardo, still in pain from the losses sustained by *Il Bidone,* was pessimistic about the chances for such a film to succeed. Fellini, nevertheless, saw Montgomery Clift as perfect for the doctor and proceeded to contact him, despite Lombardo's objections. Clift was not interested in the role, although only a few years later he portrayed a psychiatrist in *Suddenly, Last Summer.*

Fellini had the option of going to another producer, but he suddenly abandoned the project, less because of Lombardo's opposition to it than because, for the first time, he would have been using another person's source material. And, by this time, another of his ideas was taking firm shape in his mind.

It had been there, more or less dormant, since the time in 1947 when he had been searching for a story to accompany Rossellini's *The Human Voice.* Fellini had suggested a story about a pathetic little prostitute who, while plying her trade in Rome, is picked up by a famous actor and treated to a night on the town. Nothing came of the idea, but the character of the diminutive prostitute persisted and came to life again briefly in *The White Sheik.* In that film, during his search for his delinquent wife, the husband is comforted by two prostitutes, one of whom is called Cabiria, and who was played by Giulietta Masina.

"And then," as Fellini told critic Arthur Knight, "while I was shooting a scene on location for *Il Bidone,* suddenly there she was in the flesh—an independent creature with a hard cover of anger for her terrible lonely pride. We had put down tracks for a traveling shot right up to the door of her little shack [an abandoned water tank near the ruins of a Roman aqueduct]. She came out furious and ordered us to take them away. Nevertheless at the lunch break I carried one of our baskets of food to her. When she wouldn't open the door I left it on the steps. Two hours later she crept out and carried it off to the woods to eat. After that she began to come closer and closer to us, like a little animal, and finally we could talk." The real-life prostitute's name was Wanda, and Fellini was able to learn from her a great deal about the kind of life she led.

One of Wanda's fascinations for Fellini was her obvious desire, and just as obvious inability, to make contact, to communicate with others. In a way, she was a living embodiment of the thematic material that traced through both *La Strada* and *I Vitelloni*: the individual, lonely and isolated from others.

Fellini went to Pinelli to discuss the idea for a film about such a prostitute, to be played by Giulietta. Pinelli liked the idea, as did Flaiano, and daily meetings were held for discussion and development. When the story had hardened sufficiently, the three took a two-week trip away from Rome and stayed in a hotel working up an outline. Pinelli remembered the idea that Fellini had suggested to Rossellini about the prostitute's night out with a famous star, and thought it could be used as an episode in the film. Fellini, however, didn't think it fitted in with the story as developed. There were other disagreements. Pinelli wanted the story to end darkly, in tragedy. Flaiano wanted comedy and pathos in it, and to that end voted for the episode with the actor. Fellini wanted to show Cabiria's miserable life, but also wished her to have some hope in the end.

In furtherance of his research, Fellini became a kind of streetwalker himself, strolling night after night with his gifted scene designer, Piero Gherardi. They wandered along the Via Veneto and outside the Baths of Caracalla, and observed the nocturnal life of the historic area known as the "archeological quarter." Pinelli and Flaiano, too, made the acquaintance of prostitutes and pimps, all in the interest of verisimilitude.

On one of his nightly walks, this time in the vicinity of the Colosseum, Fellini encountered a man who a newspaper had referred to as "the man with the sack." Fellini became friendly with him and accompanied him on his rounds as he gave food to needy and homeless people. He had other essentials in his sack, too. When they came across a derelict who was obviously ill, the mysterious man gave him both food and an antibiotic injection.

"He did this kind of thing every day," Fellini said later on. "I saw fabulous things in his company; it was as though he raised the curtain on dark hallways of buildings, hidden rooms, abandoned houses where one would think there would be only mud and mice, but held people." He noticed an old woman sleeping in the entryway of a mansion on the Via del Corso, and learned that the building's night watchman let vagrants sleep there until five in the morning. The man with the sack knew of all such places.

"So I imagined for the film I was developing that Cabiria would meet this man on the Old Via Appia while on her way home at dawn, she complaining about a wretched client who hadn't paid her. I had her see the man with the sack get out of a car and head toward a hillside cave and call out someone's name. She gets to know him, and is deeply impressed by the stories he tells her."

When the script was in reasonably good shape, Fellini took it to Lombardo. After reading it, Lombardo asked Fellini to come in and discuss it. He had strong doubts about the story, he said. "Let's be frank. You made a film about lazy bums and queers, then one about a rascally gypsy and a half-wit, and another about swindlers. You wanted to make one about insane women. And now you come to me with a story about prostitutes. I wonder now, what will your next film be about?"

"Producers," Fellini snapped.

It was not only what he regarded as the sordidness of the subject matter that bothered Lombardo; he didn't see the Italian censors letting it pass without cutting it to ribbons. And there was a third objection—to Masina's playing the prostitute.

Fellini decided to abandon Lombardo and look around for a more sympathetic producer. As Solmi tells it, "The first was some outcast on the verge of going to prison, the second had no money, two more were afraid of censorship, a fifth was a stable owner waiting for one of his horses to win big, and the sixth gave him some development money, but limited the size of the budget to a ridiculously low amount." Richard Basehart tried to help Fellini by attempting to interest an American producer in co-producing the venture; the producer promised a share of the financing, but never came through with it. A Swiss financier showed interest, asked to see the script, and, upon reading it, lost interest.

Fellini was at home one evening, pondering how to produce his film, when Dino De Laurentiis paid him a visit. "What kind of a man are you?" the producer asked, accusingly. "You go to see everyone else, and you don't bother to come to see me!" He, of course, had been well aware of Fellini's difficulties. Soon a deal was arranged, even to De Laurentiis's offering Fellini 25 percent of the film's profits. Charity, however, began in the home office, for the profit percentage was contingent on Fellini's signing a five-film contract, a further catch being that any profits on succeeding films would be held hostage to losses sustained by the first. (This kind of arrangement was not uncommon in the world of film deal-making; it was known as cross-collaterization.)

Giulietta was unhappy with the terms and thought her husband ought not to mortgage himself so drastically to De Laurentiis, but Fellini was less interested in acquiring a fortune than in getting his films made. Already he had spent nine months attempting to get into production what was now titled *Le Notti di Cabiria* (*The Nights of Cabiria*). He had given his heroine the same name as the little prostitute in *The White Sheik.*

Fellini signed with De Laurentiis in April 1956, and pre-production moved forward rapidly. A new writer, the poet and scriptwriter, Pier Paolo Pasolini, known for his familiarity with some of the seamier sides of Roman life, was brought in to help with the dialogue. With Gherardi's help, Fellini designed Cabiria's wardrobe, buying many of her clothes at a street market. Fellini would hand Gherardi notes and little sketches about costume and set details, and these would be quickly interpreted by the sensitive art director.

Production began in the summer of 1956, and lasted well into the autumn because of a lengthy delay caused when Giulietta fell and fractured her knee. Fellini edited the film during the winter and had it ready for showing in March. It was held up, however, because of the anticipation of potential censorship, and for entry into the Cannes Film Festival in late April, 1957.

The final form of the film deviated in many details from the script. Some of this was due to Fellini's habit of changing and improvising during shooting; some to cuts made during the editing. How much had to do with the hovering problem of censorship remains a moot point.

In any case, the film that is still shown and reshown opens in a mildly idyllic fashion, with Cabiria running hand in hand with her latest lover and protector through a field toward a river bank. There, the man embraces her, grabs her purse, and pushes her brutally into the river. She has nearly drowned by the time she is rescued. For all his research into the life and ways of prostitutes, Fellini's main focus, both cinematically and in human terms, is on Cabiria, as she alternately retreats and advances toward a human relationship she hopes pathetically will be a real one.

In spite of the grim nature of Cabiria's milieu, the film is shot through with charm and humor, helped immeasurably by the grimaces and gestures of Giulietta, even to a happy little dance she does. One high point is the long sequence with Amedeo Nazzari, a famous actor (in real life as well as on screen) who picks her up after his mistress has walked away in high dudgeon. First taken to a nightclub patronized by the wealthy and celebrated, then to his luxurious villa, she has to spend most of the night hiding in a bathroom because the mistress has decided to return.

A female Don Quioxte, Cabiria's seemingly unconquerable spirit helps her survive humiliations and betrayals, until at last she meets the man who will understand her, end her loneliness, even— the unthinkable—marry her. His name is Oscar and he purports to be an accountant who is, so he says, lonely too. Cabiria, suckered in, sells her hovel of a house and withdraws her life's savings from the bank to serve as a dowry.

Taken to a lake by Oscar, Cabiria begins to perceive that he is not all that he claims; in fact, all her illusions gone by now, she assumes he is about to kill her. Oscar, from the look of his eyes, does seem quite capable of murder, but he is put off by her shrieks, and instead of throwing her into the water he tosses her to the ground and runs off with her money.

In the film's final moments, Cabiria stumbles back into the woods and reaches the road where she comes upon a group of young people singing and dancing. They see Cabiria and serenade the wretched woman. At the end, her face fills the screen, a little smile once more in evidence.

Oscar is portrayed by the French actor, François Périer. Fellini had had his usual indecisions about casting and, as he said, "I stuck Périer's picture up on the wall of my office and I would look at it now and then without being able to make up my mind. Then one day I painted a mustache under his nose and a Robes-pierre shirt around his neck and I thought the flabby nature of the accountant was just right for him."

In the film Oscar, although slightly seedier looking than a typical accountant, seems mild and sympathetic both to Cabiria and the viewer. How then to also show him as capable of murdering Cabiria? Périer, concerned about this aspect of his role, went to Fellini for advice. "Don't worry," he was told, "we'll see to it."

After Cabiria has gotten all her money together, the two are seen sitting in a cafeteria. Fellini told Périer to wear dark glasses for that scene, then, when Cabiria opens her purse to show him the wad of bills, to raise the glasses slightly to see better, thus awakening suspicion in the audience that he is a scoundrel.

Périer was impressed with Fellini's politeness and tact, and a patience he found amazing in comparison with other directors. "During my big scene with Giulietta," he said, "we took, both she and myself, too quick a rhythm. Without reproaching us, Fellini asked us to begin again . . . several times. He tired us out completely and after several takes we were forced to slow our pace. It was just what he wanted."

Before *The Nights of Cabiria* was shown at Cannes, another honor came Fellini's way in the United States, where *La Strada* was chosen by the Motion Picture Academy as Best Foreign Film of 1956. He and Giulietta made their first trip to the United States, primarily to pick up his Oscar. "Nice show," he told reporters, "a big show, but I don't know if the prizes are right." De Laurentiis had a publicity man look after the Fellinis while they were in Hollywood, and once his presence and whereabouts became known, the telephone in his hotel suite rang often with calls from producers asking him to direct in the United States.

Fellini was willing to listen, but not to commit himself. One producer wanted him for a western that would have artistic qualities. Fellini paid him a visit, and was taken into an office where, on a desk, was a contract, a check for $250,000 made out in his name, and a pen. He was left alone for ten minutes. "When they came back," he said, "and found I hadn't signed, they couldn't believe their eyes."

The three weeks of their American visit were spent in California and in New York, where Fellini was asked if he would make a film in the U.S. "Not a horse western," he said. "I would like to do a lyrical diary on American life—like pages out of a diary. It would be the United States as I see it."

Their next stop was Cannes, where Giulietta's artful performance as Cabiria, composed of gesture, droll and pathetic glances, and mimicry, won her the award for best actress.

Prior to the release of *The Nights of Cabiria* in its home country, the rumblings of censorship became loud enough to cause a stir in film circles and to reach the press. Powerful elements in the Vatican, word had it, were attempting to bring influence on Italy's censorship board to deny the film approval for exhibition. There were complaints, too, about Fellini's showing prostitutes frequenting the famed and tourist-trodden archeological quarter of the Via Appia.

"I didn't want the negative to be burned," Fellini recalled, "so, following the advice of a friend, Padre [Angelo] Arpa [a Jesuit Father], I went to Genoa, to the home of a famous cardinal [Cardinal Siri] to show him the film in a little projection room. He had set up a couch, a kind of throne, with a huge red cushion, on which to view the film."

The showing was set for midnight, and Fellini was not permitted to be in the room during the projection. "I don't know if the great prelate saw the film or fell alseep," Fellini said. "Probably Father Arpa woke him up at the proper moments—when there were holy processions or scenes—and at the end he said, 'Poor Cabiria, we must do something for her.' "

The cardinal made a phone call, apparently signifying his approval of the film, and the threat of censorship was ended, but not without one strange condition. Fellini must remove the sequence that dealt with Cabiria and the "man with the sack."

Fellini's explanation of this demand was that "evidently it bothered certain Catholic circles that there would be this kind of homage paid to an anomalous kind of philanthropy, free from ecclesiastical mediation.

"Someone," he went on, "accused me of being a kind of Richelieu who, instead of fighting it out in the open, did everything behind the scenes. But in the end the film was saved."

Only those who were at the Cannes showings saw "the man with the sack" sequence. Among them was the French critic, André Bazin, who wrote a lengthy, searching, and highly laudatory essay on the film, in which he discussed the meaning of the episode in the context of the film as a whole. When he saw the film again in Paris, after its general release, he was surprised that the entire episode was gone. His admiration of Fellini was such that he now decided the cut had occurred because Fellini regarded it as useless within the structure of the film.

Italian critics and intellectuals were less kind. Alberto Moravia attacked the Catholic hierarchy for its sometimes devious ways of censorship, and the government for setting up a censorship commission that operated on the principle "that they were Catholics first, and citizens second."

Bazin's essay on the film, aside from that minor bit of mis-interpretation, was an influential analysis of Fellini's style and meaning. It was his theory of cinematic "auteurs" that provided the seedbed for the French "New Wave" of directors such as Louis Malle, François Truffaut, and Jean-Luc Godard. For Bazin, Fellini had the "inspiration that connotes a true author." He was the first of many to see *La Strada*, *Il Bidone*, and *Cabiria* as related thematically, a trilogy of "renunciation and salvation." Significantly, he titled his essay: "The Voyage to the End of Neorealism."

About the film's final moment in which Cabiria seems to be aware of the camera, he wrote: "Here she is now inviting us, too, with her glance to follow her on the road to which she is about to return. The invitation is chaste, discreet, and indefinite enough that we can pretend to think that she means to be looking at something else . . . (but) enough, too, to remove us from our role of spec-tator."

Fellini had already demonstrated a fondness for little parades and processions, and here at the end of *Cabiria* was one more (the young singers and dancers). But this one, he claimed, was central to the film's conception.

Critics had been regularly accusing him of taking an evasive position toward reality, of failing to offer a solution to his characters' problems. He decided, he said, that the criticism might be justified, that he hadn't indicated a way out for his characters— "Now you must read such and such a newspaper, or get married, or go to church"—that, in fact, he ended up not saying anything to them.

So, for Cabiria, he wanted to offer some comfort, say to her in effect, "I can't explain to you what's wrong, but I'm very fond of you and I'll even offer you a serenade." Thus, in ending the film about the little prostitute with a heart of woe, "I have her meet a group of exuberant young people who, a bit jokingly, express their appreciation by singing her a song. It is from this idea that, ultimately, the entire film was born."

When *The Nights of Cabiria* opened in Italy in the early fall of 1957, it was an immediate success, and its popularity followed wherever it was shown. Fellini and Masina frequently traveled with it, for publicity and financial reasons. Giulietta had won recognition as one of the screen's finest actresses, and Fellini was now regarded as one of the greatest of the newer directors. He rewarded himself with a new car, a very special black Mercedes.

IX

AMERICAN critics and reporters had the opportunity to meet with Fellini when he went to New York again in October 1957 for the opening of *Cabiria,* as the film was retitled for American release. For Fellini, it was an opportunity to explore the city, both out of curiosity and for possible ideas that might allow him to consider the offers being made to him by American film companies.

Familiar as he was with the captious ways of critics in Italy, he was surprised by the diversity of American critical opinion about *Cabiria.* Much of it was favorable, but the *New York Times* reviewer, Bosley Crowther, said the atmosphere of the film was sordid, that it ran on too long, and that Masina's costume—a striped shirt and ragged little fur piece—was "weird and illogical." In the *Saturday Review,* however, Arthur Knight offered the opinion that Fellini was now Italy's greatest film artist.

Richard Wald, a reporter for the *Herald Tribune,* interviewed Fellini in the director's suite at the Hotel Carlyle and reported him to be "a tall, heavy man with black hair graying at the temples and a poetic manner of speech and hand. Talking in a soft voice with a heavy accent and occasionally lapsing into Italian to express himself more clearly, he explained his several ideas in search of an embodiment."

These ideas had less to do with film-making than with his reactions to American life. Fellini had gotten a sense that relationships here were different from those in Europe. People in the U.S.

were more distant, drier, whereas in Europe "a stranger on a train will tell you what troubles him, his secrets, his wife's pregnancy." America was exact and scientific, while in Europe the tendency was more toward abandoning oneself to imagination and the feelings. But how to convey that sense of America? Since he hadn't found the form of expression for it, he could not see himself accepting any offers to do a film here.

After two weeks in New York, Fellini flew to Hollywood for another week. The previous June, the Screen Director's Guild of America had voted him a special award for outstanding achievement in the cinema, and now a dinner was held in his honor, with director John Ford doing the presenting. Fellini flew back to Rome still unconvinced that he could direct films anywhere outside Italy.

A year before *Cabiria* was released, Urbano Fellini suffered a fatal heart attack. While at the funeral in Rimini, Federico could not help being aware of his lack of closeness to his father, and of the physical and spiritual distances he had traveled since leaving Rimini for Rome and the larger world. One reason for his lack of real interest in making films in America was that he had been thinking seriously of a film idea triggered by the illness and death of his father.

With Pinelli's aid, he wrote a narrative treatment of a film to be titled *Viaggio con Anita* (*Journey with Anita*). Certain elements were clearly autobiographical, but not to the degree of *Moraldo in the City*. In the story, a famous and successful writer, Guido, after learning that his father is seriously ill, decides to drive from Rome to his home town, Fano. Guido is bored with his marriage, and on the spur of the moment, he asks his secret girlfriend, Anita, to make the trip with him. During the journey, the writer, who is in his mid-thirties, finds himself consumed with passion for the much younger woman. Soon after they reach Fano, the father dies, and while awaiting the funeral Guido rediscovers the town he had left, meets old friends and, in a welter of new feelings and emotions, proposes marriage to Anita. Although disappointed by Anita's sensible refusal, Guido does discover during the journey something of the simplicity and fullness of life he was lacking in cosmopolitan Rome.

Fellini allows Guido a measure of consolation. The last line of the treatment reads: "The image of Anita waving good-by, however, is so gentle and loving that his sadness is not without its shimmer of joy."

In the treatment, as though in response to the rising frankness in films of the period, or perhaps because of a release in his own inhibitions, there are sequences more vividly erotic than in any of Fellini's previous work. During the journey, Guido and Anita are given a hospitable supper at a farmhouse. It is the Night of San Giovanni, and the farm girls have a ritual on that night of "frisking nude in a meadow." The scene is described, and later Anita, stimulated by having joined in the frolic, leads Guido back to the meadow. "Still intoxicated, now she repeats the game delightedly, childishly and provocatively in front of Guido. Anita strips off her clothes and begins to roll again, nude, on the heavy dew of the grass. . . ." Just how Fellini would have filmed this scene in view of the still prevalent strictures of the time is not clear, but what is clear is the contrast between Anita's simple, almost pagan freshness and the sterility Guido feels, in spite of what he has achieved.

When Fellini returned from America in November 1957, he decided that *Journey with Anita* would be his next film project, and immediately began negotiations with Sophia Loren to play Anita. He also contacted, rather strangely, Gregory Peck for the role of Guido. Negotiations with Loren ground to a halt, mainly because she was far more preoccupied with the problems resulting from her marriage to Carlo Ponti, which was regarded in Italy as illegal. (Ponti's divorce had not been recognized by the church.) Another script, *Fortunella,* a picaresque comedy written with Pinelli and Flaiano, and obviously designed for Giulietta, he turned over to his friend and colleague, Eduardo De Filippo, who directed it competently enough but with virtually none of the distinguishing Fellini characteristics. Fellini, it is likely, felt he would have been repeating himself by doing another story that depended on Giulietta's clownish and waiflike performances.

Journey with Anita could have made a fine film in Fellini's hands, as a reading of the recently published script indicates. The rights to it were sold many years later to producer Alberto Grimaldi who, in 1978, gave it to Mario Monicelli to direct. The highly sensitive, even poetic story became a comic vehicle for Goldie Hawn and Giancarlo Giannini and came to New York in 1981 as *Lovers and Liars*. The misadventures of an American girl in Italy taking a trip with a banker to his working-class father's funeral in Pisa served, in this mediocre transformation, as a demonstration of the vast differences between a film by Fellini and one by a less talented counterpart.

Professor John C. Stubbs, who translated the Fellini script into English (from a manuscript in the possession of Fellini's Swiss publisher) was curious about the amount of autobiographical material in the screenplay, and wrote to Fellini, who refused to comment.

But parallels to his own life abound in the story, even to the description of the protagonist, Guido: ". . . a fully mature man in his late thirties. A sanguine, self-confident, irreverent, and amusing fellow, he has the look of an intellectual who is successful and well-known. . . ."

Guido has a younger sister. (So does Fellini.) The telephone call alerting him to his father's illness comes from Fano. (Very near Rimini.) The house of Guido's parents "stands on one of those interior streets of seaside towns. . . . Actually the house sits right on the corner of the main street that runs toward the station and the sea." (Fellini described similarly a house he had lived in.)

Anita, in the story, is full of admiration for Guido's fame and success (as were numberless women in Fellini's case), but Guido feels joyless and empty. Ecclesiastes-like, he finds no permanence or solidity in the "torn, factious, skeptical world of today." The father's funeral is described vividly: "In the splendor of the summer morning, the funeral seems like a festival. A swarm of photographers have come down from Bologna. . . . The crowd includes relatives, friends, acquaintances, and curious onlookers. . . ." Would there have been that much excitement about the father's funeral without the famous son's presence?

Stubbs, in an introduction to the screenplay, points out

some of the determining factors in Guido's estrangement from his father: a lack of understanding between them because the father wants his son to live conventionally, while the son is set on a less secure intellectual career; Guido's resentment of his father because of his infidelities and the pain they caused his mother. Fellini, in his youth, quarreled with his father about his career path, and was aware of and pained by the older man's infidelities.

Fellini, by abandoning *Moraldo in the City* and *Journey with Anita*—two very good screenplays—revealed that he was hesitant about bringing to the screen the intimate material of his life's experience, although increasingly fascinated by it. He felt the urge and the need, too, to widen possibilities, to expand and explore a richer cinematic universe. The films he had made until now were on a relatively small scale, with stringent budgets. He was not made wealthy by *Cabiria*—there were still debts to be paid off—but it was proving a commercial success, and enhancing his prestige. For several months he was indecisive about what to do next. He considered an Italian-American epic, *Barabbas*, flirted with *The Decameron*, and with a farcical treatment of *Don Quixote*, the latter to star the French comic actor Jacques Tati. He was more serious, however, about *Casanova's Memoirs*, with Orson Welles playing the great seducer. Pinelli was also in favor of this project.

Instead, Fellini took another look at the Moraldo story, wondering if it might be transferred from its 1938 setting to the present. But the Rome that had both dazzled and discouraged the youthful Moraldo had become a quite different city. The political and social climates of 1958 were vastly different from that time of prewar fascism.

The year 1958, in the view of Peter Bondanella marked the beginning of "the golden age of Italian cinema." Film production was on the increase, aided certainly by a decline in Hollywood's output and fewer American imports into the native market. Meanwhile, the foreign market for Italian films was expanding, largely due to the aura of artistic quality imparted by men like Fellini, De Sica, and Rossellini.

Rome was now something of a film mecca. Tax benefits made it advantageous for American stars, directors, and writers to live and work abroad, and epics cost less to make because of lower wage scales and fewer union restrictions. Fellini was an occasional onlooker at Cinecittà while MGM's *Ben Hur* was in progress. Gore Vidal, a writer on the film, met Fellini there one day and they became good friends.

In comparing the Rome of 1958 with the one of twenty years earlier, Fellini noted the hordes of tourists, and the mounting traffic that assaulted the ears and jangled the nerves. Now, sitting at cafés on the Via Veneto, one could see famous faces of the international set.

He was famous, too. Publicity people cajoled him into attending premières of his films and paraded him at festivals. There were dinners given in his honor and prizes presented at award ceremonies. In this "Tower of Babel of different languages" he tried "to define a certain sense of unease and bewilderment that these ceremonies communicated to me." At the same time he, too, was a participant in this new, fast life. Famous people wanted to meet him; there were those he admired whom he wanted to meet. He developed a liking for good, special, fast cars. Often he would leave the clamor of Rome for drives alone, or with a good friend or colleague, to the seashore or to the countryside.

He met with Pinelli and Flaiano to consider a new approach to the Moraldo story: make him a man in his mid-thirties who was still in Rome after those intervening years. They sat deep in armchairs at Rosatti's café mulling over a contemporary Moraldo. He would have become a journalist, they decided, of the sort that went after gossip and sensation, the kind who would frequent the Via Veneto. They gave him a problem: the struggle between his instincts to be a serious writer and the necessities of his daily work.

Pinelli recalled their talk sessions. "While developing our new Moraldo we weren't thinking about social problems, or a particular moment in history—other than as a setting—but only of a journalist in Rome who was facing a personal crisis. Everything we brought into the story related to that crisis. We saw Moraldo as bemused, filled with contradictory impulses. He didn't know what to do, what to think, how to act. It was through looking at him in this way that we came quite naturally to examine the atmosphere of his milieu."

A new establishment called the Café de Paris had opened on the Via Veneto and, like the others, put out tables and chairs on the sidewalk. Fellini, who had not spent much time on the avenue for several years (although it had been for him a symbol of success and acceptance when he had first come to Rome) was now going there more often—after all, it was where Moraldo would spend much of his time. He was sitting this afternoon at one of the tables, just as the sun was sinking over the gardens of the Villa Borghese, when he noticed a fat man nearby, accompanied by a pretty girl of lush proportions. He recognized the fat man; he was Farouk, the deposed king of Egypt. The former king was sipping mineral water and enjoying the sunset.

Then Fellini noticed a group of photographers slowly approaching Farouk's table, moving closer and closer like beasts stalking their prey. The closer they came, the more their flashbulbs popped, until Farouk, provoked beyond his endurance, leaped to his feet, his bulk causing the table to overturn. Now more people rushed up to see what the disturbance was about, and the photographers had a field day.

Fellini was intrigued by the method behind this apparent madness, and managed to get to know one of the photographers, Tazio Secchiaroli, who introduced him to some others. Over drinks— which Fellini bought—and once over a dinner he treated the photographers to, he learned their tricks, the way they fixed on a victim, goaded the person, sometimes provoked a commotion or a fight. They waited in ambush if a potential victim tried to outwit them, and were ready with cars and Vespas for a pursuit. Their assignments came from editors of newspapers and magazines; sometimes they worked in tandem with a reporter.

Fellini decided that his contemporary Moraldo would work with a photographer like Tazio.

* * *

Ennio Flaiano kept a journal in which he wrote occasionally. An entry made in May 1958 began: "This evening I went walking along the Via Veneto, trying to see it clearly, how it has changed from 1950, from the time when I would go there by foot every morning through the Villa Borghese and stop at Rosetti's bookstore, and there meet such as Marcari and Cardarelli the poet. The air was clear, the traffic was light, Brancati went around on a bicycle, the odor of warm brioches wafted from the bake shop. . . ."

He noted the difference between the present and the time, only eight years before, when there had been a countrylike gaiety to the avenue, when writers and journalists had come for an aperitif at one or another of the cafés. "How a street can change. Now that summer is close, it seems more like a beach than a street. Cafés spill out over the sidewalks. How many are there? Six, seven? Each has its own design of an umbrella, like at a seaside resort. Cars jerk along, people take the air, moving along with the indolence of seaweed, as though our destiny really is on the sea."

In June, Flaiano wrote: "I'm working now with Fellini and Tullio Pinelli, dusting off an old idea of ours about a young fellow from the provinces who comes to Rome for a career in journalism. Fellini wants to make the film a sketch of the café society that fluctuates between eroticism, alienation and boredom . . . and good living. The film's title will be *La Dolce Vita* and we haven't yet written a single line of it. One of our locations will definitely be Via Veneto, and yes, our destination will be the sea."

A later entry mentions that the three collaborators were considering an early scene in which Moraldo, new to Rome, is walking up Via Veneto, no money in his pockets, gazing with fascination at the crowd. But this notion was dropped when it was decided that a more mature Moraldo would make his first appearance on the job by entering a nightclub. Pinelli has mentioned that at about this point in the development of the story Fellini changed Moraldo's name to Marcello. "Once the protagonist grew older," he said, "Fellini decided that no one but Marcello Mastroianni would play him."

Marcello, Flaiano records in June, "becomes one of those writers that our present-day civilization of sensation produces. That is to say, he writes about scandals." Continuing their building of the character, Fellini, Pinelli, and Flaiano agreed that Marcello had been an idealist at first, who by the time the story opens had "allowed himself to be taken over by the society he scorns. He is seduced into giving up his earlier ideals."

At this point in the journal, Flaiano says that Fellini wants the photographers "who invade Via Veneto" to be made part of the story; one of them will be Marcello's companion in his work. "Fellini has the idea for this person very clearly in mind. He claims to have the model for him. But we must give this person an exemplary name, because the right name will help his personality come alive."

Several names for the photographer were considered and discarded, until Flaiano found one they all thought appropriate. He had come across it in an obscure opera libretto. "In it," Flaiano records, "we find our perfect and prestigious name: Paparazzo." They had no idea at the time that the name would eventually go into the dictionaries of many languages.

Throughout the month of June the story continued developing and taking on a larger dimension. Before settling on Via Veneto as a principal setting, Fellini had toyed with an idea for a film set at a film festival such as the one at Cannes. An important element in that idea was the fuss created by the arrival of a blonde, bosomy, and glamorous star. He had seen the prototype of this woman in a full-page photograph in an American magazine. "My God," he recalled. "I said to myself, don't ever let me meet her. I was incredulous." The atmosphere of the Via Veneto was not dissimilar to that of Cannes—the cast included some of the same producers, actors, starlets, and hangers-on. The notion of a movie sex goddess descending on Rome fitted the Via Veneto story just as neatly. This is probably what Fellini meant when he said that "The idea of the film is inseparable from the idea of Anita Ekberg." As more dimensions were added to the story it began to take on the form, in his words, of "a vast fresco, with characters and incidents emerging to fill it out."

Some of the incidents were suggested by real life occurrences, the kind that Marcello might report on. A few years earlier the infamous "Montesi affair" had caused great shock in Italy.

The body of Wilma Montesi, an attractive young woman, had been found on a beach after an all-night drinking and sex party. There had been other sex scandals. Marcello, it was decided, would participate in such a "festivity."

Marcello, searching for a more meaningful way of life, most admires an intellectual writer named Steiner, who seems to have everything Marcello might want: writing talent, music, interesting artistic and intellectual friends, a wife of sterling character, and two charming children. To live like Steiner, to be literally above the strife and frenzy (he lives high up in an apartment building) might be what Marcello is seeking. But Marcello was not to find his answer from Steiner.

"For the Steiner episode," Pinelli explained many years later, "we wanted to show the desperation that can lie behind happiness. In a French newspaper I came across the case of a professor who, for unknown reasons, had killed his children and himself. Like Steiner, that professor had seemed to have everything that would make life worth living. Steiner, we decided, perhaps like the professor, was too happy, too fulfilled, but only seemed so, because inside he was despairing, facing a private terror that there was nothing more but emptiness. Life had lost its meaning for him. One comes across these seemingly incomprehensible cases. What accounts for them? For Marcello, the shock he feels is conclusive, and he is cast in the role of a journalist whose duty it still is to report on the grisly affair. It is an irony, and a final disillusionment for him."

Fellini was also communicating, separately from Pinelli and Flaiano, with Brunello Rondi, another writer, and close friend. In a letter to Rondi he discussed the Steiner character: "Did you read about that tragedy in France some years ago? A young wealthy fellow, with a promising career, a beautiful home, who loved his wife deeply and was very attached to his daughters, comes home one day, beats his two children to death with a club and then jumps from the tenth floor. Now, what if this guy were Steiner?" Fellini goes on in the letter to describe an evening in Steiner's "gorgeous apartment," where Marcello senses "the deep calm of family feelings."

The first conception of Steiner, the intellectual writer, had come from the character of Gattone in the Moraldo screenplay. The person Gattone was based on had died of a dreadful disease, and the manner of his death had frightened the youthful Fellini. Through continual discussion (and the newspaper story Pinelli had come across) the much more complex and elegant Steiner evolved. Later, when the script was completed, a shocked producer said to Fellini: "Dear master artist, I beg you, tell me you, with that kind face, are not the one who thought up this thing. It is not possible."

Borrowings were made from previous scripts. Marcello is identified as being from Fano, as was Guido in *Journey with Anita*. Like Guido, Marcello is portrayed as having a distant relationship with his father. A father appears briefly in the Moraldo script—he comes to Rome to urge Moraldo to return home. In *La Dolce Vita* he is given an entire episode during which he visits Marcello and is entertained at a nightclub by his son, who also provides him with a female companion for the night. While making love with her, the father suffers a heart attack (another echo of the Anita story), but recovers sufficiently to leave for home, even though Marcello wants him to stay and talk.

In *Journey with Anita*, Guido's companion does a wild, "pagan" dance during the festival on the Night of San Giovanni. Somewhat similarly, the sex goddess, now named Sylvia, dances un-hibitedly when, accompanied by Marcello, she visits a baroque night-club set among the ruins of the Baths of Caracalla. In the earlier screenplay Guido has a quarrel with Anita while on the road, berates her about her behavior, and orders her out of the car. He drives off, but soon turns around and finds Anita sitting calmly on a wall filing her nails. Almost the same scene takes place in *La Dolce Vita*, in this case with Marcello berating his mistress, Emma, for what he re-gards as her restricting possessiveness and love. He pushes her out of the car, drives away and, returning later, finds her at the side of the road with a bunch of flowers she has picked while he was gone.

Moraldo is echoed again in an episode eventually excised from the script. The young Moraldo, it will be remembered, has an affair with the literary Signora Contini, who takes him to her bosom and bed. For *La Dolce Vita*, an episode was written involving a ma-ture writer, Dolores, who while encouraging Marcello to actually get down to writing his novel, keeps him sexually captive for a time in a remote old tower in the country. (When the episode was removed, another was hastily added that came from a news story about two children in a provincial town who claimed to have seen the Virgin Mary.)

When it came to the detailed fashioning of the script, the writers, late in the summer of 1958, settled in for several weeks at a hotel in Fregene, a seaside resort about a half hour's drive from Rome.

X

WHEN Dino De Laurentiis was shown a first treatment of the screenplay for *La Dolce Vita* he was not very impressed, and it was with reluctance that he advanced Fellini about one hundred thousand dollars for preproduction costs. His dismay increased when he received a completed script comprised of nine seemingly diverse episodes, linked only by the presence of journalist Marcello Rubini in each segment. "He finds the story," Flaiano noted in his journal, "incoherent, false, and pessimistic. The public [he says] desires at least a little hope and some entertainment."

Yet, De Laurentiis was willing to finance the production if an important international star could be obtained for the role of Marcello. He felt that someone of the stature of Paul Newman was needed to "carry" the film.

"Fellini can be passionate in his convictions," Pinelli said. "Not only did he insist that Marcello be played by an Italian, but specifically that the Italian had to be Mastroianni. Fellini and De Laurentiis had fierce arguments over this and finally De Laurentiis saw a way of settling their quarrel. He proposed that the screenplay be given to some prominent critics to read and judge. Fellini agreed, mostly out of curiosity to learn their opinions."

The three experts chosen by De Laurentiis were Ivo Perilli, Gino Visentini, and Luigi Chiarini. The first two found the story structurally unsound and too complicated. Chiarini largely agreed, but thought the subject might be saved if balanced with "healthy forces"—perhaps another character who would not have come to "a dead end." De Laurentiis made the mistake of either trusting the critics' judgment, or using it as a way of bowing out as the producer. In any case, a loud argument between him and Fellini could be heard throughout the building, after which De Laurentiis stormed out.

The situation hardly being new to Fellini, he continued with preparations for filming while at the same time looking for a new producer. He simply put the project on the open market, so to speak, and indicated his willingness to talk to potential buyers. His position was one of some strength, for *Cabiria* was still doing well in many countries, and the word had spread that the new film would center around the high life of the Via Veneto, and would be filled with spicy and scandalous material. What happened, in effect, was a seller's market. Talks were initiated during the next few weeks with seven would-be producers, among them Goffredo Lombardo. The negotiations with him were serious, one of the sticking points being that De Laurentiis wanted his advance money back immediately. Serious, too, were the negotiations with Angelo Rizzoli, the Milanese financial and publishing tycoon, and his representative, Giuseppe Amato. At one point, Fellini discovered he had made agreements with three producing entities, and he had to wriggle out of two of the deals after putting his faith in Rizzoli and Amato.

Legends have arisen about Fellini's hectic dealings with producers. Some were known to back off just at the moment of signing a contract. One such is said to have raged, "Rather than sign such a contract, I'll eat it." Upon which, he began chewing huge mouthfuls of the paper. On a second meeting, he yelled, "You want to reduce me to starvation! I won't have a thing left to wear!" This time he stripped to the buff, causing Fellini to race out of the office. At a third meeting, all seemed calm until: "Look, Federico, rather than signing this death warrant, I'll first swallow the ink." Fellini, so the story goes, attempted to stop him, but the producer gulped the contents of a whole bottle of ink. Pinelli was not certain the story was entirely apocryphal.

Fellini was still in the midst of his negotiations when he went off to London in search of Anita Ekberg, and tracked her down in a nightclub where, he reported afterward to Pinelli, she danced without her shoes, and was indeed the living embodiment of Sylvia, the blonde sex goddess of his story. He began negotiations with her agent. While De Laurentiis was still the ostensible producer he had interested Henry Fonda in the role of Steiner, and Maurice Chevalier had agreed to play Marcello's father. De Laurentiis's wife, Sylvana Mangano, had been enlisted for the role of Maddalena, a rich, bored, and beautiful heiress, a card-carrying member of the Via Veneto crowd, but when De Laurentiis bowed out, Mangano, too, became unavailable.

Luise Rainer met Fellini during a visit to Rome. They exchanged mutual compliments and Fellini arranged for her a private showing of *Cabiria*. He looked in during the screening and heard her sobbing. Before she left Rome for New York she had agreed, without seeing the script, to take on the part of the aging writer, Dolores.

Lex Barker, recently divorced from Lana Turner, was hanging around Rome, acting in low-budget spectacles, and was tapped for Sylvia's boyfriend. The cast kept changing, however, partly due to delays caused by the negotiations, at times because an expression of interest did not mean a firm commitment, and sometimes because of Fellini's own change of mind. When Henry Fonda read the part of Steiner, he disliked it so intensely that he immediately cabled Fellini his refusal. Chevalier was busy at something else by the time his contract was sent to him.

In October 1958, arrangements with Rizzoli and Amato were concluded. Rizzoli agreed to reimburse De Laurentiis for the money already advanced to Fellini, and Fellini's fee for directing was set at fifty thousand dollars, plus a share of profits. Rizzoli was doubtful, however, that there would be any profits for a film without "hope, or a ray of sunshine in it." Amato had his doubts, too, and because he was the one involved in the day-to-day disbursement of as large a budget as yet laid out on an Italian film, he constantly harassed Fellini with his complaints and arguments, until these grew so annoying that Fellini called in Rizzoli as arbiter.

With contracts signed in November, Fellini began to work with Piero Gherardi on the costume and set designs. As did the writer, Brunello Rondi, Gherardi had a special genius for knowing

what was in Fellini's mind—and certainly an aspect of Fellini's genius was his ability to find and work with gifted associates. One evening, Fellini took Gherardi for a long drive and talked with him
about the kind of picture he envisioned. He wanted the film to look
like newspaper photographs, with sharp contrasts of black and white
and, as often with newspaper action photos, a mixture of sharp focus and blurred shots. He discussed what Steiner's apartment ought
to look like, and he even gave him a clue about the ending: a sign
would appear before Marcello on the beach of Fregene after the orgy
at the villa. "A revolting sight, halfway between mythology and science fiction." It was to be some kind of fish; to design it Gherardi
had to rely on an intuitive reading of Fellini's mind.

Contemporary female fashions were to be stylized. Fellini
was fascinated by the changes in women's clothing. "One day," he
said, "I saw women walking along dressed in a fantastic and extraordinary way, so fascinating that it set light to my imagination."
It was the new style of the sack dress that struck him most; suddenly
women looked different to him, presumably missing the attractive
bulges and curves that set them apart from men.

Gherardi's first meeting with Fellini occurred in September
of 1958. In November, the designer was at a house he kept near
Bangkok when Fellini cabled that he was ready to start production.
An Oriental influence apparent in the film comes from Gherardi's
residence in Thailand. Soon after the opening sequence, a Siamese-
style ballet is performed in a nightclub. Maddalena's bedroom is
furnished with oriental pieces.

Gherardi's task was complicated not only by the need to con-
struct eighteen sets, but by the director's constant second thoughts.
"Until I have said we'll film here," Fellini explained, "I feel free to
change, to keep inventing things." This freedom extended to costuming. There were times when Gherardi improvised clothing right
at the scene; he kept Cinecittà's seamstresses working overtime: a
costume called for at nightfall would have to be ready by morning.

The monumental task of casting 800 small and extra parts
continued up to and during the production. By this time Fellini had
a collection of photographs of actors and nonactors numbering in
the thousands, and he would pore over these faces in anguish at the

necessity of having to make a choice. Sometimes it was a matter of deciding what a character should look like; at other times he searched for an image already in his mind.

He had such a mental image of the character of Paola, a teen-age girl who reminds Marcello of one "of those little angels in the churches of Umbria." The last moments of the film were to show Paola, across a breakwater, attempting to say something to Marcello, who is unable to hear her. Marcello had met her earlier when she waited on him at a seaside restaurant while he was trying to work on his novel, and in contrast to his associates she had seemed to him a symbol of purity and innocence. She was not only important to the meaning of the film, but hers would be the last face seen on the screen.

After failing to find a Paola in his collection of photographs, Fellini went on radio and television to describe the girl he was looking for. The right one didn't turn up, so he took an ad in a Rome newspaper, inviting mothers to bring their teen-age daughters to meet him at a Rome theater he had rented. Although 5,000 mothers and daughters turned up, he was unable to find a suitable girl.

Paola was still not cast when filming was underway. An old friend invited him to dinner one evening at his home. When the host's fourteen-year-old daughter came down the stairs to say goodnight to her father, Fellini had found his Paola! Her name was Valeria Ciangottini, and Fellini signed her to a contract the next day.

A few weeks before the start of filming on March 16, 1959, Anita Ekberg had arrived in Rome and Fellini arranged to meet her in the rooftop garden of the Hotel de la Ville at the top of the Spanish Steps. He saw her approaching, followed by a retinue that included her husband, her agent, and her publicity man. Ekberg, physically, was in the mold of a Marilyn Monroe, but of much more heroic proportions. As a star and an actress, she was of far less moment, having decorated some films made in 1955 and after. Still, Fellini was vastly impressed. "I said to myself, so, these are the earlobes. . . . I felt her to be phosphorescent." Was the character she would play *positive*, Ekberg wanted to know, sipping at a cocktail, and who were the other actresses? There would be Luise Rainer, Fellini told her, and the French actress Anouk Aimée (Françoise

Sorya), whom he had just cast for the part of Maddalena, and another French actress, Yvonne Furneaux, as Emma, Marcello's mistress. Mastroianni wanted to meet Ekberg, but Fellini thought he ought to wait until their scenes together began. But Mastroianni, nevertheless, persuaded him to arrange an introduction.

Fellini asked Mastroianni to join the Ekberg group for dinner. "When Mastroianni was introduced to her, she distractedly held out her hand, looked to the side, and said not a word to him for the whole evening," Fellini reported. Later, Mastroianni remarked that Ekberg was really not such a great thing; in fact, she reminded him of a Wehrmacht soldier who had forced him onto a truck back in the war days. "Perhaps," said Fellini, "he felt offended by that glory of elemental divinity, that health, the echo of a sun force which, instead of exalting him, nauseated old Snaporaz."

Mastroianni and Fellini had known each other since the actor and Giulietta had worked together in a play at the university's experimental theater, but during the long months of filming *La Dolce Vita* a strong comradeship grew up between them, a kind of mutual identification with the character of Marcello. Fellini nicknamed Mastroianni "Snaporaz," a name he used two decades later for another character played by Mastroianni.

Born in 1924, Mastroianni worked in his father's carpentry shop after finishing high school, then studied surveying, an ability that caught the attention of the Germans during the war. He drew maps for them until 1943, when he was sent to a forced labor camp. He managed an escape to Venice and headed for Rome as soon as it was liberated. There he joined the university theatrical group Masina was part of, and found a job with an English film company.

His film career meandered along through the fifties with undistinguished roles. In 1956, he was featured in a film starring Sophia Loren, playing the part of a taxi driver. He assumed he would be playing similar roles for a long time to come, but the Italian public had become aware of him and so had Luchino Visconti, who in 1957 starred him in a moody film, *White Nights*, where Mastroianni distinguished himself. So strong was his relationship with Fellini during the making of *La Dolce Vita* that during one two-week period on location they roomed together.

*   *   *

While waiting for filming of *La Dolce Vita* to begin, Luise
Rainer went to New York, and managed to persuade Fellini to give
her a copy of the script to study while she was away. The more she
studied, the more she disliked her character. She wrote Fellini a distressed letter, saying that Dolores was "sordid and hateful." Fellini
cabled back a soothing and flowery message to the effect that her
presence in the film would add to it "a miraculous luminosity." All
would be worked out when she returned. In May 1959 she was back
in Rome, ready to discuss the changes she wanted. Production languished while the two argued in Fellini's Cinecittà office for several
hours. Rainer headed back to New York. More cablegrams, with
compromises from both parties. She returned to Rome, and Fellini
changed the concept of the character to conform more closely with
her wishes. She was still not satisfied, and took it upon herself to rewrite her part, an action not calculated to please any director. As
time grew near for Rainer's scenes, with Rainer still molding Dolores to her own vision, Fellini solved the problem by deciding that
the Dolores episode was not really needed and eliminating the entire segment, and with it Rainer, from the film. He quickly substituted an episode involving the two mischievous children who provoke
a near riot with their supposed vision of the Virgin. Marcello travels
with Emma to the site of the "miracle," and is saddened and sick-
ened by the spectacle of hordes of believers taken in by the hoax. So
hasty was the writing of the episode, that much of it was improvised
on location, with screams of anguish from Amato and Rizzoli, who
saw the budget increasing alarmingly.

Because Anita Ekberg's availability was limited, her scenes
were scheduled early, and since most of them were outdoors and
many took place at night, filming had to be done in chilly March
weather. Marcello, who has become enchanted with the voluptuous
Sylvia, follows in her phosphorescent wake, and manages to be
alone with her for several hours during a nocturnal Roman odyssey.
The "goddess" decides she wants to bathe in the waters of the Trevi
Fountain, and Marcello gamely follows her in—a teeth-chattering
scene to shoot. Another scene set in a baroque (and imaginary)

nightclub in the Baths of Caracalla was shot on a huge Cinecittà set fancifully designed by Gherardi.

Also shot outdoors was the nighttime ride in Marcello's little sports car during which Sylvia "rescues" one of Rome's innumerable stray cats and insists that milk be found for it. Another scene took place on the busy Via Veneto, where filming was allowed by the city authorities only between two and six in the morning. They managed well enough for the scene on the avenue, near the entrance to the Excelsior Hotel, in which Marcello is "laid out" by Sylvia's fiancé, and she gets a chastening slap herself, but word got out among the populace, and things were a good deal less peaceful the next time the film crew came around, this time to shoot the scenes in which Maddalena drives Marcello along the avenue in her white Cadillac convertible amidst heavy traffic. The police agreed to allow the "takes," so long as traffic wasn't snarled. Fellini, in a lead car, led the way for the Cadillac with the two actors. Anouk Aimée was not an experienced driver, nor had she ever driven a car as huge as the Cadillac. Behind and beside her were camera and production cars. Not only was her nervousness showing, but a sizable crowd had been attracted by the procession, late as the hour was. People lined the sidewalks as the parade of cars turned into a side street and made its way around again for another trip up the avenue. Some ugly epithets were yelled at Fellini by one troublemaker, infuriating him enough to go looking for the man afterward with two husky crew members.

The restrictions and the behavior of the onlookers was too much for Fellini. He told Amato that future Via Veneto scenes would have to be filmed in the studio, which would mean reproducing the avenue on the Cinecittà lot, an undertaking so expensive that the budget would have to be increased by 50 percent. Amato flatly refused, and it took an appeal to Rizzoli to get the additional financing, but with a condition. Fellini agreed to give up his percentage of the profits.

Gherardi went to work taking meticulous measurements of the stretch of Via Veneto that Fellini wanted to use. Then he recreated a replica at Cinecittà that was a marvel of exactitude except for one little thing: Via Veneto rose upward from Piazza Barberini to the gateway of the Villa Borghese gardens. The Via Veneto of the film was flat, a circumstance that bothered Fellini not at all.

During July and August, the production moved to locations in the vicinity of the seaside resort of Fregene. One of the scenes shot there, though brief, is evocative because it reveals Marcello's confusion of impulses. He is attempting to write his novel on the patio of a beach restaurant. His typewriter and some blank sheets of paper are on his table. He makes a telephone call to the possessive Emma, loses his temper and hangs up. It is then that he notices the young waitress, Paola, the epitome of the innocence that he, presumably, has lost. He stops writing, and telephones Emma again—a defeat of sorts.

Lengthier were the scenes shot in a luxurious villa that occur toward the end of the film. At this point in the story the by now thoroughly disillusioned Marcello has left journalism for press agentry. A large group of party goers has swept in from Rome to celebrate the divorce of Nadia (Nadia Gray), a matronly beauty. Marcello appoints himself a sort of master of the ceremonies, which include a striptease performed by Nadia. One of the onlookers is a pretty starlet, whom Marcello humiliates by riding her like a horse, then covering her with feathers from a pillow he has torn open. Then, as the party goers leave toward dawn, he "blesses" each of them with more feathers.

The "orgy," as filmed, is more symbolic than real. Nadia, during her striptease, is never entirely uncovered, and whatever sexual acts might be transpiring are left largely to the viewers' imaginations. However, Fellini, ever the stickler for verisimilitude, decided he needed some expert advice.

"Believing that Pasolini [who had been brought in to help with the dialogue for *Cabiria*] was familiar with orgies," he told Giovanni Grazzini, "I invited him to dinner, but Pier Paolo told me he didn't like middle-class orgies and knew nothing about them. He was sorry, he said, but he had never participated in any, and didn't know anyone who had. So I started the sequence with no idea in my head, got the actors arranged, and suggested we invent some debauchery. I had a beautiful Dutch assistant who kept her eyes on me in anticipation of seeing me produce who knew what crazy scenes of turpitude. After two hours I heard her saying to another disappointed assistant, 'He wants to play the pig, but doesn't know how.' "

Two of the segments filmed did not appear in the finished version. One took place at an awards ceremony (another vestige of *Journey with Anita*), and the other at sea, where Maddalena and Marcello are picnicking in a boat. A girl who is swimming near the boat is burned to death when a cigarette tossed into the water ignites some gasoline that has seeped from the engine. The film was already overlong, and the murder-suicide of the Steiner episode seemed starkness enough. Still, Fellini claimed he could have made a ten-hour film with the available material. As it was, he continued improvising within the confines of the script and without it. Many of the party scenes taking place at the Castle of Bassano di Sutri were improvised and shot while retakes were being made. Fellini gives credit to Brunello Rondi for suggesting much of this material. Rondi, he said, was an avid partier and had tales to tell of goings-on that took place in the abodes of patrician Romans.

It is at one of these patrician parties that Marcello re-encounters Maddalena, for whom he has conceived an infatuation. In one of the most remarkable scenes of the film, Maddalena, although she has been willing to sleep with Marcello (in a prostitute's bed, of all places!), is not willing to commit herself to a serious relationship—and yet she enjoys playing with him and leading him on. This penchant of hers is almost surrealistically illustrated in a conversation between the two. She leads Marcello to a large room, empty except for a chair in the center, and tells him the room is called "the chamber of serious discourse." She has him sit in the chair, and leaves. The camera follows her to the end of a marble hallway where there is a shell-like fountain beneath the statue of a nude woman. "Marcello," she whispers into the fountain, "can you hear me?" He does hear her, mysteriously but clearly, and is moved to declare his love. She admits she loves him, too, but feels unfortunately that she has whorish instincts. This doesn't faze him, and while she continues to seduce him verbally, a young man appears, and in a moment, while Marcello is still foolishly pouring out his heart, Maddalena makes love with the stranger.

The role of the intriguingly amoral Maddalena provided an important turning point in the career of Anouk Aimée. Twenty-six, not a classic beauty, she could nevertheless stir a critic to write, "she is an actress with a haunting quality, so delicately suggestive of the Modigliani portraits that her presence stirs a sense of wonder." Fellini managed to coax from her an erotic quality, along with a cold, suppressed hysteria and the suggestion of a lost, sympathetic woman. But it wasn't easy, Aimée never having displayed those qualities before.

He spent hours patiently explaining to her the nature of the woman she was playing. With the camera turning, she would tighten up, and wouldn't bring out what he wanted. Finally, he resorted to performing a crazy little jig behind the camera just as she started a scene. He made funny faces, he waved his arms wildly. Aimée kept on, but her effort to keep from laughing gave him the quality he was seeking.

"She can be absolutely shy," he remarked, "and in the next moment she's as tough as a shark in deep waters. She always maintained with me her little-girl persona, but behind that facade there was a bit of what I wanted her to have in Maddalena—an almost metaphysical sensuality."

He succeeded with Ekberg, too—better than any director before or since. With her, he took a more flirtatious approach, gave her little hugs, intimated a passion for her that could not be given real expression. He inspired Gherardi to costume her not only glamorously, but at times outlandishly. In one of her scenes she climbs the narrow, winding staircase (re-created at Cinecittà by Gherardi) to the dome of St. Peter's, garbed in an adaptation of a cardinal's robes, complete with hat. "Federico," Ekberg complained, "I think you are making a fool out of me."

As a shortcut to emphasizing the characters, Fellini concentrated on the faces of his huge cast. For many of the smaller roles he selected faces that would evoke an immediate audience identification. Others were there to add to the mood, as in the case of an old clown, who appears in the scene in which Marcello entertains his father at a nightclub. The clown pretends to be taming three "tiger" girls with his whip, but as he does a little dance with a balloon he directs sad glances at Marcello's father, who has taken a fancy to one of the "tigers." This scene foreshadows the orgy in which Marcello will "ride" the starlet.

Otello Martelli, Fellini's photographer, was given difficult tasks to accomplish.

"Because," said Martelli, "what was important to him was the focus on the characters. He wasn't concerned how this might affect the depth of field. I would tell him that the use of a particular lens contradicted the principle of its use. 'What can that possibly matter?' he would say. He turned out to be right. The film was given a certain style, severity to the images, concentration within the frame, along with some distortion of the characters and the settings."

Fellini, in considering the score for the film, had at first thought of adapting period music, but working again with Nino Rota, he took a more grab-bag approach in line with the varied moods and atmospheres. There were themes original with Rota, along with snatches of "Stormy Weather," "Arrivederci, Roma," and "Patricia," a song Marcello first hears played by Paola on a jukebox, and again when it is used to accompany Nadia's striptease. For the next few years, "Patricia" became a favorite accompaniment for striptease artists in London and Paris. It was by now noticeable that Fellini had a penchant for circus-type march tunes, and he used one again.

Rota was known for his absent-mindedness, and Fellini was nervous about losing the themes they had developed. He insisted Rota keep a book of musical notation during their work together in Rota's home, an old Roman palazzo with peeling plaster and a huge skylight, not far from the Pantheon. The book was kept on top of Rota's piano, and each theme in it was carefully labeled and identified according to which film it had appeared in. For further security, Fellini brought a portable tape recorder along to Rota's home.

Fellini was unsure about keeping his "monster fish" at the end of the film. Gherardi had started with a formless lump of material. "I made a kind of huge beast," he later explained, "with blobs of plaster all over it like veal tripe. For eyes I gave it convex enlarging lenses." Two endings were shot: one with Marcello left drunk and alone on the beach, following the all-night orgy, and another with the orgiasts trooping at dawn to the beach, where fishermen are just pulling in the monstrosity. The bloated sea creature seems to stare upward at Marcello with a dead, accusing eye. In both endings, Marcello hears Paola calling to him from across an estuary, but can't make out what she is saying. Fellini had taken a dislike to his "fish," but ultimately kept it in.

Filming ended toward the end of August 1959. By then Fellini had changed and departed from the original screenplay to such an extent that the script kept by his secretary was said to have grown larger than the Rome telephone book. After two months in the editing room—punctuated by frequent quarrels between Fellini and Amato over what should be cut or kept, a first version ran more than three and a half hours. By mid-November, what Fellini said was his final version came to just under three hours. The length was needed, he said, for an "arrythmic quality" that would reflect the kind of life portrayed. His original conception had taken on a grandiosity beyond his early intentions. "I wanted to shoot with the camera," he said afterward, "a conflagration in the culminating moment of its splendor, just before its disintegration."

XI

THE screenplay begins:

A vast panorama of the Roman countryside. To one side are the ruins of the San Felice aqueduct, towering arches that come striding across the land. Two thousand years ago these arches brought water to the city, but now there are many gaps where whole sections of the aqueduct have fallen in. Directly in front is a soccer field; the goal posts dwarfed by the height of the aqueduct. In the distance the sound of motors is heard. A speck in the sky grows rapidly larger. It is a helicopter, and beneath it is a hanging figure. A second helicopter follows closely behind. As the copters pass over the field the figure suspended below can be clearly seen. A larger statue of Christ the Laborer swings from a cable. The shadow of the copter and this incongruous figure flashes across the walls of the aqueduct. . . .

From these startling images the scene changes to the roof of a modern apartment building on which four young women in bikinis are sunbathing. The copter carrying the Christ figure passes on, but the second copter swoops low, and Marcello and Paparazzo, his photographer, make their appearance. Marcello silently indicates that he would like to make a date with the girls, who are airline stewardesses from another country.

With this beginning, Fellini makes clear some of his intentions: the contrast of Rome's 2,000-year-old past with the present—helicopters, modern-day journalism, stewardesses relaxing between flights, a reporter seeking an unusual story, the luxury of a sun bath amidst the bustle of the city, an ever-present photographer, a statue being airborne to the Vatican.

Commentators, favorable or unfavorable, can be forgiven for seeing in the film a morality tale, the story of a man on a spiritually barren path that leads him toward a private hell. The film also seems to indicate that society as a whole is on a downward spiral. Fellini has denied any overtly moral purpose or parable in the work, but he has also said that at one point he considered titling it *Babylon, 2,000 Years After Christ*. Even while developing the screenplay, when Marcello was still called Moraldo, he said publicly that his film would be about "Moraldo, no longer as he was when he arrived in Rome, but twenty years later, already a little hardened, already on the edge of shipwreck." And that he would be seeking a change in his life, a "transfiguration."

Thomas Mann once said about his novella, *Death in Venice*, "I, the creator, am dazzled by its many facets," and while Fellini never appeared to be dazzled by *La Dolce Vita*, he must have been at least somewhat dazed by the varying interpretations of his film. "The author," he said, "is the last one who can talk consciously about his work with knowledge," and at times he seemed to have as much difficulty in analyzing the layers of meaning as did the many others who tried.

Oddly, the film, viewed a quarter of a century after its birth, doesn't seem fully to merit the amount of explication it has engendered, and the fact that it has, over time, inspired so much analysis would seem to be a tribute to the power and allusiveness of its images. The interpretations have been many and varied.

For instance, Professor Donald P. Costello of Notre Dame wrote in his book *Fellini's Road* (1983), "Marcello is never just a journalist in Rome. He is modern man faced with modern life, and even, behind the modernity, eternal man faced with eternal life—or death."

Costello sees mythical elements in the very composition of the images. In describing the first of the episodes with the rich, bored Maddalena, in which she leads Marcello to a tryst in the bedroom of a whore she has had him pick up, Costello sees more than a simple attempt on Maddalena's part to escape from boredom: rather, he says, Fellini is ritualizing the approach to the prostitute's apartment. "He creates a cinematic dance. Circled in the spotlight of the car's headlights, Maddalena floats along a wall, the camera picking up the gliding motion, gliding itself and then varying the Maddalena and camera rhythms with Marcello's twirling of a rose. This dance introduces us to the central compositional figure of the film: the twirling spiral."

The spiral is there again in the staircase that Sylvia, the film star, ascends with Marcello to the roof of St. Peter's. But for others, such as the French critic Gilbert Salachas, it is dawn's early light that is the key to Fellini's meanings. "In Fellini's world," Salachas wrote, "dawn signals the moment of truth. The spell is shattered, and a person finds himself once again alone and shivering, abandoned, pathetic, left with neither energy nor illusion." Almost everyone saw meaning, but not always the same.

Alfred Hitchcock, borrowing from early Russian theorists, liked to say that cinema's effects came from the director's juxtaposition of images. Couple a shot with one image, and it would convey a meaning; substitute a second image and a different meaning would result. Fellini's approach was more intuitive, as though meanings were to arise not from juxtaposition alone, but from the nature of the composition of a particular shot or grouping of shots. His actors—all details—were to conform to the "life" his imagination infused in the scene. "Choosing a setting," he said once, "forces me to bring into being an indistinct world, to deal with real possibilities. . . . That's why I am tremendously afraid of that moment." In *La Dolce Vita* critics often saw more than actually met the eye, as when a swarm of photographers on motor scooters follow Marcello in a sports car and Sylvia in her large car on her way to Rome. Realistic as it was, film historian Edward Murray would say about the sequence: "Secular processions take the place of sacred ones. A long line of cars containing devout worshippers of the flesh, followed Sylvia from the airport into Rome. . . ."

Many saw spiritual and religious implications. Fellini's

friend, Father Angelo Arpa, a professor of theology at the University of Rome and one of the few clerics in Italy to approve the film, said, "Never has cinema included in sin such a profound sense of bitterness and weariness, or misfortune and desolation."

If discussion about *La Dolce Vita* made anything perfectly clear, it was that its meaning lay in the mind of the beholder. There was no doubt in the mind of reviewer Moira Walsh, writing in the Catholic magazine *America*, that "Fellini intends this film as a salutary moral warning." But she worried, rather immodestly: "What will the effect of this film be on someone without my advantages of intelligence and training?"

If John J. Navone in *Commonweal* regarded it as "the most Christian film in years," Michael Roemer in the *Reporter* saw it in secular terms: "Implicit in the film is the suggestion that if most of us had money, and therefore time, we would stand face to face with the unresolved emptiness in which we live; that it is only the strait jacket of the daily struggle that saves many of us from a continuous experience of chaos."

For critic John Simon, the film implied "the impossibility of loving." Dwight Macdonald seemed to want more from the vaunted orgy scene, which disappointed him. It was "embarrassingly dull," he wrote. Beyond that, he said, the film was "a sermon against upper class corruption, but one that exploits its gamy subject matter as much as it exposes it." Macdonald was one of the à la mode critics who chose Antonioni's *L'Avventura* as superior to *La Dolce Vita*. When *La Dolce Vita* was entered in competition at the Cannes Film Festival in May 1960, Antonioni's *La Notte* was also entered, and a spirited kind of partisanship—Fellini versus Antonioni—developed. Novelist Georges Simenon, the presiding juror that year, became *La Dolce Vita*'s most enthusiastic supporter. He also met Fellini and was impressed by his honesty and simplicity; their friendship continued for many years.

In his *Intimate Memoirs* Simenon wrote: "Thanks to the vote of Henry Miller, who doesn't have an opinion and has decided to vote as I do, and one other juror, *La Dolce Vita* wins [the Golden Palm], and I go out with the list of awards to Fabre-Lebret [the festival director], who is waiting out in the hall. He is not alone. A representative of the Ministry of Foreign Affairs is there with him, but aren't both of them being told what to do by Paris? Our list of winners does not delight them." When Simenon fulfilled his duty by reading the names of the prize winners at the gala evening that closed the festival, he was "hissed, whistled at with police whistles, while Giulietta waits in the wings and [afterward] sobs on my shoulder."

There were those who had developed or espoused particular film theories, and with film-making in one of the most fertile periods of its history, they struggled to fit into their critical framework each new work of extraordinary originality. Andrew Sarris had his "auteur theory" to defend from the battering assaults of the feisty Pauline Kael—but here was *La Dolce Vita*, with a seemingly loose structure—events related to each other thematically instead of by plot—and the films of Antonioni, whose approach was influenced as much by the new-wave novel as by abstraction generally in the arts. And soon enough came *Last Year At Marienbad*, directed by Alain Resnais from a nonlinear script by Alain Robbe-Grillet, which mingled past and present in an enchanting puzzle that was never completely resolved. How to deal with these when one's theory is based on the kinds of films directed by John Ford and Howard Hawks, and others who had managed to stamp their individuality on their films while staying within the confines of a studio system?

So Sarris conceded that *La Dolce Vita* was important because of its "social impact," but then he proceeded to deflate it, saying that Fellini had "enlarged his material without expanding his ideas." The film's failures, he went on, were formal as well as intellectual and, in general, the film was as bloated as that infamous monster fish of the ending. Meanwhile, in the *New Yorker*, Edith Oliver advised her readers "to ignore the forced irony . . . and take the movie as it comes." And, she asked, "What is wrong with some pretty girls sunbathing in bikinis?"

Robert Richardson, in his study, *Film and Literature* (1969), described a striking correlation between *La Dolce Vita* and T. S. Eliot's masterful poem *The Waste Land*: "To put it simply, Fellini's films depend heavily on what are usually thought to be solely poetic techniques, while Eliot's poetry makes frequent use of certain cine-

Young Fellini, contemplative, in 1940

and as portrayed by Bruno Zanin, furtively groping Magali Noël in the Fulgor Cinema (*Amarcord*, 1973)

Young Masina in *Variety Lights*, 1950

and (with Anthony Quinn) in *La Strada*, 1954

Alberto Sordi as the White Sheik

Giulietta Masina and Peppino De Filippo in *Variety Lights*

Giulietta Masina and Peppino De Filippo are at center taking curtain calls in
Variety Lights

Fellini directs Anita Ekberg, above, and Mastroianni rides bareback, below, in *La Dolce Vita*

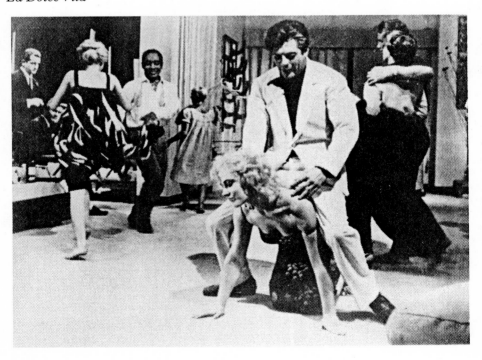

Anouk Aimée (left) and
Sandra Milo, wife and
mistress, as fanta-
sized by Marcello
Mastroianni playing
Guido, below, in *8½*

The director at work on *City of Women*

and *Amarcord*

Amarcord: A painted ship upon a painted ocean

matic techniques." He then finds that both the film and the poem
are "twentieth-century versions of Ecclesiastes, visions of the hol-
lowness of contemporary life." The Tiresias of the poem and the
Marcello of the film are, therefore, ideologically related.

Quite wrong, Charles B. Ketcham, a professor of religion,
would seem to be saying when he claims that "Fellini uses the sacra-
mental system of the Roman Catholic Church as the theological for-
mat [Ecclesiastes having made his lament long before there was a
Catholic Church]. . . . It is the belief of the Church that the sacra-
ments spiritually cover or provide for each important stage or phase
of life—from birth to death. In *La Dolce Vita* the spiritual life of
the protagonist covers just such a progression, but in this case, because of the choices and lifestyle of Marcello, each 'sacrament'—
each decisive action—moves Marcello toward his spiritual death
rather than salvation. . . . It is this theological mythology which
binds the seven main episodes of the film together into a meaningful whole."

The mystical number seven intrigued other analysts of the
film, and although there were at least nine episodes during the writing and editing stages, much significance was attached to the fact
that as finished there were seven. Although the screenplay, as published, breaks the film into fifty distinct scenes, the episodes referred
to are presumably those that involve Marcello with Maddalena,
Sylvia, his father, Steiner, the aristocrats' party, the false miracle,
and the final orgy.

For her analogy, Barbara K. Lewalski, in the *Massachusetts Review*, called upon Dante. "Fellini has consciously under-
taken . . . a contemporary *Divine Comedy* in a modern medium
for modern times. . . . The characters and situations make fairly
obvious allusions to their Dantean prototypes in *The Inferno*."
Much like "a journey through the various circles of Hell, Marcello
observes and only passively participates in the various evils and perversions of modern life. . . . The scale of evil extends downward
from the natural sins of the flesh to the much more reprehensible
perversions of intellect." For Lewalski, Fellini's imagery was also
transposed from Dante.

Richard A. Duprey, in *Catholic World*, agreed that Marcello inhabits an earthly hell, but he also drew on the number seven to link the film with the Book of Apocalypse, because of the seven dawns, which bring "the harsh light that dismembers dreams and delusions." Duprey multiplied his allusions to include Marcello as an "Italian Peer Gynt" and, in a later article, as "an unwitting Faust."

The Steiner episodes bothered many critics. Henry Hart in *Films in Review* could see little point in the meeting between Marcello and Steiner, which takes place in a church, and immediately follows Marcello's hectic night of adventure with Sylvia and his humiliation when her fiancé knocks him to the ground with the photographers gleefully catching the action. Marcello, in a dismal mood, has entered the church and finds in Steiner a sympathetic, encouraging friend, someone interested in his developing himself as a writer. The scene is basically one that characterizes, but that also provides a calm interlude between the frenzy of the night with Sylvia, and the near madness of the "miracle" scenes that follow. It contrasts, too, the peace of the old church, in which Steiner plays a Bach fugue on the organ, with the religious delusion deliberately encouraged by the press, radio, and television reporters covering the story told by the silly children. Moreover, it shows Marcello looking for an answer to his psychic dilemma, wondering if it is here in the church, in the music Steiner plays, in Steiner's very life style. But there are hints of something else; a touch of pretentiousness in the literary Steiner's playing Bach in this ancient church, and at the end of the scene, a foreshadowing that comes when the camera closes on Steiner's face as he stares grimly into some other realm. It would be hard to imagine a scene with more meaningful overtones, and Alain Cuny, who played Steiner (Fellini had discovered him late, when he saw the actor as the cuckolded husband in Louis Malle's *The Lovers*) gives it a sensitive reading.

Whether this is what Barbara Lewalski refers to as "the reprehensible perversion of intellect," or whether she means the intellectual gathering that takes place at Steiner's apartment, an examination of that scene shows several motifs, one of them being a gentle poking of fun at the pretensions of the guests, among whom are a mannish woman, Margherita ("You know her abstract paintings"); an Indian girl who plays the guitar and sings; Repaci, a novelist ("He has written dozens of books—you know their importance"); and Iris, a woman poet dressed in an odd monk's robe. Then, too, in this scene Steiner acts rather strangely, describing himself as smaller than a thimble. Talking with Marcello, he indicates his dissatisfaction with "a sheltered existence in a world where everything is organized," and at the end of the scene he has a long speech in which it is evident that he is filled with fear and anguish, that "peace makes me afraid," that he distrusts it, that it hides a danger, and that his fear is tied in with what the world will have in store for his two lovely children. By this time, it is clear that Marcello has found in Steiner a role model. He has brought his mistress, Emma, with him, and when she takes in the handsome apartment, the seemingly happy home life of the Steiner family, she tells Marcello that this is what they ought to have together. Oddly, Emma was overlooked by most critics as part of the "seven episode" scheme, yet she appears throughout much of the film.

The Steiner scenes, including the one in which Marcello learns that Steiner has killed his two children and himself, struck many critics as unmotivated, although one wonders how much more clearly Fellini could have indicated a forthcoming tragedy without telling the audience about it in advance. But the tragedy is not the Steiners' alone; it is also one more disillusioning shock and failure, cataclysmic for Marcello in his search for a meaningful life.

Naturally enough, Fellini, who had brought on this avalanche of interpretation, was asked for his own explanation of his intentions in *La Dolce Vita*. He went to Paris in April 1960 for the press screening. With him were his collaborator, Pinelli, and his assistant, Dominique Delouche, to help him through the interview session, which was held in the suite he shared with Giulietta in the elegant Hotel Plaza-Athenée. By this time, with the enormous commercial success of the film in Italy, he was being treated very well by his producers. The suite was brightened with vases of roses, carnations, and lilies. Seated on a couch, Fellini pondered questions asked by Martine Monod of *Les Lettres Françaises*.

"I am not a man who dashes off messages," he told her. "I don't have a very precise ideology. When you describe your epoch, no matter how impartially, you notice that there are emergencies, events, attitudes that strike you more than certain others and that are more important. . . . So you unconsciously become a moralist. If *La Dolce Vita* has a meaning it came all by itself; I did not go after it."

Fellini, Martine Monod said, got up from the couch and looked out the window. He was tired of hearing about the scandal the film had caused in Italy. "Do you know what the Milan upper bourgeoisie could not tolerate? The orgy. It upset them; they were in agony at seeing themselves in the mirror."

The new film, he wanted to make clear, was linked to his preceding ones. "Contemporary life is filled with contradictions: a frantic, tense, exciting life and, in fact, a terrible emptiness, an immobility. Men, for example, going from one woman to the next, from adventure to adventure. And all this, only to end up revolving around oneself without really budging."

It was Rome, he said, that was really the star of the film. "The Babylon of my dreams. I chose it for its permanence. Rome is there like a symbol. Any big city in any epoch would have served as a background for my film."

In another interview, he attempted to clarify his "Christianity." "If by Christian you mean love toward one's neighbor, yes, all my films revolve around that idea. There is a priest who came up with a fairly accurate definition when he said: 'When the silence of God falls upon mankind.' Aside from what is solemn and biblical in this definition, yes, *La Dolce Vita* could be viewed in this light. Indeed there is the silence of God, for love is lacking. They only talk about love, but they are barren, unable to give it. Thus even *La Dolce Vita* is a deeply Christian film."

At other times, in discussion, Fellini would edge away from any too obvious moral meaning, including too close a connection with a "Christian point of view." When speaking with students of the Centro Sperimentale (the film school adjoining the Cinecittà studios) he said he didn't want the film thought of as a kind of trial, but if taken as such, it was "not a trial seen by a judge, but rather by an accomplice."

In a later interview with an American professor, Charles Thomas Samuels, he made an even stronger denial about showing corruption, and said there had been no polemical intentions in the film. The title, he went on, "came to have a meaning exactly the opposite of what I had intended. . . . I wanted (it) to signify not 'easy life' but 'the sweetness of life.' "

"That's not the way it comes out," Samuels objected. "Marcello looks like someone wallowing in trouble. Think of that scene in which he sees an angelic girl . . ."

"That is a result of the myth produced by a Catholic upbringing," Fellini replied. "A wish for some purity, something morally complete and angelic—stamped at the bottom of our minds and leaving us with a nostalgia for something rarified."

"If he could attain that would he be better off?"

"No," said Fellini, "he likes *la dolce vita*, [finds it] very fascinating."

"At the end, he makes a gesture of resignation."

"No, he says, 'I don't hear. I don't understand.' It could also be considered a bantering gesture: 'I don't hear you because I don't want to hear you.' "

Fellini found himself doing more and more explaining, always seeming to want to simplify, while others were complicating. It became a matter of seeing in the film what one wanted to see. Moralists saw sin and corruption. Theologists saw a soul in torment. Easy pleasures were equated with evil; unsanctified sex led to perdition. Where Fellini left ambivalence, viewers wanted definition.

The last scene has this ambivalence. Most viewers took it as symbolic of the corrupt state into which Marcello has fallen. But a closer look at the scene reveals some ambiguity. When the fishermen haul in the amorphous monster, one of the onlookers says, "Oh horrible!" But a woman, peering at the "fish" more closely says, "My God, the splendor!" The fish, meanwhile, seems to stare at all of them, in close up, with its round, unmoving eye.

Then, hard upon this view of the "fish," its mouth dribbling jellyfish, comes the sound of children playing on the beach across an inlet. The girl, Paola, is standing there, calling to Marcello. He can't make out what she is saying. But we hear: "Me and you—in the car . . . don't you understand?"

But he can't hear, he can't understand, gives a weary little shrug and turns away. The last shot on the screen is of Paola waving and smiling. It is an aching and evocative moment. The viewer is left feeling that Paola perhaps does have a message for him, but that unfortunately (or willfully, as Fellini suggested) he can't hear it. Fellini said that in the case of *Cabiria* he wanted to give his audience a gift at the end, and here, perhaps, he was again reminding them of "the sweetness of life." He had searched hard and long for the right girl to play Paola. The sea monster, he has said, came from a childhood memory of something like it that a storm had thrown up on the beach at Rimini. Was Paola the memory of his Rimini love, Bianchina? That has to remain in the realm of speculation, but when asked at the time what his next film would be about, Fellini said that he might attempt to explain the mysterious message Paola was trying to give Marcello.

XII

FELLINI was not made rich by *La Dolce Vita*, but its enormous success enabled him to form his own production company—not with his own resources but with the backing of Angelo Rizzoli. The new company was named Federiz. The plan was to produce films by Fellini and others by carefully chosen, talented directors. Clemente Fracassi, Fellini's able and trusted production manager for *La Dolce Vita*, was given the responsibility of finding worthwhile projects for the new company.

A small office, consisting of a large outer room and a smaller inner sanctum for Fellini, was opened in central Rome. Piero Gherardi did the decorating. For Fellini's office he provided orange curtains, green lampshades, and large couches. The main feature of the outer room was a huge table, on which Fellini's constantly expanding collection of photographs could be sorted and cataloged.

Federiz, in spite of good intentions, made no films by other directors. But a new Fellini film was germinating. During the summer of 1960, he and Guilietta were invited by Rizzoli for a stay on the island of Ischia, near Naples. Rizzoli was the owner of the luxurious Regina Isabella hotel on the island. Ischia is noted for the jet set crowd it attracts, as well as for its radioactive springs, which are supposed to be effective in the treatment of rheumatic illnesses. Rizzoli's hotel was also a spa that featured baths from the springs and mud baths. If there was a moment of germination, it

happened there, for when he returned to Rome Fellini began to discuss a new idea with Flaiano and Pinelli.

Fellini later told John Gruen of the *New York Herald
Tribune* how the idea had come about: "The conception came after
a process of lengthy self-examination. I went for a rest cure, at a
moment when things were at a low ebb. I was in limbo, taking stock
of myself. I needed to reconcile my fears. I asked myself the usual
questions: 'Who am I? What am I doing? Where am I going?'

"I felt I needed to find the answers to countless questions.
And that is when the idea took root. Thus, a journey into the inner
self. It would be a summoning up of dreams, recollections, forgotten
feelings, shadowy doubts, and a kind of eternal quest for self knowledge and acceptance. It would be a catalytic film—for myself, for
the actors involved and, I hoped, for the people who would see it."

The first inkling of the notion was, however, a vague one,
"A confused desire to sketch out a man in a day out of his life, the
picture of a man in his contradictory, unclear, sum of diverse reali-
ties, in which you could see all the levels of his being, the planes
superimposed on each other like a palace of which the facades have
crumbled and which reveals its internal structure, still intact, stair-
ways, hallways, rooms, the furniture. . . ."

Mostly to clarify the idea for himself, he talked about it
with Flaiano during a drive to the beach at Ostia. Flaiano listened
quietly, without comment, but Fellini had the feeling that he was
thinking the theme wasn't cinematic, that if it was anything, it belonged to another, literary dimension.

Several days later, he talked about it again with the usually
more sympathetic Pinelli, but he, too, remained quiet, and seemed
rather perplexed as to how such an idea could be expressed in a
film. When next Fellini talked with Brunello Rondi he found the
perfect listener. Rondi responded with his usual enthusiasm; in
fact he was ready to start on the collaboration at once.

They began without a clear-cut direction, or an exact idea
of who the protagonist was. Perhaps he was a lawyer or an engineer,
or a journalist. And even though Fellini had begun to mull over the
idea while at the spa in Ischia, it was only after he began exploring

themes and situations with Pinelli, Flaiano, and Rondi that he decided to use a spa for the setting. He chose Chianciano Terme, in
Tuscany, as the kind of spa where his hero would be taking the cure.
He and Pinelli went to Chianciano and spent ten days there. It was
a pleasant place that catered to well-off Roman society. The sulfur
and calcium springs were thought to be good for disorders of the
liver and bile ducts. Medical treatments were available. Amuse-
ments included concerts on the tree-shaded grounds, tennis, and a
gambling casino.

From Chianciano he wrote to Rondi saying that the new
film would be "a fantastic, enchanted ballet, a magical kaleido-
scope." Another time he described it as a "tortuous, changing, fluid,
labyrinth of memories and sensations, tying together daily happenings, feelings, nostalia, imagination." Both still and volcanic, life
would appear to be a long waking dream. Enough of what Flaiano
ironically titled "The Beautiful Confusion" was on paper in October
1960 for a production to be planned. There was a sequence in an
imaginary harem; another that involved a hypnotist; others that
took place in the baths. The hero was given both a wife and a lover.
No beginning or ending had yet been decided. Pinelli kept asking,
"Just what does the protagonist do for a living?" While attempting
to resolve these matters, Fellini kept postponing the date for production to begin.

While in London during December 1960 he considered casting Laurence Olivier in the role of the protagonist, and if not
Olivier, perhaps Charles Chaplin, whom he had long admired. "I'm
beginning to get the feel of it," he told a writer for the *Times* of
London, "but really there's nothing clear enough to talk about. All
I know is that it probably will seem even more arbitrary and disor-
ganized than *La Dolce Vita*."

When he returned to Italy, however, he telephoned Mastroianni and said he wanted to talk to him about an idea for a film.
("He always had Marcello in mind for the role," Pinelli said. "We
knew it, even if he didn't.")

When he met Fellini after the call, Mastroianni said, "He
told me he wanted to do a movie about a man seeking to find him-

self. It would be the story, played on many levels, of an inner search. A reconstruction of a life that had come to a stop—artistically, morally, and spiritually."

Before embarking on the film, he had agreed to participate in a Carlo Ponti project that had materialized from a Cesare Zavattini suggestion: to capture on film the droll, earthy spirit of the fourteenth-century Italian poet and scholar Giovanni Boccaccio in a series of modern tales. Others who had agreed to take part were De Sica, Visconti, and Mario Monicelli. Now, while Fellini was still attempting to work out the story of the man at the spa, Ponti was becoming insistent that he honor his commitment to *Boccaccio '70*. Fellini decided to get "this distraction" out of the way.

The distraction was, in fact, welcome. His own life was in a somewhat confused state. As he put it, his principal worries were "God, wife, women, money, and taxes." As far as money was concerned, the $50,000 fee he had received for *La Dolce Vita* was running low; with Mastroianni he explored the burgeoning car market. "We liked to have a good time with a new car," he said. "If he bought a Jaguar, I would buy a Porsche, and then he would buy a BMW." He took trips in the cars, often enough with Mastroianni as a companion. If his wanderings seemed idle on the surface, they bore fruit in the images in his films. To the cars, he said, he owed "ideas, characters, even dialogue. Often I would stop wherever I was and take notes. The wanderings didn't have to have a specific destination. It was enough to see trees, sky, colors, faces that passed by silently."

There were women, undoubtedly, and the rumors about them were echoed in the press. Pinelli admitted that at the time of the writing of the as yet untitled film, all three of them—he, Fellini and Flaiano—were undergoing strains caused by marriages and mistresses. Angelo Solmi, in his biography of Fellini published in 1967, made delicate reference to Fellini's problems in this area when he wrote that Giulietta "like Luisa in the film [*8½*] understood and forgave Federico in the end . . ."

In his contribution to the multi-part *Boccaccio '70* Fellini found an opportunity to vent his spleen against censorship. A Jesuit magazine had made a violent attack on him, going so far as to suggest he ought to be jailed, so he mounted an attack in return. Early in 1961, with his usual collaborators, he wrote the script for *Le tentazioni del dottor Antonio* (*The Temptations of Doctor Antonio*). The story dealt with a crusader against vice (Doctor Antonio Mazzuolo) whose targets included enticing displays of the female form in periodicals. But to his horror, he encounters one day a huge billboard that features a reclining film star holding a glass of milk. The caption reads: "Drink More Milk."

The good doctor mounts an attack on the poster, first by badgering the authorities, then, when no action is taken, by physically assaulting the billboard with ink pellets. His victory is short-lived, for the woman on the billboard comes to gigantic life and tempts him not only to distraction but to insanity with her ample charms. Eventually the doctor is placed in a strait jacket and taken off to an asylum.

For the embodiment of the abundance and healthfulness of milk, Fellini chose Anita Ekberg and, as her would-be nemesis, Peppino De Filippo.

Making the film took up most of the summer of 1961. The night scenes were shot in a neighborhood near the Old Appian Way. It is at night that the woman leaves her billboard and roams the doctor's neighborhood as a fifty-foot-high giantess. The scenes were done in literally two dimensions. At the studio, Piero Gherardi built a miniature set that represented the doctor's neighborhood. Its fire hydrants were one-inch high. Thus, when Ekberg walked on the set she loomed above the buildings. "Real life" sequences were done on the actual streets. For Fellini, the undertaking represented a kind of holiday. So delighted was he with his fantasy enchantress and the mental demolition of the vice crusader that he filmed enough for a full-length feature and had eventually to carve thirty minutes out of it so as not to overburden the omnibus film of which it was a part. Even so, it ran for more than an hour.

At its opening in Milan on February 22, 1962, *Boccaccio '70* included well over three hours of diverse episodes that did little to capture the spirit of Boccaccio. Fellini's broad satire was in marked contrast to the elegant sophistication of Visconti's episode (with Romy Schneider) and the country humor of De Sica's segment (with Sophia Loren). Monicelli's contribution was a slight bit of comedy that was excised when the film went into foreign release.

If Fellini fared better with the critics than the other directors, the response toward his episode was lukewarm at best. Some thought it more burlesque than satire; one critic said it was "more naught than naughty." But there were those who saw brilliance in Fellini's direction, even if the story lacked his characteristic freshness.

When the film was shown at Cannes a storm blew up over the excision of Monicelli's episode. He protested, and was supported by the Society of Italian Film Authors. Fellini ignored the fuss and made no protest over the cuts made in the *Doctor Antonio* episode. In the United States, the Catholic Legion of Decency gave *Boccaccio '70* a "C," or "condemned," rating. In Kansas, the state censorship board asked for certain deletions in Fellini's segment. It was thought that when the woman of the billboard came to life, her breasts "bobbled too much." The lawyer employed to defend the film's integrity stated that the woman in question was Anita Ekberg, and that when she ran through the streets "breast bobbling" was unavoidable.

Doctor Antonio marked Fellini's first use of color. He had previously gone on record about his opposition to using color, stating: "There are only two colors you can use in cinema—black and white." But in this case he'd had no choice in the matter, because the producers had stipulated that the entire film was to be in color. Also, the "playful air" of his part in the project had enabled him to experiment with color "without too great a commitment."

"I had thought," he told critic Tullio Kezich, "of Dr. Antonio as a small man, all in black, in the midst of the huge, white buildings of the EUR [a modern area of Rome fostered by Mussolini]. When I saw the projection, the marble was no longer white, it had become blue. The sky had reflected on the smooth parts of the buildings, and there was nothing to do about it."

With Ponti's film out of the way, Fellini resumed his relationship with Rizzoli. His own production company, Federiz, went into limbo, and for his new film he established production offices in the old Scalera studios that were now under Rizzoli's ownership. The new and as yet untitled film would be produced jointly with Rizzoli. When pressed for a title, he gave it a temporary one, 8½. By his calculation, he had made, to that point, seven and a half films. There were the six feature films beginning with *The White Sheik*, and he counted his share of *Variety Lights* and his episodes in *Love in the City* and *Boccaccio '70* as half films.

By the end of 1961 he was still deliberately vague about the film. A reporter wrote: "Trying to piece together the story has become the favorite guessing game on the Via Veneto." The existing script was kept under lock and key; in any case, it was being rewritten on an almost daily basis. "It contained episodes that were never made," Pinelli said. "We were all good friends and we saw each other nearly every day."

"Every morning," Fellini said, "he would ask me what profession our hero was, and I continued not knowing it."

Pinelli said: "Flaiano and I knew that Federico was doing something that had not been done before—he was breaking down the traditional way of making movies. It was not going to be a 'novel' film, a connected story, but instead a perfect correspondence between the images and the story—and stories rather than *a* story."

Finally, with the nature of the hero's profession still unclear, Fellini decided the writing process had gone about as far as it could, and that to resolve the vagueness he would have to begin seeing the characters in person, so to speak, to choose locations and, in effect, to go looking for the film.

Early in 1962, he began testing actors at the Scalera Studios. He announced that filming would begin on April 1. He asked Anouk Aimée to come from Paris to test for the hero's wife, Luisa, but was having more difficulty finding an actress for the equally important role of Carla, the mistress. His production manager, Clemente Fracassi, busied himself with contracts, dates, set building, and finding the location for the spa, the film's principal setting. The interiors of the main spa building were erected on the Scalera sound stages.

Meanwhile, in his office at the studio, Fellini was "still un-

able to find my film. It just wasn't there any more. It had gone off."
The office had a huge desk with its usual clutter of photographs,
wall panels—also covered with photographs—arm chairs, and a
couch. On the same floor was Gherardi's large design studio. Two
other offices were occupied by Fellini's assistants, Lina Wertmuller
and Guidarino Guidi, and by Deena Boyer, a Philadelphian living
in Italy whom Fellini had appointed his "on-set press officer." As
she wrote later, preparations for filming appeared to be proceeding
normally.

But Fellini knew he was in dire creative trouble. He had
named his hero Guido Anselmi, and knew that Guido's own creativity was blocked. But more and more that question of what the hero
did, who he was and what "self" he was searching for, had become
of critical importance. Fellini was inclined toward making Guido
an art director, because that would put him in a field comparable to
his own, and he would be able to understand his dilemma.

Meanwhile all his associates and assistants worked with
confidence because, even though they knew little about the story,
they trusted him. As he recalled, "They thought I knew what I was
doing and that my keeping the plot a secret was a publicity stunt."

From his office at the studio he could hear the carpenters
below hammering away on a set. It was nearing the end of the work-
day and he decided he couldn't go on with the film. He took pen and
paper, and began writing to Rizzoli, saying that he knew what he
was about to tell him would end their relationship, and their friendship, too, and it was a letter he should have written months ago,
except that he had assumed he would be able to solve the film's
problems.

While writing he heard his crew chief calling him from the
courtyard below, asking that he come to the set. One of the carpenters was celebrating his birthday with Asti spumante. Fellini
left the letter unfinished and went to the stage where he joined in a
toast to the carpenter, who then raised his glass in return: "To your
health, dottore, and a great film. Viva 8½!"

Fellini remained on the set after it emptied, thinking. Here
he was, a director, preparing a movie that now seemed to have vanished from his mind. "It was in that moment," he said, "that I

found the heart of the film I was looking for. I would tell exactly what was happening to me. I would make it the story of a director who no longer knew what he wanted to make."

During his period of indecision, he had postponed the start of filming several times. It was to have begun on the first of April, then the eighth, the tenth, the sixteenth. On the evening of April 21, filming not yet begun, he asked his press assistant, Deena Boyer, to drive him home in her car. During the ride he talked to her about the film in more detail than he had before. By now she knew that Guido had become a director, but she did not know that he had received his identity only ten days before. Fellini also revealed that he had considered making Guido a screenwriter unable to write the screenplay he had been commissioned to do.

Boyer knew that one of the sets being constructed was a mock-up of a launching platform for a spaceship. Would it now remain in the picture? When he had envisioned his protagonist as a scenarist, Fellini said, the launching-pad site was to be used in an imaginary sequence depicting man's abandonment of the earth—all humanity, led by the Catholic Church, would pile into a gigantic spaceship. Now the mock-up would be featured in the climax of the film about a creatively blocked director. "In the end he doesn't make the picture, and the unfinished sets are abandoned to the wind and the rain and everything disintegrates," Fellini told Boyer.

Earlier in the month, Boyer had watched a series of screen tests. One was for the part of Maurice, a magician who entertains at the spa—Fellini chose an English writer, Ian Dallas, for the role; another was for Saraghina, a huge prostitute who came directly from a Fellini boyhood memory. Boyer had also watched him testing one of his collaborators, Brunello Rondi, for the part of a writer who criticizes Guido's scenario for a film. "If you want my opinion," Rondi said, improvising the scene, "you should wait awhile longer before you begin this picture." In the test, Fellini seemed to consider taking the advice. "But who's going to tell Rizzoli that?" he asked. In the end, Rondi did not get the part.

The postponements continued, with several parts still remaining to be cast, and with the closely guarded screenplay still being rewritten. Claudia Cardinale, then a nineteen-year-old beauty, had been signed before Guido was made a director. An early version of the script had identified "Claudia" (Fellini, who had trouble finding names for his characters, would often use the name of the actor) as a museum guard's young daughter whom Guido meets at the spa. A later version of the script removed the identification with the girl he had known during his early days in Rome. It is possible to see a relationship, too, between Claudia and the Paola of *La Dolce Vita* whose message, Fellini had intimated, would be made clear in his new film. In the development of Cardinale's role, however, the more Claudia was redefined, the more ambiguous she became.

Finding someone to play the critical role of Carla, Guido's mistress, had occupied Fellini for nearly a year. He had considered Anita Ekberg, keeping her on tenterhooks, but had finally ruled her out. While revising the manuscript with his writers in a hotel near Lake Bracciano, he spent several evenings interviewing possible Carlas. Earlier in the year, he had resorted to one of his ploys— placing newspaper ads describing the kind of woman he sought: "Someone old-fashioned, with a pink and white complexion, a small head on a Rubens body, very soft, flowery, maternal, and opulent."

There were those who took the ads as a joke, but Fellini, who needed this woman and would travel, went as far as Milan and Trieste to see women of Rubenesque proportions who might be suitable. Thousands answered the ads. Also, during these travels he kept an eye out for the even more opulently figured Saraghina. Camilla Cederna, a jouralist present at some of the screen tests, wrote about the applicants: "Enormous women; they were like enormous chests of drawers, like elephants on two feet." Fellini tested dozens, but found his Saraghina in Milan, as he told the author. He saw her walking along the street, approached her, and learned she was a young opera singer, an American of Czech descent, who was on her way to a music lesson. Blonde and shy, her name was Edra Gale, and it took some convincing before she agreed to be tested and was given the role.

A May 1 start date was postponed because Fellini still had not found Carla. Recently, though, he had been leaning more and more toward a young actress, Sandra Milo, whom a colleague had once brought for dinner to his house at the seashore. She had appeared in a few films, but her most recent one, Rossellini's *Vanina, Vanini,* had been a failure. Depressed, she had announced that she was leaving acting and would henceforth devote herself to poetry and other forms of literature.

On May 1, Fellini gave French writer Jean Rougeul the part of a caustic critic who represents Guido's conscience. Then, suddenly making up his mind, he telephoned Sandra Milo. He had been searching, he said, for an actress to play a man's dream of a woman, someone beautiful, sexy, full, and voluptuous. As it happened, Milo had recently lost a considerable amount of weight and wasn't happy about gaining it back. She wavered, telling Fellini she didn't think she wanted to go back to acting.

The next day, she was still in bed in the apartment she shared with her husband, when the doorbell rang. A housemaid opened the door, and saw a delegation led by Fellini. She ran to the bedroom exclaiming, "It's Fellini, it's Fellini!" Milo hurriedly got into a dressing gown and went into the living room, which was already being turned into a miniature studio. With Fellini were Piero Gherardi, cinematographer Gianni di Venanzo, a make-up man, and two lighting assistants. Reluctantly, Milo allowed herself to be dressed in a costume and made up.

"Suddenly," she told Maria Pia Fusco, a well-known Rome newspaperwoman, "the lights blazed and everything exploded in me. I felt like flowers under artificial light that bloom with the pleasure of offering themselves."

The test proved positive for Fellini. Sandra Milo was put under contract, she agreed to gain ten pounds, and a new and absolutely final start date was announced.

On May 9, 1962, the filming of *8½* began.

XIII

FELLINI'S shooting script for *8½* departed from normal practice by not including directions for camera movement or descriptions of individual shots. It begins as follows:

A STREET IN A CITY. EXTERIOR. DAY.

Guido is at the steering wheel of a car that has just stopped moving. On the other side of the windshield, the view is almost completely blocked by a multitude of all kinds of cars, all of which have ground to a halt. . . . A few inches from Guido's face, in a car stopped next to his, is the face of another man, a middle-aged stranger, with hard features, fresh-shaven, with little indecipherable eyes behind his glasses. . . .

It becomes clear, after a time, that Guido is in the midst of a dream, but the script does not describe precisely what is seen in the film: the traffic jam that Guido is caught in occurs in an underpass. Fellini was again changing and improvising, no matter how hectic the concerns and problems of the production staff. And while the screenplay served as the basic architecture of the film, it was seldom used as a precise blueprint. On the other hand, he did place on the title page, as a reminder to himself, the words: A COMEDY.

He didn't want the script to be too complete, he said; otherwise, for him, the picture would be dead. "I'd feel that the thing had already been accomplished in the writing—I'd have no interest in trying to film it. I love to improvise; something lucky and un-expected in one scene opens the door to another and another."

There were never more than two copies of the script on the set at any time, and neither of these was available to the actors, who were given their lines typed on a sheet of paper—sometimes the evening before, and often only a half hour before going on camera. Brunello Rondi was on the set much of the time, and would write or change dialogue the evening before shooting. Mastroianni had had the benefit of talking with Fellini about his part for several months, but even he hadn't read the script when filming began. And while San-dra Milo was told to grow fatter, Mastroianni's orders were to grow thinner; Fellini wanted an older, hollowed look to his face. Since Mastroianni enjoyed his food as much or more than Fellini, absten-tion from his favorite pasta dishes was one of the trials he was forced to endure.

For Sandra Milo, it was eating that tested her endurance. Her first appearance in the film shows her arriving at a train station near the spa, where she is met by Guido. The costume she wore in this scene and in several others was to identify her as the quintessen-tial "other woman" for years to come. As described by Deena Boyer, who was on the set with her, it consisted of a black velvet redingote worn open over a crepe dress with generous decolletage; a white ermine collar, muff and pillbox hat; white gloves; a little silver eve-ning bag, and violets at her bosom. To complement the buxom and sensuous personality Fellini had specified, he asked Piero Gherardi to create an almost literally new face for her. Ordinarily Milo wore her brown hair short; now she was given a blonde wig with a low chignon. Her brown eyebrows were shaved and replaced with pale blonde lines. Her turned-up nose was made less prominent, her wide mouth round and delicate.

But Carla was supposed to enjoy eating, and she was hungry when she arrived at the spa for her illicit liaison with Guido (both are married). Milo's first day on the set involved a scene in which Guido takes Carla to a little restaurant, where she is supposed to be eating, drinking, and talking.

"That first day was awful," Milo told Maria Pia Fusco. She

had to work with unfamiliar lines while biting away at the chicken and interspersing her eating and words with sips from a glass of mineral water.

"It's hard. I can't seem to do it," she told Fellini.

"It'll all work out," he encouraged her, as he had her do take after take.

As the day wound on, she consumed sixteen chicken legs, interrupted by several trips to the restroom to vomit. After the sixteenth chicken leg she informed Fellini that she could go no further. They stopped.

But the next day, as she passed the projection room where Fellini was looking at rushes, he called to her. "Let's do that scene again," he said, "and this time just do it the way you feel like."

"I ate only two chicken legs," Milo said, "and now he liked the scene and the way I did it very well. And with it, my new fat personality was born, representing carnality with no problems, no thought, blonde, white, red mouth always ready to be kissed."

About her relationship with Fellini, she said: "I think we immediately developed a sympathy for each other, and I mean a physical sympathy, because we seldom spoke very much. I admired him, I adored him, as all women do—although at first I was sensitive to his yelling on the set. There's a scene in which I get off the train [filmed several weeks after the chicken-leg scene] and call to Guido. Fellini screamed at me, 'go forward. Stop! Go forward. Stop!' I burst into tears.

"Marcello helped me a great deal, always encouraging me. I was in a kind of trance, because of the great power Fellini had. After a scene in a bedroom, where I'm in bed, having gotten a fever, and supposed to be a little delirious, Marcello said to me: 'You're going to get the Silver Ribbon for that. You really are good.' When it happened, I think it was because of that scene."

Milo commented, too, on the harmony that existed among the many women who played in the film. In addition to herself, Anouk Aimée as Guido's wife, and Claudia Cardinale as both a dream image and the star whose role in the unmade film is undefined, there was the important stage actress Rossella Falk (as a friend of Guido's wife), Barbara Steele as Gloria, the youthful

fiancée of Mezzabotta, an old friend of Guido's, and Madeleine
Lebeau as a French actress. In fact, Fellini as director was surrounded by more doting women in real life than Guido was in the
film. For a so-called "harem" scene, he enlisted the voluptuous
Jacqueline Bonbon, a starlet called Hedy Vessel, and Hazel Rogers,
an American dancer. In the scene, Guido cracks a snake whip to
get all the women in his real and fantasy life to do his bidding and
serve his needs. When Tullio Pinelli was once asked about Fellini's
relationship with women, he answered: "See the harem scene in
8½; it's like that."

"This harmony on the set was his doing," Milo said. "He
distributed his attention among so many of us, and all of us. For
example, he would sit down at a table during a lunch or dinner
break, and he would be brought those large slices of Parmesan
cheese that he loves. He would cut up the slices into smaller pieces
and would feed it to us, like a bird with his nestlings. I thought that
he must be happy with all these women, these creatures of his, but
I doubt that he was."

A friend and one-time associate of Fellini's likes to tell a
story about one of the women in the film who became determined
to seduce her director. She invited him to drop by for a drink one
evening, and made sure to be at her seductive best when he arrived.
Fellini, said the friend, sat quietly for a time, taking in the situation,
then asked where her bathroom was. The actress waited several
minutes for him to return; then she grew worried. When she went to
look, she discovered that Fellini had simply left the apartment.

"I am Guido," Fellini once said, when he was asked by a
critic if his own problems corresponded to those of the hero of the
film. Several writers have wondered to what degree Fellini's inner
or psychological conflicts influenced the substance of *8½*, and have
commented on elements in the film that they interpret as both
Freudian and Jungian. One writer stated that Fellini was in Jungian
psychoanalysis shortly before and during the making of *8½*.

A clue to the reason for the speculation can be seen in a
section of the film in which Guido, at the spa, meets the entertainer

one evening. He is Maurice, a magician who claims to be able to read minds. The magician has an associate who will write on a blackboard what she receives from his reading Guido's mind. She chalks out the mysterious phrase "asa nisi masa." Yes, that's what he had thought of, Guido admits. The incident acts as a trigger to Guido's childhood memories. As a boy, he and a friend used to play a word game involving a made-up language in which the vowel of each syllable of a word is preceded and followed by the letter "s." In this case, the word is "anima," Italian for soul but also an important word in Jungian psychology.

The word "anima" was used by Jung to characterize every male's unconscious female identity (for a woman's unconscious male identity he used "animus") and it was, of course, seized upon as an indication that the meanings of 8½ could be found in Jungian theory. The correspondences do intrigue. Without going into the abstruse byways of Jung's many volumes of theory, it is possible to see Guido as an example of his "extraverted" type, a man oriented toward external reality. A man such as Guido, Carolyn Geduld, a professor at Indiana University, wrote, would retreat into fantasy, a "typical reaction of the extravert who fails to adapt to external conditions." She mentions also "the mother archetype. . . . For Guido, the reproachful—yet dangerously sexual—woman who is his biological mother (and in later life, his wife Luisa) is also an unpleasant synthesis of the two types of women he knew in childhood." (Meaning the kindly nun and the prostitute Saraghina.) For Guido, then, the archetype takes on a whore-nun dichotomy. He must resolve and synthesize the problem with his anima and will then, presumably, find his way back to wholeness and mental health. Or, in Ms. Geduld's words, he will achieve "an inner unity."

In 1984 Fellini told me that in spite of his great interest in Jung and his theories, he had never undergone analysis. Rather, he had had many talks with a prominent Jungian analyst in Rome, and learned much about Jung's thought from him.

From early on, Fellini said, he had maintained a deep interest in parapsychology and psychology. The year after he made *La Dolce Vita* a friend and colleague, Vittorio De Seta, told him about Dr. Ernst Bernhard, a Jungian analyst. "I became curious to meet him," Fellini said, but it took unconscious field forces for the meeting to occur.

"One day I dialed a number that I thought belonged to a very beautiful lady. A man answered. 'Who is speaking?' I asked him. 'This is Bernhard,' he answered. 'Bernhard who? Who are you? I am trying to reach the number of a beautiful lady.' 'I'm sorry,' he said, 'but I'm an old man.' I discovered he was the very Ernst Bernhard De Seta had told me about, and I told the doctor I wanted to meet him. He was surprised, because he thought I was still trying to get to the beautiful woman. Anyway, we met, and became good friends."

Several people, Fellini said, have asked to speak with him about his interest in Jung. One of these was Dr. Suzanne Wagner, a Jungian analyst who resides and practices in Malibu, California. She and her husband were preparing a documentary film on Jung, and having heard of Fellini's interest in the Swiss psychologist, she wrote to him in Rome and he agreed to meet with her.

Fellini, by then, had stated: "I have complete faith in Jung, and total admiration for him."

His discovery of Jung, he told Dr. Wagner, had less do at the time with *8½* than with another idea he was exploring that had to do with death. He would start on it, pursue it for a time, then lose the thread. Sometimes he was distracted by an outside interference, but he had the feeling that his failure to bring the idea to fruition had something to do with his own inner condition.

Fellini also told Dr. Wagner about another incident that had occurred shortly after he mistakenly called Dr. Bernhard. He was walking in the vicinity of the Spanish Steps and encountered a friend who seemed pale and in a state of shock. The friend told him he had just been to see his analyst, Dr. Bernhard.

"This struck Fellini," Dr. Wagner said, "that mysterious forces were at work, drawing him toward Dr. Bernhard, truly a leader then in Rome of what might be called the Jungian community."

Fellini's fascination with Jung is further documented by the fact that he visited the strange tower that the psychologist had built in his home village of Bollingen, Switzerland, and that he became friends with Jung's son. But Dr. Wagner, a charming and attractive woman, believed that with her Fellini was being more than a little whimsical. Even so she had the impression that he made frequent visits to Dr. Bernhard and gained some relief from what he referred to as "a depressed state of mind." Nor did he strike her as someone who had been "analysed"; rather, he seemed somewhat anti-analysis.

He told her a story about leaving the office of Dr. Bernhard one day, still in his state of depression, and noticing a beautiful woman standing at a street corner. He hailed a cab, and on the spur of the moment invited her along. Simply the sight of the woman banished his depression, he told Dr. Wagner, and the encounter was fully as helpful as any analysis. "He did not add anything more about the incident," she said.

In placing Jung among those he most admired, Fellini gave Dr. Bernhard credit for "explaining his thought to me in an incomparable way. It was like the sight of unknown landscapes, like the discovery of a new way of looking at life; a chance of making use of its experiences in a braver and bigger way, of recovering all kinds of energies, all kinds of things, buried under the rubble of fears, lack of awareness, neglected wounds. What I admire most ardently in Jung is the fact that he found a meeting place between science and magic, between reason and fantasy." It would seem logical, in view of this statement, that 8½ was not only influenced by some Jungian indoctrination, but that the meeting with Dr. Bernhard was an important element in the film's origination.

While Deena Boyer was trying to make sense out of what was occurring under Fellini's direction on the set, he did give her a brief explanation of what he was trying to portray—the three levels, he said, "on which our minds live: the past, the present, and the conditional—the realm of fantasy." What might otherwise seem puzzling in the film becomes reasonably clear when it is realized that Guido exists simultaneously in all three planes, beginning with his fantasy of being caught in the jam in an underpass and freeing himself to sail upward—only to be brought down on a beach by a man who turns out to be his assistant on the film he is supposed to be creating.

When he wakes in a bedroom at a thermal resort, attended by doctors, the viewer might assume that Guido is now back in the real world, but wait—the sound-track noises are unnaturally loud— the kind of buzzing sounds that are heard on a movie set—and the lights, too, are the arc lights of a sound stage. Guido, it appears, is the "hero" not only of the film the audience sees, but also of a film being made about him. One can take this further, almost to an infinite dimension.

Christian Metz, a French film theorist with a semiotic approach, saw the film in terms of "mirror construction," and said it belonged to the "category of works of art that are divided and doubled, thus reflecting on themselves." Another French critic, Alain Virmaux, also noted that this was the first time a director had constructed his whole film, and ordered all its elements, "according to the repeating mirror images."

Metz went on to explain that *8½* was "a film that is doubly doubled. . . . It is really a double mirror construction one should be talking about. It is not only a film about the cinema, it is a film about a film that is presumably itself about the cinema; it is not only a film about a director, but a film about a director who is reflecting himself onto his film." A similar interpretation can be reached by anyone who takes the trouble (or privilege) of viewing the movie more than once.

Most who saw the film, however, regarded it as the story of a man searching for the causes of his midlife crisis, his desperation as a director reflected in the confusions of his emotional life. A fuller appreciation resulted when the film was seen on the three levels mentioned by Fellini. Many people wondered why Guido and his associates were dressed in contemporary (1962) clothing, while on the grounds of the spa the guests wandered about in fashions of the 1930s. Deena Boyer asked Fellini for an explanation.

"My childhood memories go back to that time," he told her—and it's a fantasy. Anyway, the spas haven't changed much."

He was being offhand about it, but the film reveals that he knew precisely what he was doing—establishing the simultaneity of

Guido's levels of perception. He was careful, too, to provide the clues—or triggers—to indicate which mental state Guido was residing in at a particular moment.

Walking the grounds of the spa, Guido is in the so-called here and now, but, haunted by the past, he sees the spa in terms of memory. The music played by an orchestra on the grounds is the kind played at such spas in the 1930s. Young girls are serving mineral water, triggering in Guido a third state, a fantasy vision of an idealized young woman, Claudia, who tenderly hands him a glass of water from the spa. She will appear again in other guises. Time present intrudes when Carini (also called Daumier), Guido's constant critic, asks him about the meaning of the film he is supposed to be making. Carini's clothes are modern.

The blending of time and mental states continues throughout the film. The past intrudes into the present, the present into the past, imaginings into one or the other. The shifting takes place smoothly—an accomplishment in itself, considering that the sections of various sequences were often filmed weeks and months apart, and in different locations.

By the time Sandra Milo made her (film) arrival at the spa she was in her third month of pregnancy and, to Fellini's satisfaction, pleasantly rounded. Much of the studio work was done at Scalera, but some was done at Cinecittà. The spa was built in a wooded area of the EUR. Four large buildings from what Mussolini had planned as a great exhibition in 1940 (cancelled because of the war) still survived, and Fellini used one of them for the entrance and main lobby of his spa's "Grand Hotel."

The baths were built in a basement of another of the buildings. Fellini found his film theater for the viewing of the screen tests (in the film) on the main square in Tivoli. The beach at Fiumicino, near Ostia, was used for the scenes in which Guido, as a small boy, encounters the woman who sells herself to fishermen for sardines. The trigger for the scene occurs when Guido notices a fat woman at the spa. The transformation of Edra Gale into the gross, almost devilishly wanton Saraghina has its place as Guido's first erotic experience, and by the very grotesqueness of the exhibition she provides (her lumbering rhumba on the sand, her sly and leering look at little Guido) makes it memorable and significant in the story structure.

From the melange of time levels and mental states, a literal story can be sifted, and does emerge by the film's end. Guido is at a spa attempting to get himself physically and spiritually together so that he can continue the work on his next film, the sets for which are already under construction. His relationship with his wife, Luisa, has become strained; he is in a state of confusion about the film he is about to make; he is being badgered by his producer and production associates, a writer friend, and by the stars (with their agents) who are being interviewed or are already contracted for the film. Among these are the young and beautiful Claudia and an older French actress, both of whom want to know more about their unspecified "roles."

Essentially, what has happened to Guido is that he has lost for the time being the *elan,* the vitality, the motivation behind his creativity as a director, and without being too consciously aware of it, he is delving into his past in an attempt to find the wellsprings of his current malaise. But with the memories certain dreams and fantasies also emerge to consciousness, representing what he would like his life to be.

His young married mistress, Carla, joins him at the spa, but since he is maintaining his facade of married respectability, he places her in a nearby hotel, where he visits her and asks her to play sex games that will make her seem like a whore. Carla, however, does little to ease his distressed state of mind, so Guido asks his wife, Luisa, to come to the spa. In a dream, Guido's mother and Luisa become confused in his mind. It is clear that Luisa represents the pressure of conformity and Carla the unsatisfying lure of carnality, and that he finds it impossible to reconcile the poles they embody. There is a famous cardinal taking a cure at the spa, and during a visit with him in the steam baths, Guido asks for guidance but gets little advice other than that it is man's fate to be unhappy. Perhaps the "real" Claudia will be an answer for him, but a would-be romantic meeting between them goes flat when it is clear that Claudia is far less interested in him than she is in the role in his film, a director's not unusual dilemma. He has to admit that he doesn't know what the role is; there may be none at all.

The production staff, in spite of Guido's reluctance, is gearing up. Screen tests of the leading players in the "film" are shown to an audience that includes Luisa, who by now has strong doubts that her relationship with Guido can be salvaged. To her shock, she sees herself portrayed by others in the screen tests, and it now seems that Guido's film is not about what he professed it to be, but is dealing with his own life's drama. Nevertheless, a press conference is held on a beach near where a spaceship gantry has been erected, and at this point Guido's anguish has become so acute that he envisions himself committing suicide. When he emerges from this dream fantasy he has not ended his life, but he has ended all hope of his making the film. The spaceship structure is being dismantled.

Throughout the film, fantasies intrude, some having to do with the way Guido imagines he would prefer his life to be. He would like Claudia, the star, to be the dream Claudia—comforting, caring, forever devoted to him; he imagines Carla and Luisa happily dancing together, adjusted to sharing him; and he fantasizes a scene in which he is the master of a household containing all the women in his life and can cow them into submission by cracking his snake whip.

Once Guido has seen his film collapse and becomes aware of his own failure, Fellini gives up all pretense of literalness and takes the story into another realm. His first scenario for the ending describes it as follows:

DINING CAR.

As the train rolls across a quiet countryside, Guido once again enters an unreal world. Around him, the other passengers become people out of his life. They smile sympathetically at him. He recognizes that he cannot deny them. Greatly moved, he rises and searches for a way to tell them that, at bottom, he can be happy this way. The waiter and Luisa are dumbstruck. Guido takes Luisa's hand and tries again with his eyes to "tell her something," while the train rolls on through the night, comforting him with its sound.

Fellini shot this much as he described it above. Then, while the production continued he decided to shoot a trailer to be shown in theaters in advance of the opening. At least that was what he said he was doing, perhaps to justify the extra costs. Rizzoli agreed to let him bring back the entire cast, as well as a small circus troupe. Fellini used seven cameras to film the troupe dancing around in a circle, led by Guido as a boy. It is likely that he was considering an alternate ending, and not merely a trailer.

As the production moved toward its conclusion, Fellini worked on both endings, doing retakes of the scene in the dining car and of the circus procession on the beach. In both versions, Guido makes a speech to Luisa indicating that he has decided to accept his confusions, must settle for what he is, and can only be accepted as such. More than that, those who have contributed to his confusion are of vital importance to him, to be accepted for what they are, too. Back in control once more, Guido is able to command his actors to do his bidding. He has rediscovered his creative powers and will presumably now be able to make his film—not the one about the spaceship and humanity deserting the earth but, presumably, the one the audience has just seen.

It was not until late in January of 1963 that the second of the two endings was decided upon. The meanings were essentially the same, Fellini felt, but the ending in the dining car, although quite beautiful, struck him as a more intellectual than emotional expression, and as a result less moving. The audience's response to the "circus" ending vindicated his judgment, although it was to cause some critical dissension.

With the première of the film hardly a month away, the provisional title was made the final one, after waverings over others such as *I Confess* and *The Confessions of Snaporaz* (the latter now fixed as Fellini's nickname for Mastroianni). Gherardi designed the title in a florid style reminiscent of Fellini's advertising posters for the Fulgor cinema in Rimini. And, for the first time, Fellini's name went over the title. ("It was a smart thing for him to do," Alberto Lattuada, the director who had hired him in the early days at Lux Film, commented rather sourly. "It made him more important than the stars—it made *him* the star.")

At the première in Milan, the last week of February 1963, and simultaneously in Rome, there was scattered applause but no enthusiastic call for the director to take his bows. A shower of critical praise gave the film a boost as its showings spread throughout the country, but there was little in the way of controversy, as there had been in the case of *La Dolce Vita*, to lengthen the runs. Sergio Frosale in *Cinema* was one of the film's few detractors, and his criticism focused mainly on what he deemed Fellini's snobbishness in using actors with foreign accents and personalities. He objected to Ian Dallas as the magician, Jean Rougeul as the intellectual, and Barbara Steele as the self-centered fiancée of Guido's friend Mezzabotta. "Fellini," he said, "would have been more truthful and precise if he had substituted Italian types for these characters."

In contrast, other critics rolled out the names of Proust, Joyce, and Ingmar Bergman for comparisons to "this chief work of a magician of genius."

"It may not be a film in the current sense of the term," Gian Luigi Rondi the brother of Brunello, rhapsodized, "but it is certainly cinema—in fact, the utmost in cinema, the like of which the screen has not offered us with such suggestive power, such impulsiveness, such free and light-hearted simplicity."

Almost at once, Joseph E. Levine responded with a handsome offer for North American rights to the film, and while Rizzoli tooled up his palatial yacht in preparation for the Cannes Film festival, Fellini was already thinking about and planning his next work.

XIV

I DON'T know if Jung's thought influenced my films from *8½* on," Fellini said some years later. "I only know without question that reading some of his books encouraged and favored the contact with deeper and more stimulating areas, and provoked fantasy in me."

He added, "I have one great limitation, I feel—of not having general ideas about anything. Reading Jung has freed me from the sense of guilt and the inferiority complex this limitation gave me."

His lack of general ideas not withstanding, Fellini was able to express himself with more and more fluidity as *8½* moved into release outside Italy and caused interviewers to ask him for clarification of its meanings. He would say he disliked interviews and that they made him uncomfortable, but he was usually ready and willing to submit himself to questions, the answers to which he would expand into thoughts on life, art, religion, sex, marriage, and morals.

Guido's search for a kind of personal liberation was similar to his own "attempt to throw off my back the upbringing I have had; that is, to try to uneducate myself, to recapture a virginal unavailability and a new type of person with an individual education—thereby not to find myself plunged again into the collective whole, nor to remain subject to laws which are not my own, which are not anyone's, because they are collective."

To another interviewer, he said, "Self acceptance can occur only when you've grasped that the only thing that exists is yourself, your true, deep self which wants to grow spontaneously, but which is fettered by inoperative lies, myths and fantasies that propose an unattainable morality or sanctity or perfection—all of it brainwashed into us during our defensive childhood." The more he discussed the meanings of *8½* and his ideas about it the more he appeared to identify himself with Guido—to be saying what Guido might have said if he had stepped out of the film and into the real world.

"Woman," he said, "is mother, sister, saint, and virtue, and the other side is whore, vice, corruption, and sin." But it was presumably Guido who saw women in these black and white terms— almost literally, for the women in the film are dressed in white, black, or combinations thereof.

Guido had a problem, Fellini said, with his Christianity. He was a victim "of medieval Catholicism which tends to humiliate a man rather than restore him to his divine greatness." Fellini's friends said he was a "worried" Catholic himself. But he was able to achieve his own state of grace when making a picture. "He feels reborn," said Mastroianni. "When I make a picture," Fellini said, "I am healthy, happy, don't need anything except sex. I live in a dimension in which I am absolved, taken by life. My crisis begins when a picture finishes, when I am again with my real problems—God, wife, women, taxes—until a new light comes to announce a new game and it takes me again."

Experimentation with the effects of LSD was in vogue around that time, and Fellini was asked by a scientist friend to try the hallucinogen under controlled conditions. The scientist and his colleagues were interested in what might happen to an artist such as Fellini when under the drug's influence. Fellini consented, but then had his doubts. "I had committed myself," he said, "and didn't want to seem a coward."

The experiment took place in an apartment not far from his own in Parioli on a Sunday afternoon. With him were the scientist, two nurses, a cardiologist, and stenographers with tape recorders. After an electrocardiogram was taken, he drank a mixture of LSD and water, the effects of which were to last for seven or eight hours.

Fellini remembered little of what happened, but was later told that his hallucinating had gone on much longer than was usual and that he had been injected with tranquilizers so that his friends could take him home late that night. A nurse stayed with him. He awakened in the morning as though nothing had happened, but learned he had spoken for many hours without pause while pacing continuously around the room. The experimenters interpreted the results as "a flight, the impossibility of standing still—that my natural condition is to be in motion, on the move."

In this period, too, his preoccupation with magic and the occult increased, and his library of esoteric books grew larger. He took an interest in astrology, graphology, and palmistry. One of his favorite companions, while making *La Dolce Vita*, was Marianna Leibl, a Roman parapsychologist; and, in fact, he gave her a small part in the film. He liked to call her "the enchantress."

About his attraction to astrology Fellini said, "I like to believe in anything that stimulates the imagination. Astrology is a suggestive and diverting way of interpreting the direction of things, the why and the how."

He became fascinated by and a good friend of Gustavo Rol, a magician from Turin. "Rol," he told me, "from what I've seen is a man who has some extraordinary power. I have met others with it, but he is one of the strongest. It is a power over the material—and it's hard to give a rational explanation for it. Our rational point of view acts like a prison, and it's impossible to talk with rationality about the irrational. I do think, though, that Rol has a control over certain laws and forces. There is certainly the power to control the wind, the rain. There are forces that control these kinds of phenomena. Rol is someone, it seems to me, who can make these forces pass through himself like a medium, or channel. He's a man who has developed powers every one of us could have."

Although known for being mischievous during interviews, Fellini, in this case was not only serious, but almost defensive in his espousal of the natural nature of magic.

While accompanying *8½* on its travels to other countries, he was asked about his next project; he admitted that he had something in mind and said that it would deal with certain strange and mysterious manifestations that were of great interest to him. His preoccupation with the esoteric and the occult, the realms of dreams and fantasy, was leading to a more or less concrete conception of a film. And he was already discussing it with his collaborators.

But real events were occupying him, too. In late April of 1963, *8½* was shown at Cannes to almost universal acclaim, but no prize was awarded because it was shown outside the competition. Cannes rules demanded exclusivity in competition entries, and *8½* was already earmarked as Italy's official entry in the later Moscow festival. In June the American première was held in New York, the rights to the film having been obtained by Joseph E. Levine.

The afternoon before the opening, Fellini accompanied Levine to the recently constructed Festival Theater to check the projectors and the sound. The first images of the film are silent, and Levine exclaimed, "That's how it starts?" Only then did Fellini realize that he had not seen the film before buying it. This only endeared him to Fellini all the more.

Following the première, Levine threw a lavish party at the newly opened and elegant Four Seasons restaurant. Even though a crowd of celebrities surrounded Fellini, exclaiming their congratulations, he was worried. Ugo Stille, the American correspondent for a Rome newspaper, overheard him remarking to Mastroianni, "The people at the première parties are always the same in every country. You can't get a real reaction. But what about the real American public that doesn't go to premières, but to the movies?"

For the women at the party the real show was Mastroianni. They all wanted to meet Marcello, and he obliged by turning on his charm.

Reviews ranged from the ecstatic to the benighted. For the *Newsweek* critic, it was "beyond doubt, a work of art of the first magnitude." Brendan Gill, in the *New Yorker*, saw it as a comedy, a "marvellous" one—"his innumerable intricate tricks are enchanting."

Judith Crist in the *Tribune* didn't think the film touched the heart or moved the spirit. Bosley Crowther in the *Times* enjoyed the wit and noted "a bit of a travesty of Freud," but doubted that Fel-

lini had thought his film through to the end. But his disappoint-
ments were mild compared to John Simon's; for him the film was "a
disheartening fiasco," its originality mitigated because the "dance
of life" at the end was suggested by Bergman's dance of death in
The Seventh Seal (which Fellini had not seen).

Discussion of the film widened and writings on it prolifer-
ated as the months went by. Dwight Macdonald revised his opinion
of Fellini and found *8½* "the most brilliant, varied, and entertain-
ing movie since *Citizen Kane*," even though it pained him to disagree with his friend, John Simon. And so it went, as the film
became an intellectual cud to chew on.

Leaving the critical hubbub behind, Fellini, with Giulietta,
went to Moscow, where *8½* was Italy's official entry in the eastern
bloc film festival. Giulietta was perhaps even better known to the
Russians than Fellini, and when they stood on the stage together in
the huge hall that held more than 8,000 people, they were greeted
with thunderous applause. The end of the film, too, brought an
ovation.

The festival jury had fifteen members, the majority from
socialist countries. Italy's representative was Fellini's former colleague, Sergio Amidei. Since *8½* was clearly the hands down favorite among the entries, it was the prime candidate for the grand
prize. Nevertheless, eight of the fifteen jury votes went against it,
word apparently having been received from on high that it would be
against official policy to vote for it. This caused a ruckus among the
remaining jury members, the rebellion being led by Stanley Kramer,
the American representative.

Finally, the Czech member of the jury came to Fellini and
asked him if he would receive the prize as a brilliant director, but
one whose film, unfortunately, did not contribute to peace and friendship among nations. "I might accept," Fellini told him, "if I wanted
a funny story to tell for the rest of my life . . . accepting a prize
and a scolding at the same time."

Eventually a compromise was reached. He was given the
prize for a film that bore "witness to an artist in search of the
truth," while the Russian public was informed by the press that
the film's ideas were "pessimistic and remote from the people."

Throughout the spring, summer, and fall of 1963, Fellini firmed up the elements of his next film, which, he stated, was born as a film about and for Giulietta. One Italian writer suggested that perhaps he was feeling "a subtle but deep remorse for his neglect" of the wife and actress who had contributed so much to his early successes; rumors had abounded that the wife/husband relationship revealed in *8½* had as much basis in autobiography as anything else in the film. If the gossip was true, the new film, *Giulietta degli spiriti* (*Juliet of the Spirits*), was a magnificent means of making amends.

Fellini claimed, however, that the film had had a long period of gestation, going as far back as the time of *La Strada*. He had come across the diary of a nun in a convent library and had been intrigued by the sweet, saintly woman, her visions and fantasies. As his own interest in the fantastic and magical widened, he saw another approach in the autobiography of the rich American medium Eileen Garrett, but gave this up because, he said, he would have felt hampered by being tied to a real story. What he wanted above all was to give Giulietta the opportunity to play many roles in the same film.

His fame was now such that it seemed everyone knew where he lived on the Via Archimede. Keeping their apartment for the time being, he and Giulietta moved to a house set in the pines near the beach at Fregene, not much more than thirty minutes by car from Rome. He began meeting with his familiar band of writers—Pinelli, Flaiano, and Rondi—and the story was clarified into one about a woman who hallucinates, driven to distraction and to a reordering of her life's purposes by her husband's infidelities. The influence of the more grotesque elements in *8½* was apparent; so were Fellini's researches into paranormal experiences.

The idea, he said, finally took form when he had a vision of a lonely woman waiting in a villa for her husband's return on the night of their twentieth wedding anniversary. "This woman," Pinelli recalled, "was to have peculiar supernatural sensations, but in a realistic way. That is, she was disturbed by these strange capacities of hers. Then, we started to have problems."

The writers were not seeing the story in the same way—that is, Fellini's way. Pinelli and Flaiano would go off on the tack they

thought was correct, only to discover that Fellini was somewhere
else. "We were thinking of one kind of woman," Pinelli said, "and
Federico of another." It was the first time in all the years they had
worked together that there was no intuitive agreement among the
three of them about the interpretation of the story.

It was not until Pinelli saw the finished film that he realized
the extent of the divergence that had occurred between himself and
Fellini. "*Giulietta* was the beginning of a new phase for him," Pinelli said. "His concern was less with human feelings than with images."

Flaiano's problems with Fellini, Pinelli said, were more on
a personal level. "[Flaiano] was becoming more and more famous
for his own work, his plays, essays, novels. And it bothered his ego
always to be considered second to Fellini, on a lower level."

It was in this atmosphere of disharmony (the only exception
being the faithful Rondi) that the screenplay was completed, and
the exhaustive work of casting begun. The advertisements went
out, the countless photographs were pored over, and the applicants
streamed in. Fellini had first thought a February 1964 start date
would be possible, but ultimately, filming was postponed until November. He was once more tied together with Rizzoli, and with a
handsome profit percentage arrangement, similar to that for *8½*,
which left him and Giulietta comfortably off.

In February 1964 Fellini learned that *8½* was a nominee
for the Best Foreign Film Oscar. Rizzoli grandly arranged an ex-
pedition. Among those he invited on the trip to the Academy Award
ceremonies were the Fellinis, Sandra Milo, Pinelli, and Flaiano. Pinelli declined. He had made two previous trips, and by now he felt
himself to be merely a part of the Fellini court. Flaiano accepted. It
was because of that trip that the long relationship between Flaiano
and Fellini blew apart. It may have seemed a comedy to some, but
it wasn't.

"I went to the airport to see them off," Pinelli related, "and
while waiting in the lounge I heard sounds of a strong argument between the two. Flaiano looked pale, almost as though he was dying.
What had happened was that everyone else, including Gherardi, the
art director, had been given first-class tickets—and Flaiano was

handed one for tourist class. Fellini refused to take the blame. It was not him, but Rizzoli who had dispensed the tickets. Flaiano spat out an insult at him. It was inconceivable, he said, that Fellini should have allowed an author of his, Ennio's, calibre—not to mention the collaborator on his films—to be treated on the level of a company press agent. 'Don't go!' Fellini finally shouted back."

Later, on the plane, Fellini left the first-class section and sat with Flaiano for a while in tourist—but everyone on the trip, Sandra Milo later related, heard "the sound of broken glass" and knew that "a glorious relationship had been broken because of a green instead of a red ticket."

"But that," said Pinelli, "was only the tip of the problem. The roots went deeper. Flaiano could not abide his underclass status with Fellini, and his own work was taking precedence."

Sandra Milo's version of the event is taken from a book published by her in 1982. It deserves mention, even though she, herself, has disclaimed it as a reliable source of information. If nothing else, however, her book, titled *Caro Federico*, published by the Rizzoli firm in 1982, is an interesting piece of Fellini speculation.

The book, she declared, was a novel, a fantasy, about an actress named Selana and her director, Fellini, a fairy-tale really about a relationship between the two. Selana in the story bears a remarkable resemblance to the author. Details of Selana's work in Fellini's films, and of her continuing relationship with him, are similar to accounts given to interviewers by Milo. What created something of a scandal in Italy were several passages that vividly describe an intermittent love affair between Selana and the supposedly fantasized Fellini. There were mentions in the Italian press of rewriting done by another on Milo's original manuscript, which she was said to have created in a hideaway in Abruzzo. Indeed, the passages dealing with Selana's sexual intimacies are inventive enough to have been written by a professional pornographer. (When Fellini was asked for comment, he said, "I don't even want to smell it.")

April 1964 was an important month for Fellini. Not only did he take the Oscar for *8½*, but Gherardi was given the award for best

black and white costuming. In Italy, meanwhile, a congress of critics voted the film a record seven Silver Ribbons. Sandra Milo won
one of them. As a result, she found herself a successful actress and,
as she said, a rather unwilling international sex symbol.

Fellini apparently saw her in this way, too, for he approached
her to play the important part of Suzy—as florid and fantastic a
woman as he had yet envisioned—in *Juliet of the Spirits*. "It wasn't
right for me," she told Maria Pia Fusco. "It was a wonderful role,
but it seemed to me I was going backward. Federico convinced me,
though."

Suzy is first seen in the film as she is glimpsed by Giulietta
coming out of the sea like a bizarre Venus. She is Giulietta's neighbor, her life a round of psychedelic parties with a bevy of young,
attractive men. As Fellini described her in the screenplay, she is
"like an apparition of a superb feminine divinity." On the realistic
level, it was indicated that Suzy might be the girlfriend of a Greek
armament maker, but in her larger than life flamboyance she symbolized female sexuality incarnate, the embodiment of the pagan impulses buried by the force of religious upbringing in Giulietta's sub-
conscious. Suzy lives luxuriously in an atmosphere of disarray. She
is all sensuousness. A slide from her bed leads down to a shimmering
blue pool, in which she cavorts nakedly, urging Giulietta to do the
same.

As in *8½*, Milo was almost literally remodeled to Fellini's
specifications. She was given beauty treatments, massages, and dance
lessons, because "Fellini wanted me to move a certain way. Piero
Gherardi shaved my eyebrows completely. To me I was ghastly ugli-
ness, a monster, but Gherardi was blissful, as though now that he
had destroyed my face he could begin to rebuild. First came the
blonde cotton-candy wig, then re-created eyebrows, red hair. Fellini
said to me, 'You must be absolutely pretty. Remember, inside of
you—you must repeat it constantly—you say to yourself, "I am
beautiful, the most beautiful woman in the world." ' That is Fellini's
magic, the fact that he can wrap the actor up in the role he has
to do."

In his wife, Giulietta, he had a less willing and subservient
disciple. Once production was underway at Rizzoli's Scalera studios

in the Palatine hills, she participated in a séance held in their apartment—Fellini was still avidly researching psychic phenomena—but
balked at attending others. "I believe in it," she said, "and am considered a good medium, but that's why I don't want to do it. It reveals a fascinating world and a dangerous one." Fellini, at the séance, was convinced that his father had appeared and spoken to him.

On the set, there were shouting fights between the two as
they differed about how Giulietta should interpret the role of a woman
whose ordered world has collapsed following the discovery of her
husband's infidelity and his desire to leave her. "I needed to erase
everything Masina had portrayed before," Fellini told writer John
Gruen. "That engaging and poignant clown of *La Strada* and *Cabiria*
had to go. We worked endlessly. And all along I knew what I was
losing—but not what I was gaining. She found a thousand objections. This or that did not 'feel' right to her. And I became angrier
and angrier. But don't you understand, I would tell her, I want you to
play *yourself*. What I'm asking you to do is what you *always* do—
what I'm asking you to feel is what you *always* feel."

Gruen heard a whisper on the set: "All the defects of Federico's own marriage are in it. He hasn't left out a single bizarre and
unhappy detail."

But Fellini said to him, "It is the least biographical of my
films. My wife just happens to be in it." He gave credit to Giulietta
for aiding him in "penetrating certain areas of reality. She was the
perfect guide. A number of times on the spur of the moment I just
asked Giulietta what she would say, what she would do, and I accepted her solutions without the slightest change."

With *Juliet of the Spirits* Fellini went full-blown into the use
of color, as though once having decided to do it, he would employ
its possibilities to the fullest. When he was asked by Tullio Kezich
about his earlier aversion to color photography he said, simply, "I
have changed my mind." In fact, he said, "color is an essential part
of this film," and he doubted that he could have done it in black and
white. "It is a type of fantasy that is developed through colored il-
luminations."

But, then, in talking with John Gruen, he contradicted himself: "Color is basically immobile, and yet it must move. Color is

wrong for a film that tries to be as subjective as mine. I struggled with myself about using it until I came to the conclusion that the only way to use it is subjectively."

The moment Fellini left, one of his co-workers said: "He comes up with a new interpretation of his working methods every time someone asks him about it."

By late August 1965 Fellini was working on the final editing of the new film, and Rizzoli was busy arranging for its release. But relations between the director and producer had become something less than cordial. For one thing, the house at Fregene chosen as Giulietta's residence was not to Fellini's liking, and so he had a new one built and completely furnished from scratch. The real-life Giulietta liked it so much that she had one commissioned on a smaller scale for Federico and herself. More expense was involved when production was moved from Rizzoli's small studio in the Palatine hills to the far more commodious Cinecittà. Rizzoli was anxious to have the film premièred at the Venice Film Festival in September, but Fellini balked at this.

As reported by Lillian Ross in the *New Yorker*, Fellini declared that he hated film festivals, that the atmosphere of competition was foreign to his nature. "Festivals and New York cocktail parties, they both have the same atmosphere, with all those people who come and talk, talk, talk." Rizzoli, a seventy-five-year-old man, he said, liked to go to film festivals, with their abundance of yachts, beautiful women, and good food. To Rizzoli's displeasure, Fellini decided against going to Venice, but, on the other hand, was willing to go to New York for a grandly publicized opening and a round of appearances, parties, and talk, talk, talk.

The opening of the film in Rome in late October 1965 was an event of some magnitude in the cinema world, but the general tenor of the audience and critical response was rather a letdown after the extraordinary peaks achieved by *La Dolce Vita* and *8½*. The extravagance of the décor was praised, and Masina was favorably treated, but the film was regarded more as a display of Fellini's flamboyance than as a deeply meaningful treatment of the married woman's dilemma in the modern world. The basic plot seemed relatively simple in contrast to those of his other films. Giulietta, in her lack of sophistication and sexuality, eventually coming to terms with her abandonment and resolving to face the future unfettered by the psychological baggage of her past, was uncomfortably close to a conventional, even soap-opera heroine.

Much hoopla accompanied the film's New York opening two weeks later. Fellini arrived with Masina and Sandra Milo, declaring that the St. Regis was his favorite hotel, buying gifts for his wife at Bergdorf's, and attending with her a round of interview sessions and parties. For one of the parties, Giulietta cooked a spaghetti dinner for thirty guests. Another was hosted by Jacqueline Kennedy at her Fifth Avenue apartment. Some years later, when Mrs. Onassis was asked about the occasion, she had little memory of it, nor of who was there, but Giulietta considered it the highlight of her visits to the United States.

The film had its partisans among the New York critics, but there was also a slight air of disappointment, as though Fellini had cooked up a whole dinner of confections rather than a full, satisfying meal. In fact, this was the metaphorical focus of Robert Brustein's displeasure.

He wrote in the *New York Review of Books*: "After two and a quarter hours of birthday cake décor, appetizing costumes, spectacular memory-fantasies, yellow wigs and crimson beards, dream caravans from the sea, séances, orgies, and succulent courtesans— one emerges from the theater as from a debauch, glutted and bleary-eyed, yet with a curiously empty stomach and a flat taste in the mouth." For him, the film was specious and hollow.

Saturday Review was kinder, but declared that the "spirits" Giulietta called up were more interesting than she. Fellini's faces— his use of them—intrigued the critic the most; they gave the film its expressive strength.

The most savage attack came, once again, from John Simon, in the *New York Times* and the *New Leader*, and occasioned an outraged rebuttal on the part of Fellini adherents. Once one of Fellini's most ardent supporters, Simon wrote that Giulietta [of the film] "has become a free woman. Heaven knows why, or to what purpose." He expressed dismay about what he regarded as the film's vulgarity, and described its color and costuming as "the incestuous marriage of *Harper's Bazaar* and *Vogue*."

If he was bothered by the severity of some of the critical notices, Fellini gave no sign. His main concern at this point was the popular success of the film; it was his costliest yet, and had required outside international financing by Rizzoli.

"He is a man," writer Salvato Cappelli observed of Fellini, "not adapted to survive in a hostile atmosphere, but perfectly capable of creating around himself, with fastidious selectivity, the climate which serves his purpose."

Symptomatic of this capability was his breaking with Rizzoli and returning to Dino De Laurentiis. More and more Fellini left Rome behind for the more serene surroundings of Fregene. The apartment on Via Archimede was sold, and he purchased a small *pied-à-terre* on Via Margutta, a quaint, narrow street of antique shops and small art galleries not far from the Piazza del Popolo, whose restaurants and cafés were more likely to see him than those of the Via Veneto. His friendship with Pinelli was still intact, but they saw less of each other. Flaiano he did not see at all.

XV

EARLY in 1966, reports began to circulate in Rome that Fellini was at work on a new film, that it would star Marcello Mastroianni, and that the producer would be Dino De Laurentiis. The title given was *Absurd Universe*. For several years, Fellini had been developing a story—as his friends knew—about death. Details now emerged, through information he imparted to the critic Gian Luigi Rondi.

The protagonist of the story (soon to be named G. Mastorna) has died and is on a journey through the afterworld, his exploration of which will allow for a rich combination of the comic, the absurd, and the fantastic. Eventually retitled *The Voyage of G. Mastorna*, it turned out to be the most famous film in Italy that was never made.

Fellini contracted to make it for a fee close to a quarter of a million dollars, and De Laurentiis scheduled a production that would begin later in the year.

In search of a name for his main character, a cellist, Fellini found it by chance while looking through a telephone book in Milan. "From that moment the story called itself 'The Voyage.' " For many years, it remained a project that might someday come into being. In spite of its "integral narrative structure," he said long after the project's abandonment, "perhaps it isn't even a film, but a force, an urge, a stimulus. Something came into being not to be made, but to allow me to do something else."

Mastorna has had a curious importance in the continuing

development of Fellini's film-making; it also contributed to a physical and mental crisis that resulted in a lengthy hiatus between films. The change that Pinelli had noticed in Fellini's stylistic preoccupations during the making of *Juliet* was also reflected in the break with many who had worked with him through several films. For his collaborator on the screenplay of *Mastorna*, he chose screenwriter Dino Buzzati. Nino Rota would be retained for the music, for nothing ever disturbed the harmony of that relationship. But somehow the new film and its problems cast a pall over Fellini.

Liliana Betti, Fellini's long-time secretary and assistant, wrote, in a book-long sketch of her working relationship with the director, of his being "afflicted for some time with a paralyzing confusion, which drove him to uncertain renunciation or useless, implacable stubbornness." He was in "a state of depression," induced, she said, when he and his staff moved to "the marvelously equipped offices and studios" of De Laurentiis on the Via Pontina. He "started drooping like a plant in a refrigerator."

Through the first half of 1966, Fellini struggled to make his film on his own terms, arguing with De Laurentiis at every turn while construction of large and costly sets proceeded. So did casting. The names included several of Italy's most popular comedians, among them Toto, Macario, and Fanfulla. Others announced for the cast were Vittorio De Sica and, tentatively, Shirley MacLaine, with whom De Laurentiis was negotiating.

Fellini divulged more details of the story, which, he said, was "actually the story of a city, illustrated through the adventures of a cellist, who discovers he's lost something insignificant, but which he thought a lot of. The picture relates this search for the missing thing in which he first acts alone, then is joined by his friends, parents, and finally the entire population of the city. However, I must keep the nature of the missing 'thing' a total secret, nor will I reveal whether or not it is found at the finale." He did say that the picture would be filmed in black and white, and that there would be location work in Rome, Milan, Naples, New York, Amsterdam, and Calcutta. It further turned out that principal financing would come from the American firm, United Artists.

Filming was to begin on September 5, 1966. Then came a

postponement of four weeks caused by Fellini's indisposition. He was said to be suffering from physical and nervous exhaustion, and had been ordered by his doctor to take a complete rest for several weeks.

In mid-September Fellini dispatched a letter to De Laurentiis, with the apologetic message that he could not begin the film, "because after all the things that have happened, I will not be able to complete it." There had been too many contradictory, disturbing incidents that, Fellini wrote, had nothing to do with the film itself but which surrounded the preparations "with an atmosphere of resistance and stagnation."

As Fellini later explained to me, "The problem was myself. Before the picture could exist there was the Fellini business. No one thought about the picture I wanted to do. Instead they thought about the picture they wanted to do with Fellini, and an atmosphere of misunderstanding was created. It was difficult for me to see my picture in terms of someone else's financial vision, to take a serious interest in bankers, distributors, exhibitors."

De Laurentiis reacted with outrage to Fellini's decision. What about the nearly finished set constructions, the crew members and technicians who had been assembled? De Laurentiis made his anger public, and bold newspaper headlines resulted. The producer brought on a battery of lawyers to hound Fellini, who, he declared, had already cost him losses of nearly $1 million. In fact, he asked for Fellini's assets to be seized as partial repayment of what he said was the nearly $500,000 he was owed by the director. Articles were indeed impounded—about $5,000 worth—but Fellini had earlier had the prescience to put his house and various possessions in his wife's name.

De Laurentiis countered by claiming the percentages owed Fellini by Rizzoli for *8½* and *Juliet of the Spirits*, plus damages due to the cancellation of a second film that Fellini was to make with him. Fellini looked into producing his film without De Laurentiis. The Italian Socialist government had formed a film distributorship; United Artists was willing to continue the financing under another arrangement. But by this time Fellini was unsure whether it should be Mastroianni as the departed (from this earth) cellist, or Laurence Olivier. Perhaps Olivier wasn't right either. In any case, Mastroianni accepted another assignment, and without his star power United Artists withdrew its backing. Fellini next tried forming his own production company, which he named Fulgor Films, after the theater in Rimini where he had seen his first movies. It had a very brief life.

Fellini, wrote Liliana Betti, took on the air of a man besieged by debtors. "One morning he came from Fregene with a package containing two or three gold brooches and a small medallion" which he "sold to a jeweler on Via del Tritone." The money he obtained from the sale allowed Fellini to treat the painter and film-maker Hans Richter to lunch.

In January of 1967 Fellini and De Laurentiis met to resolve their dispute in what Fellini has described as a Mafialike atmosphere. The discussion took place in a car that slowly prowled through the dark streets of Villa Borghese, and the upshot was that Fellini agreed to continue work on the film.

But who would play Mastorna? De Laurentiis's choice was Ugo Tognazzi, a stocky comic actor then having a vogue in Italy. Fellini agreed at first, even with a certain amount of enthusiasm. Then he wavered again. He thought of Gregory Peck, Oskar Werner, Paul Newman. None seemed right. And De Laurentiis was adamant about using Tognazzi.

In a hotel room one evening in March, Fellini became ill with pains in his chest. Fearing that he was dying, he called a doctor, then scrawled a note to Giulietta, which he pinned to the door, warning her not to come in first (in case he was already dead). On the way to the hospital, his car crashed into another vehicle. After what Fellini claimed were 500 X-rays, his doctors suspected cancer. His condition was serious enough for him to be placed in an oxygen tent under sedation. De Laurentiis, perhaps suspecting malingering, sent his own doctor to check on Fellini's condition.

When word of his illness got out, Fellini's hospital room was flooded with telegrams, flowers, and good wishes. Two of the telegrams came in red envelopes, indicating that they were from heads of state. Fellini began to think he was dying. Then he got word that his former collaborator, Flaiano, had decided to let bygones be bygones, and was going to pay him a visit. "Now I *know* I'm dying," Fellini groaned.

Old friends from Rimini came to see him, among them a boyhood friend, Sega Bagarone, now a laboratory specialist. Fellini described his symptoms, upon which Bagarone muttered, "Sanarelli-Schwarzmann." He explained it was a rare form of allergic pleurisy, usually confined to animals. "But you have it."

Fellini insisted that Bagarone explain his theory to the specialists. They, he wrote later, thought it a brilliant interpretation of his illness, but refused to accept it. Fellini, nevertheless, on Bagarone's advice, stopped taking his prescribed medications and took cortisone injections instead, although it required the connivance of a nun and a nurse's aide to achieve this. "In twelve hours I could breathe," he said, "and in twenty-four I could talk." Meanwhile, his magician friend in Turin, Gustavo Rol, sent him beneficial emanations. Even so, it took another month in a convalescent home in Manzina, near Rome, for him to recover fully. Fellini had his own name for the disease: Tognazzitis.

While convalescing in May 1967, Fellini devoted himself to writing a long essay for a book to be called *My Rimini*, and also amused himself by drawing people and events remembered from his childhood and adolescence. These went into what turned out to be a handsomely illustrated volume. He not only delved into his memories, but when in good health again, paid a visit to his home town, where he noted the extraordinary changes that had taken place. Rimini had become a resort where 500,000 people—most of them Germans—came each year for vacations. And he noted another change—in the young people. The furtiveness between the sexes that he had known was gone. "I sensed the presence of something I had never had in my own childhood and youth, when we were inhibited by the role of the church and of fascism, and by our mothers and fathers, whom we venerated as if they were monuments." As with all his experiences, the recalling of his early days in Rimini and the return visit planted seeds for film ideas.

Meanwhile the struggle to get *Mastorna* made went on. In

spite of his illness and his brush with death, Fellini's relations with De Laurentiis continued to be rancorous. Finally, Fellini decided he had to put an end to the battle. He suggested to the producer that they find a way to settle the matter amicably. In effect, he offered to repay De Laurentiis with his earnings from future films. The two met with lawyers "late at night," Betti wrote, "in Dino De Laurentiis's immense, incredibly luxurious office at Castel Romano." Fellini said, "You see, Dino, you and I were stuck in a hole. . . ." "What hole?" De Laurentiis asked. Even at the end they were failing to understand each other.

Fellini opened a new office on the Via della Fortuna and gave his first interview since his illness. "I was pronounced almost dead," he said, "but now I know I'm going to live as long as I can." He acknowledged his gratitude to those "who quit speaking to me years ago and wrote me letters filled with love and affection." He may have looked tired, but he insisted he still had a lot of fire inside.

Among those with whom he met in those first days of relative freedom was the Neapolitan producer Alberto Grimaldi, who, while grinding out low-budget "spaghetti westerns," had come up with Sergio Leone's *A Fistful of Dollars, For a Few Dollars More,* and *The Good, the Bad and the Ugly*. With these films, Clint Eastwood ascended to the pinnacle of stardom, and Grimaldi became a rich man with a direct line to United Artists, then aggressively mining the international film field. Many years before, Fellini had been attracted to *The Satyricon*, written by Petronius Arbiter in the first century A.D., as the basis of a satire on fascism. He had happened to read it again during his illness and found himself still tempted by it, but this time because he saw in it certain parallels to modern society. He later said he had agreed to make it because Grimaldi stuck a contract in front of him and he needed something to put on it, but there is no doubt he saw in *The Satyricon* a stimulus to his increasingly visual imagination.

Just as important, Grimaldi agreed to repay Fellini's debt to De Laurentiis. As part of the deal, he also took over the *Mastorna* project, which Fellini eventually would bury for good.

During this fallow period something else came up. A French company was putting together a package of three short films based on tales by Edgar Allan Poe. Fellini was first told that Ingmar Bergman and Orson Welles had each agreed to do a tale, but, as it turned out, Louis Malle and Roger Vadim were the other participants.

Fellini said, afterward, that he agreed to make one of the films because with two such visionary film-makers as Bergman and Welles, "there would have been some common quality in this homage to Poe." He had not signed for monetary considerations, he said, but because of the personal crisis he was in. "I was overwhelmed with troubles, had not worked for two years. I could have broken the contract, but that didn't seem right [!]. So I proceeded." The story suggested to him was "The Telltale Heart," which failed to interest him.

He asked his assistant, Liliana Betti, to read through the works of Poe in search of another story. None satisfied him completely, although he was intrigued by "Never Bet the Devil Your Head," a humorously macabre tale of a man, Toby Dammit, too inclined toward rash betting. After a time, Fellini began to wonder why it was necessary to use Poe at all as the basis for his section of the film. He had come across a book of stories titled *Gobal,* by Bernardino Zapponi, a writer who had once contributed to *Marc' Aurelio.* The stories had a grotesque quality that appealed to Fellini, and one of them, he decided, would do better than Poe for the film. On the spur of the moment he looked up Zapponi.

In one of those coincidences that always appealed to Fellini, Zapponi was discovered living just across the street from the office on Via della Fortuna. "He rang me at eight thirty in the morning," Zapponi said to me. " 'I read your book,' he told me. 'We have similar tastes. I feel we could be brothers.' He wanted to make one of my stories, and asked me to work with him on the script. But soon he found out this was impossible, that it had to be Poe, and so we turned instead to 'Never Bet the Devil Your Head.' "

In adapting the story, Zapponi was just as willing as Fellini to play free and loose with the original. "By the time we finished, nothing was left except for the title and the ending." (Even the title was changed to "Toby Dammit" for release, and the ending bore only a vague resemblance to Poe's.) Zapponi did the writing, showing Fellini a few pages at a time. They met almost daily at one or the other's apartment, or at a restaurant.

"We wandered through deserted trattorias and luncheonettes on the outskirts of town," Zapponi told Liliana Betti. They strolled the boardwalk of Ostia, the beach empty and desolate with winter coming on. "Such hopelessness gave birth to the story of a mad, drug-addicted actor who comes to die in Rome. Fellini loves squalor. It never ages." They chatted, made absurd suggestions, took "a childlike joy in inventing stories." Zapponi understood that Fellini did not have the time to both write and handle the problems of realizing the film. But during their discussions and in changes Fellini requested, he felt he was being guided by precise, almost mathematical laws.

Grimaldi became an associate producer of the production, and Fellini moved to his offices on Largo Ponchielli. There Fellini found the production manager, Enzo Provenzale, who had worked with him on *The White Sheik*. It was a happy reunion. Provenzale, with a sure hand and knowledge of Fellini's needs and methods, gathered the production forces. Fellini concentrated on casting—for him the most important detail of all.

He thought Peter O'Toole would be perfect for Toby. Fellini charmed and wooed the actor, and at last convinced him to take on the role, but hardly had O'Toole accepted it than he changed his mind. Fellini then thought of Richard Burton, but was dissuaded by the many accounts of Burton's drunken behavior. Finally, he chose the British actor Terence Stamp. Soon enough, Stamp was made up to look like a man ravaged by drugs and alcohol, his eyes unfocused, his hair unkempt and stringy.

Fellini was not satisfied with the devil of Poe's story, described as "a little lame old gentleman of venerable aspects" dressed in black, "his hair parted in front like a girl's." Instead, in what turned out to be the most striking feature of the short film, the devil became a small blonde girl.

"I thought a man with a black cape and a beard was the wrong kind of devil for a drugged, hipped actor," he later explained. "His devil must be his own immaturity, hence, a child."

The search for the proper embodiment of this Fellinian version of the devil involved advertisements in the Rome newspapers. From the crowds that responded, Fellini was unable to find the girl he wanted. In the end, he solved the problem by making two into one: the face and the ashen hair belonged to a twenty-two-year-old Russian woman; the body to a tiny dance student.

The film that emerged after twenty-six days of shooting in January 1968 at the experimental film center (a small but well-equipped studio adjoining Cinecittà) places the actor in Rome where he has come to work in an Italian "western," made under the guidance of the Catholic priesthood. Fellini was in his anticlerical mood again. The actor sees the Roman film world through the distorted eyes of a man on LSD; the denizens resemble a "dolce vita" crowd that has become crazed and outlandish. In an airport scene, the background personages are grotesques; during the drive to Rome some of the backgrounds are real, others painted flats.

When the actor manages to finish the film, the grateful producer presents him with a Ferrari. Eventually, near a high, broken bridge he bets a little girl playing with a ball that his Ferrari is fast enough to sail over the gap. The final scene shows the girl playing with the actor's head. When the film went into release, more than one viewer noted that the angelic girl of *La Dolce Vita* had been replaced by one with the impudent eyes of a devil.

That spring of 1968, Ingmar Bergman came to Rome for a vacation with his companion, Liv Ullmann. It was understood that he and Fellini, mutual admirers, would meet, but Bergman at first was strangely shy. "We would agree to meet for lunch," Fellini told me, "and then he would cancel the appointment. It took a week before we finally met—and at once we became like brothers."

"They embraced, laughed together," Liv Ullmann wrote in her book, *Changing*. "They wandered through the streets at night, arms around each other, Fellini wearing a dramatic black cape, Ingmar in his little cap and an old winter coat." Their warmth toward each other was such that they talked of doing a film together. Word of this reached an American producer Martin Poll, who flew to Rome in hopes that he would be able to put a joint project together. Fellini was willing, Bergman was willing, and Poll was confident that he would be able to get the financing for a two-part film—one by each director—entitled *Love Duet*.

XVI

AFTER one more fruitless attempt to resurrect *Mastorna*, Fellini embarked with enthusiasm on *The Satyricon*. While reading the fragmented work of Petronius—no more than one-fourth of it has survived through the centuries—he had been struck by what he called "the darkness between episodes. Even when in school I had attempted to fill in the void with my imagination. I would invent a whole series of fragments and propose them to the professor."

Such plot as could be found in the work revolved around the adventures of the narrator, Encolpius, a youth who at times plays a direct part in the events he describes and at other times happens to be a witness to them. His principal companions are a beautiful young boy, Giton, with whom he is in love, and a young man, Ascyltus, who vies with him for Giton's affection. What connecting story there is has to do (it would appear) with an offense Encolpius has given to the god Priapus, who has put him in exile and deprived him of his potency—which he hopes to regain through magical intervention. Much of the charm and relevance of the work comes from the many digressions, including two famous examples of what are known as Milesian tales, early exemplars of the modern short story.

If anything, it was the atmosphere, the emanations from the work, that most attracted Fellini. "It made me think of the columns, heads, missing eyes, broken noses, the whole cemeterial scene on the Appian Way, the sparse fragments in archeological museums, scattered pieces of things that might have come from dreams." The film he saw in his imagination would fill the voids, the dark places, and would not be "a historical epic reconstructed from documents."

Even so, he, with Zapponi as his co-scriptwriter, did a lot of research into the times of Nero. (Petronius, a member of Nero's court, was his "arbiter of elegance," the taste-maker.) They visited Pompeii, spoke to Latinists and other authorities of the period. Liliana Betti and Fellini's script girl, Norma Giacchero, went through and digested for him dozens of texts on the customs of ancient Rome. The mass of documentation, however, served only to give Fellini a sense of the period and as a guide of sorts for his set designer and costumer, Danilo Donati.

"We took ourselves away from concrete things," Zapponi said, "and invented, often absurdly. We used none of the translations of Petronius, but did get ideas from texts about the everyday lives of those times. From one text came an idea for a kind of tenement house to collapse. The early Romans weren't able to build houses very well. Sooner or later they collapsed—like today. We wanted to suggest the cruelty of the Roman era, and invented a theater scene, but made it a theater of the common people and not the patricians."

The most famous scene in the original is the dinner, a classical example of gluttony and crassness, given by the wealthy plebeian, Trimalchio. "We knew there was no way to avoid this," Zapponi said, "and while Fellini would have liked to do without the tale of the 'Widow of Ephesus,' he knew the wrath of all the professors of the world would fall on him if he didn't do it."

Zapponi met with Fellini every day to map out the series of sequences, and to do a first treatment of some twenty-five pages. Fellini wanted a sense of the remoteness of the epoch they were re-creating. Everything was to seem distorted, strange, and dreamlike. The writing of the actual script, most of it done by Zapponi, took them through the months of September and October of 1968. Meanwhile, Fellini went into the casting with his usual furious energy, seeing just about everyone who wanted to see him, and examining thousands of photographs in search of his "faces."

One advertisement asked for "beautiful adolescent boys," but Fellini was unable to select one (for Giton) from the hundreds of applicants, and eventually found him in London in the person of 17-year-old Max Born. There was immediate interest by the press in Fellini's project, and he expansively told reporters of his plans. Was he putting them on? Groucho Marx, he said, would play a philosopher pimp; Danny Kaye a merchant of monsters. He had parts for Jimmy Durante and Mae West, both of whom he actually did try to obtain. After negotiating with Terence Stamp and the French actor Pierre Clementi for the parts of Encolpius and Ascyltus respectively, he claimed that they wanted too much money. Instead, in London, he found a 24-year-old unknown actor, Martin Potter, for Encolpius, and hired an American, Hiram Keller, who had been in the Broadway musical *Hair,* as Ascyltus. He saw his two Roman scamps as early hippies, he said.

During the preparation period, another production of *The Satyricon* got underway, this one by producer Alfredo Bini. Fellini angrily announced that he was used to being imitated, but not before his work had even begun. There were suits and counter-suits, and close guard was put on the Fellini-Zapponi screenplay. Ironically, the star of the rival *Satyricon* was Ugo Tognazzi, the actor who had caused Fellini to abandon *Mastorna.* Eventually the Bini version was impounded by the Italian courts on grounds of immorality and obscenity, and United Artists, already committed to a $3-million investment in the Fellini film, paid another million to Bini to keep his version off international screens for a lengthy period.

Just prior to beginning production on what was now titled *Fellini Satyricon* (to differentiate it from its rival) Fellini was asked by NBC television to do an hour documentary on himself and his work. He took a rather dim view of television and its possibilities at the time, but agreed nevertheless. *A Director's Notebook* ran just under an hour and seemed almost haphazardly put together, a sort of semihumorous introduction to Fellini's world of the moment, which had to do with progressing from the literal dead end of *Mastorna* to his renewed vitality with *The Satyricon.*

The film included a visit to the abandoned sets built for *Mastorna,* temporarily inhabited by a group of hippies. Fellini also pays a visit to the Colosseum, where present and past are linked. A medium claims he can contact the ancient Romans, and Fellini asks him to prove it by conducting a séance on the Appian Way. The results were not convincing. The most interesting sequences involved a visit paid by Fellini to Mastroianni—being lionized by a busload of tourists at that moment—and the casting auditions being held for *Fellini Satyricon.* In the former, Fellini jokes with Marcello about the Latin-lover image he had created for him, and in turn, the actor chides the director for his lack of faith in him for the role of Mastorna. The audition sequence is both amusing and sad; it is a parade of pathetic, wistful types, all hoping to meet the master's specifications for parts in his new film.

Fellini comments: "Yes, I know it must seem sinful, cruel, but no, I am very fond of all these characters chasing after me, following me from one film to another. They are all a little mad, I know that. They say they need me, but the truth is that I need them more." So might have Saint Joseph said at the gateway to heaven.

When shown in the United States the following year, *A Director's Notebook* elicited little comment and would have been entirely neglected by the critics were it not for Joseph McBride, an American writing in the English journal, *Sight and Sound,* who ranked it with some of Fellini's best work, and found it "actually a rigorous development of the theme of artistic stasis," which he had pursued in *8½.* Perhaps as significant was Fellini's emergence from behind the cover of an invented character to face the audience as himself. He had become, like the director Alfred Hitchcock, an identifiable character in film as well as life. "Like any artist," said Zapponi, "he is very full of himself."

Filming of *Fellini Satyricon* began at Cinecittà on November 10, 1968, and continued well into July of the following year. With the exception of some scenes shot at the seashore, all of the shooting took place in studio settings. Eileen Hughes, a journalist based in Rome and doing some work for *Life,* happened to meet Fellini shortly before the starting date, and was invited by him to visit the set any time she liked. After six months of almost daily visits, she put her observations into a valuable book about the making of the film. In it, Fellini can be observed shouting, cajoling, joking, making bawdy remarks, driving his cast and co-workers to near distraction, and also affectionately fondling, kissing, patting just about everyone within his range.

But Hughes was just part of an auxiliary industry attached to the making of the film. A German writer was also doing a book, and a photographer was compiling a book of pictures on the film. And, benevolently, Fellini had allowed an American journalist and independent film-maker, Gideon Bachmann, to make his own documentary on the making, so to speak. Fellini also opened the studio gates to a horde of journalists from Britain, France, the United States, and as far away as Japan. Whether it was from his innate sense of how to achieve the maximum publicity, or from an inability to say no, the amount of copy turned out on *Fellini Satyricon* surpassed that of any of his previous films.

Probably never before had any film been so thoroughly explained in advance. If a particular journalist wanted to be serious and intellectual, Fellini treated him to seriousness and intellectuality, but he was just as willing to be engaging and modestly charming with someone less pretentious.

A group from the French magazine, *Lui*, asked him, "What is a film-maker?"

He answered solemnly, "A film-maker is someone who possesses and has total control over that means of expression and that art we call the cinema. . . ."

Then, to an American writer who asked him how he reacted to all the critical attention paid him, he said: "I find the American critics the most practical. They do not try to see too much. The French, on the other hand, are the craziest. They sometimes strike me as delirious. But if they say good things I am happy. I don't want to appear morbidly humble, but it sometimes seems to me I am received with too much respect."

The people from *Lui* asked how he liked critics, and to them he answered less diplomatically, "Eighty percent of film criticism comes from illiterates and deficient mentalities."

In spite of this attitude, Eileen Hughes reported that adverse reactions to his work caused him pain, and Zapponi said that though he pretended not to read or be bothered by much that was written about him, he was too vain to disregard it. All these seemingly contradictory aspects of Fellini's personality bewildered Hughes at times, and Gideon Bachmann, who had obtained his own contract to write a book about the director, had worked for years without being able to finish it. Fellini was forty-nine when he made *Satyricon* and already he was larger than life and near legendary.

Having been granted access to make his documentary, Bachmann became an annoyance to Fellini, who realized that he was being caught in unguarded moments, and that he was not exactly projecting the image of a director seriously at work. Bachmann had shown him some of his footage. "I want to portray the essential Fellini," he told him.

"That is an essential that can never have an answer," Fellini replied. "I can only be understood through my films. What you are trying to do is very pretentious. You have shown me gesticulating and screaming for three hours. I might be flattered to see myself on television for so long, but the spectator would just turn to another channel."

He suggested that Bachmann interview the people concerned with various aspects of the film, and not just hang around with his personal factotum, Ettore Bevilacqua, who would only cover up for him anyway. Bachmann remained with the production, but well outside the director's good graces.

The completed sixty-minute film had few showings, and according to Bachmann could not be used on television because its language was too frank. What the film did reveal was Fellini's impression that Bachmann had made prior arrangements for it to be shown on American television, which in itself would account for his objections to Bachmann's much-too-prying camera. "We told him that," the unremorseful Bachmann later admitted. "We told him lots of things. We let him think the microphones weren't working when they were." Ever afterward, the mention of Bachmann's name brought an expression of distaste to Fellini's face.

"What private life do I have?" Fellini complained to Hughes, saying that most of it was work. Giulietta confirmed that he seldom got home until ten or twelve at night, and then slept only four restless hours. On Sundays he slept until ten, but lunchtime was spent with his scene and costume designer, Donati, or with his all-important make-up expert, Pierino Tosi, whose task it was to create faces and hairdos that would seem like apparitions out of a museum or tomb.

The completed screenplay envisioned the film as a large and incomplete mosaic, or, as put another way by Fellini, a series of frescoes loosely tied together by the adventures of Encolpius and Ascyltus, and their rivalry for the affections of the boy, Giton. The nearly five-hundred-page script, interlarded with precise descriptions of every prop, costume, and background, was made up of nine major sequences broken into sixty-eight scenes. Fellini then had the enormous task of translating his dreamlike and often nightmarish vision of the world of decadent Rome onto film. It was spectacle of a kind, but unlike any that had ever been done before.

Fellini would claim that the end result was only 20 percent Petronius and 80 percent Fellini. In truth, he and Zapponi had invented episodes—or taken them from myths in other ancient sources—but much of Petronius remained, most notably the events and dinner at the villa of Trimalchio. Filming of this long section and the tales told within the course of the long dinner took several weeks, and if such a thing as historical fidelity were possible for Fellini, he came closest to it in these scenes.

Trimalchio's banquet hall took up the better part of a sound stage and was populated by the most decadent group of dinner guests that had ever been assembled. They indeed looked like all too real apparitions that had sneaked out of a museum. They lolled on large cushions, with huge trays of sweetmeats in front of them (none of which the actors dared touch until Fellini gave them the signal) while, for atmospheric effect, a slave kept beating monontonously on some odd-looking cymbals.

A visitor present during the filming reported:

> Fellini seemed particularly proud of a huge roasted sow—a facsimile made by the production department—that waited on a barrow for its carving by Trimalchio's cook, standing ready with upraised sword. Incenselike smoke from salvers

drifted over the setting as an assistant with a clapboard that said merely FELLINI and the number of the scene and the take moved in close to the camera, then withdrew. On Fellini's signal, the cook raised the sword and chopped down on the sow's head, which fell away on an ingenious hinge. It took several such cleavings and several camera positions before Fellini was satisfied the sow was properly decapitated, after which a wondrous feast of tiny roasted birds, goose livers, roasted bits of lamb and beef, and other delicacies was brought steaming from the belly of the sow. It was at that moment that Fellini called for the lunch break.

By the time he was three months into the filming, Fellini was having doubts that the budget for the picture was large enough to accomplish all that he wanted to do. Production costs for the myriad of details he was insisting on—the hundreds of extras, their wigs and costuming, the huge sets (including an entire wall of a building that was to collapse), the "art" objects fashioned by Donati and his assistants—were mounting and, along with delays in the schedule, were fast depleting the rumored $3-million outlay.

"I don't think this picture will ever be finished," he said to me over lunch at Cinecittà. "There is not enough money. United Artists is—how do you say it?—too cheap. They have given us such a small amount of money, really a mortifyingly small amount, enough to make the credits. Well, *buon appetito.*"

In a moment he returned to the subject. "There are rumors of a $3-million budget. Lies, just lies."

When, later, a United Artists executive was questioned about the matter, he sighed and said, "Financing Italian films has a way of being incredibly complicated. We made our arrangements with Grimaldi, but the money allotted to Fellini is tied in with others on Grimaldi's schedule. However they choose to interpret it, the picture *will* cost three million." (By the time of its completion, costs, it was said, had risen to four million.)

But Fellini could also see the Americans' point of view. The Italian film industry hardly existed anymore, he said, and so he, like many others, was dependent on American financing. "The one who takes money from the other has to prove, in a sense, that he is not a thief. We are good friends, but I think they are a little fearful. They don't trust us. For this reason, maybe, they have given my producer less money than what, in a real way, the picture costs." His mood continued to be gloomy. "The picture industry," he said, "is still so vulgar that if the film author tried to oversee what happens to his work he would quickly die of a broken heart. Between censorship, the vulgarity of the advertising, the stupidity of exhibitors, the mutilation, the inept dubbing into other languages—when I finish a picture it's best to forget I ever made it."

Once again he explained what he was trying to do. "It is impossible to know what life was really like in ancient Roman times," he said, and since the Petronius work represented only a small fragment of the original whole, the book served as a pretext "to make a fantasy, almost a science fiction." He had had to hold himself back before. The present-day stories he had done previously had prevented him from transfiguring everything in the way he would have liked, including the very faces of the actors. Now, using costumes and color (and avoiding togas and chariots, and other vulgarizations of the past) he was free to invent, virginally, so to speak, the phantoms of 2,000 years ago.

He explained the nearly 500-page length of the script. "Now that I've imagined my fresco of ancient times, my job on the set is to materialize what I've imagined. Previously I allowed room in my scripts not for improvisation necessarily, but for suggestions that would come from being filmed. For example: the aristocrat's party in *La Dolce Vita*. We worked in a real castle, we used real aristocrats. I was able to take blood from them, so to speak. I kept myself open for what could arise during the filming of the situation—as when we made up dialogue for the scene between Marcello and Anouk in those two separate rooms in the castle—but here that isn't possible. Every detail must be known in advance. Having to invent what I don't know is exacting, even dangerous. The concentration required from me is greater."

He was insistent, as he continued to explain his film-in-progress to interviewers, on the strangeness, the unknowability of those ancient Romans, whose consciousness was not in any way the same as that of the present. Under Hadrian, he pointed out, 15,000 were massacred in two days "just for pleasure—to us a massacre, sheer almost incomprehensible barbarism."

Alberto Moravia, a good friend of Fellini, questioned the unknowability of the times of Petronius, reminding him that there was a good deal of understandable psychology in his treatment of his characters, not to mention the enormous amount of scholarly study of the period. It was Christianity, Moravia said, that wanted "antiquity to become alien and unknown, to be denied, ignored, thrust into obscurity. It gave antiquity the face of sin and damnation." He compared Fellini's view of it to that of Christians of the year 1000.

Fellini seemed to be aware in advance of potential criticisms of the film, with its emphasis on cruelty and monstrosity: A theater in which a man's hand is chopped off for the entertainment value; a dead poet's relatives eating his corpse as a prerequisite for inheriting his goods; a nymphomaniac whose sexual torment must be satisfied every hour; a brothel catering to known and unknown perversions; a one-eyed emperor's pimp who insists on marrying Encolpius; a struggle with a monstrous minotaur . . .

"I have no idea how the audiences will react," Fellini told *Lui.* "Maybe people will find the film scandalous, or maybe cold and clinical. For me it is a sexless film—made as if I were filming rats or birds in the act of copulating. I am completely detached. I am creating a universe, and I let it develop according to its own rules in front of the camera. It is like a trip to the origin of human beings, of our consciousness."

Statements such as this were more revolutionary, where the developing art of film was concerned, than any manifestos made during the heyday of neorealism. Here was a film-maker, using large sums of money—theoretically to attract millions of spectators and to earn a profit—declaring that he had no desire to engage the audience with his play. He was concerned with creating, dreaming up his own universe. He was the artist attempting to stand above all the exigencies of the medium in which he created. At the same time, one could only wonder why this clinical detachment was so necessary, why an "unknown planet" had to be created when so much evidence

of the real one existed all around him. The answer had to be that
Fellini, at that moment, was less interested in exploring an ancient
world than in exploring possibilities in the medium of film.

After my lunch with Fellini, we walked to the sound stage
where the huge sow had been recently decapitated. The innards referred to earlier were being heaped on brass platters and carried
triumphantly to the guests. Trimalchio (played by a restaurateur
friend of Fellini) was now part of the scene, and he watched the
gluttony with plump and self-satisfied solemnity. Takes were done
from several angles, while Fellini, belying the serious frame of
mind he had displayed during lunch, debated volubly with his
cameraman, Giuseppe Rotunno, embraced a friend who had come
to pay a visit, joked with crew members. Over it all, smoke swirled
and cymbals sounded. The director was hugely enjoying himself at
his work.

"It is not a colossal picture," he told me between takes. "I
must work very, very carefully with the money they give me. But I
am happy—because with this one I have the feeling I am making
my first picture. I have always done what I wished to do and I am
very lucky. I am told I should not have said anything about the
cheap money, so if you mention the money, add that Fellini said
it smiling, but with sadness." He hesitated. "Yes, smiling, but with
very sad eyes."

Later that spring, Ingmar Bergman came to Rome to discuss
their joint film. Such spare time as Fellini had he was giving to his
half of the project. Without saying what it was, he mentioned to reporters that he was already thinking of his next work.

In addition to those reporting on or filming the artist at
work, Fellini kept around him a loyal and devoted corps that consisted of Liliani Betti, who put aside her own directorial ambitions
to assist him; Mario Longardi, a charming trilingual publicist who
graciously and diplomatically handled the constant requests to see
the master; the previously mentioned Ettore Bevilacqua, a former
boxer who was to keep him in shape with a regime of morning exercise and evening massages; Eugene Walter, an American living in

Giulietta Masina with François Périer (Oscar) in *The Nights of Cabiria*

and with Sandra Milo (Suzy) in *Juliet of the Spirits*

Fellini preparing the "miracle" scene

and inspecting the "fish" for *La Dolce Vita*

Casanova tête-à-tête with Madame D'Urfé: Donald Sutherland and
Cicely Browne

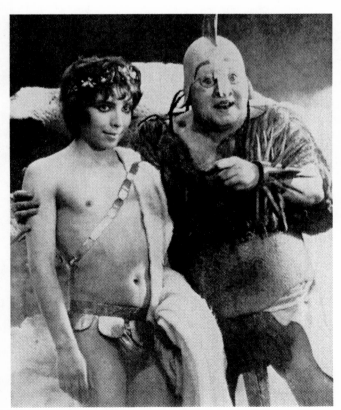

Two free spirits: Above,
Hiram Keller (left) as
Ascylto and Martin
Potter as Encolpio.
Below, Max Born (left)
as Gitone, love-object
of Ascylto and Encol-
pio, with Fanfulla as
Vernacchio, an early
Roman showman—
both from *Fellini
Satyricon*

Fellini perfects the table setting for *Casanova*

Snaporaz (Marcello Mastroianni) dwarfed by a city of women

Fellini, above, and
Baldwin Baas, below,
direct *Orchestra Rehearsal*

The director in action

Rome who acted as dialogue coach for the English and Americans
in the cast; and a Swiss Jungian psychoanalyst, Peter Ammann,
who was a volunteer assistant on the film. Fellini had met Ammann
through Doctor Bernhard and, when he learned the analyst was also
a cellist, had asked him to show Mastroianni how to play the cello
for a test Fellini was then making for *Mastorna*. Like others who
had approached Fellini for one reason or another, Ammann had felt
the pull of his magnetism, and became a part of the court. These
associations would last for an indefinite period of time; some would
fade and others take their place, depending on how much time inter-
vened between projects. Almost all the members of Fellini's court
threatened to write books or articles about him and a good many
did, the result being a constantly expanding library that attempted
on the one hand to explain his films and on the other his personality.
Many directors owe their jobs to charisma as well as skill, but Fellini is far more charismatic than most. If the warmth that distinguished his earlier films was being replaced by a chillier detachment,
he continued to exude warmth in person.

As the filming of *Fellini Satyricon* was completed during the
last week of July 1969, Fellini made a final change in the script. He
had decided to end the film on a note similar to the beginning, which
showed the reddish wall of an ancient ruined villa. Frescoes of the
characters are now seen on the wall; they slowly fade until they are
unrecognizable scrawls from the distant past. It was Fellini's way of
returning his audiences to the world of their reality.

The film was edited in time for the Venice festival in September. Eileen Hughes reported: "Fellini, accompanied by his wife
and several of the more important actors in the film, proceeded
down the Grand Canal like a conquering hero." The première, held
at the Cinema Palace on the Lido, created a scalper's bonanza. Tickets went for as much as $100 each. An Italian journalist suggested
that it was now the director who was the star of the star system.
Certainly Fellini was a star above any in his films.

The audience sat in stunned silence through the first showing, as though waiting for the critics to tell them how to regard the
film. The critics in Italy responded favorably. They wrote of its
"magical, dreamlike atmosphere," and of its being "a journey

through the fairy tales of adults." Some equated the phantasmagorical nature of the film with Fellini's personal obsessions. Some thought it a step forward for Italian cinema, while others regarded it as a Fellini film, pure and simple, to be treated in terms of the artist's development. There were those who noted that the director had little new to say in it, and a few who took exception to its "unchaste" qualities. But the treatment of the film in Italy was gentle, on the whole, and gave little indication of the sharp critical divergences that would occur when it went into international release.

XVII

IN Hollywood, during the early autumn of 1969, Paul Mazursky was preparing his second film, *Alex in Wonderland,* after achieving success with his first, *Bob & Carol & Ted & Alice. Alex* was to be a satire on the ways of the movie colony; it dealt with a director whose first movie had been a success and who is now unsure about what to do next. He fantasizes different kinds of movies, one of which he will make in a Felliniesque style. A scene in the screenplay that Mazursky wrote with Larry Tucker involves the director's going to Rome for a conference with a producer. While there he encounters the great Fellini, who pleasantly dismisses the gauche Hollywoodite. Mazursky was an admirer not only of Fellini's films but of the total creative control he was able to exercise.

He thought: why not try to get Fellini to play himself? He happened to run into Anthony Quinn, whom he knew had acted in *La Strada,* and asked him how to get in touch with Fellini. "Send him a telegram," Quinn suggested.

"So I sent him a wire," Mazursky recalled, "saying I was Paul Mazursky, who had just directed *Bob & Carol & Ted & Alice* [which had opened the 1969 New York Film Festival] and that I had written this movie and would he take a small role in it. I got back from him a funny telegram saying, in effect, 'I don't know who you are, I've never heard of Bob and Carol and whoever, and I have no interest in being in anyone's movie. But if you're ever in Rome, let us meet.' "

Mazursky and Larry Tucker flew to Rome the next day, checked into a hotel, and learned the best way to contact Fellini was through his public relations representative, Mario Longardi. Mazursky telephoned him.

"You are who?" Longardi asked.

Mazursky explained that Fellini had suggested a meeting when in Rome, and here he was with his co-writer. Longardi told him that Fellini was very busy preparing a new film, and it was not easy to see him. But he would communicate with him, and call back. The next day he telephoned Mazursky, and said that Fellini would see them at the Grand Hotel on the Via del Corso at eight o'clock in the evening.

"And sure enough," Mazursky said, "at eight o'clock, Fellini with Mario Longardi—a handsome, charming young man— entered the lobby of the Grand Hotel. Fellini looked . . . exactly like Fellini, the black hat, the black coat, smiling. We chatted a few minutes, with Longardi translating, and then Fellini said to Longardi, 'It's all right, I don't need a translator. You can go.' That was the beginning of five days during which we spent a great deal of time together. He was quite obviously amused by us. We had lunches and dinners together. Whatever he happened to be doing, he would say, 'Why don't you come along?' There was one evening we drove from place to place looking for Mastroianni, but we didn't find him.

"When we would bring up his appearing in the movie, he said, 'It's a mistake. Don't use me in your movie. Get a giant, or a dwarf, or even better, use a puppet that looks like Fellini.'

"At the end of the five days, as Larry and I were preparing to return to California, he finally capitulated. 'All right, I'll do it,' he said wearily. I told him I would return to Rome when I was shooting the picture, and we'd do the whole thing in a day, two days at most.

Several months later, with Donald Sutherland playing Alex, the director, Mazursky was close to the end of his California shooting schedule, at which time he would head for Rome and the scene with Fellini, when a call came from Mario Longardi. "Fellini is very sorry," Longardi said, "but he has changed his mind. He does not wish to appear in your picture."

"I was startled," Mazursky said, "more than that, shocked and depressed. The whole story scheme was wrapped around Alex's dreams and fantasies of being a great director like Fellini. I had even taken Fellini's advice, and given Alex a vision in which he sees a whole schoolyard filled with puppet Fellinis in all sizes and shapes.

"Soon after hanging up, I made the biggest decision I had yet made in my life. I didn't let MGM, my studio, or anyone know that I had gotten the call. I wrapped up the shooting in Los Angeles, and went to Rome as though the previous arrangement still held. With me were Sutherland, the cameraman, sound man, and my assistant director. I called Longardi and said, 'We're here and ready to shoot.'

" 'But I called you,' Longardi said. 'I explained . . .'

"I pretended I hadn't understood his message, that it had not occurred to me that Fellini would change his mind. In any case, here I was with my camera crew. 'But Fellini will not do it,' Longardi insisted. 'If he must tell you himself, he is at Cesarina's eating. But he doesn't want to do it, I assure you.' "

Mazursky went to the restaurant where he found Fellini eating spaghetti. He looked up, and they stared at each other. "Ah," he said, "you're here."

"He knew everything," Mazursky said, "without my saying a word. He laughed. 'You didn't hear, of course, that I wasn't going to do it?' I said, 'I guess I didn't understand too well what was said on the telephone, but I have to finish the movie.' We went back and forth on it, he saying he couldn't do it, I telling him how necessary and crucial the scene was, how easy it would be to do. Finally, he said, 'What do you want me to do?' I had the pages of the script with me that concerned him, and soon the tenor of the talk between us changed, as though he had assumed the role of the actor. He objected to a line, saying he would not say something like that. 'What would you say?' I asked him. He told me what he might say, and I said, 'That would be great.'

"By the end of the meal he told me to come to Cinecittà the next day, and we would do the scene in his editing room there, and he would bring his assistant, Norma, to give it more realism. I felt he had enjoyed being pursued."

The following day, Mazursky arrived at Cinecittà with Donald Sutherland and his small crew, and found Fellini had already facilitated matters. He had arranged to have a corridor cleared, down which Sutherland would come and find Fellini, outside his own editing room. "Sutherland," Mazursky said, "was gaga with awe, but Fellini outdid him as an actor. More than that, he played along with the whole thing, as I did [Mazursky had begun his career as an actor]. I would say, 'Don't tell me how to handle this, don't direct.' 'Would you mind,' he asked, 'if I were to step over here? And may I go here?'

"We got the scene done, and if *Alex in Wonderland* has any historic significance, it is because of his scene with Donald Sutherland, in which you see him as an actor, and also as surprisingly true to the way he might have handled the intrusion in real life. As for the film, when it came out it was an unmitigated disaster, and I was so depressed by this that I decided to move myself with my family to Rome, where I would find out what it would be like to live in a civilized society. There I renewed my acquaintance with Fellini, and we became fast friends, almost like brothers."

During this period, Fellini worked on the sound tracks for the various launchings of *Fellini Satyricon* abroad and, with Zapponi, wrote the screenplay that would be his contribution to the joint Fellini–Bergman film, *Love Duet.*

Martin Poll, the American producer of the film had, in fact, attempted to broaden it into a trilogy that would include a contribution by Akira Kurosawa, a director also admired by Fellini. Kurosawa, however, had already committed himself as co-director on Twentieth Century-Fox's *Tora! Tora! Tora!*

No sooner had Poll announced the signing of Fellini and Bergman than Universal Pictures, in the person of executive producer Jennings Lang, asked to take it on as financier and distributor. All seemed harmonious. Poll had his financing and a "hands off" promise from Universal. In other words, Fellini and Bergman would have the creative freedom each had insisted on.

Fellini's contribution, about an hour in length, was titled

City of Women; Bergman's was to be called *White Walls*. Before
long, however, Universal wanted a say in the casting and suggested
Warren Beatty as the star of *City of Women*. Fellini, however, insisted on Marcello Mastroianni. Bergman had less difficulty with the
studio, and willingly accepted Katherine Ross for his female star.
The two-part film would be made at Cinecittà and in Stockholm, and
a start date for filming was set for early November, 1969.

Then, no one seemed to know why, everything fell apart.
Neither Poll nor Lang would discuss it. Nor would Bergman. Fellini
talked to reporters in December: "I was prepared to start filming,
when all communication with Bergman, Poll, and Universal ceased."
His last communication with Poll, he said, had to do with the possibility of his doing *City of Women* as a feature without the participation of Bergman.

Martin Poll broke his silence in 1985, and explained some
of the circumstances of the rift. It had been a dream of his, he said,
to bring the two preeminent directors of Europe together, and he
had fought the good fight for a year to accomplish the project. The
essential fact of the matter was that Universal had taken a dislike to
the script for *City of Women*. Apparently undismayed, Fellini and
Zapponi had quickly come up with another along similar lines—a
comedy involving a man's relationship with several women. This,
too, Universal disliked. Poll, trying desperately to hold it all together, looked for financing elsewhere, and might have succeeded,
he said, if schedules and obligations of the parties could have been
worked out.

Meanwhile, Universal entered into negotiations with Berg-
man to make his film as a solo feature, and it was at this point that
Poll suggested Fellini's doing his alone, too. Fellini pointed out to
him that his next feature was already under contract to Grimaldi.
"A year and more of work on it went down the drain," Poll said.
"My dream turned into a sour nightmare." Bergman never made
White Walls. His negotiations with Universal ended when the studio
insisted on having the privilege of the final cut—all too usual in
Hollywood but anathema to Bergman.

*   *   *

Fellini did not stay idle for long. In January 1970 he made a trip to the United States with Giulietta and his producer, Grimaldi, to promote *Fellini Satyricon*, which was already doing well in Italy and France but needed the lucrative American market to justify United Artists' investment. The Universal deal having fallen apart, he was seriously considering a continuing invitation from NBC to make a series of specials that would deal with contemporary subjects. Around the same time as Mazursky's visit, Peter Goldmark, an NBC executive, visited him and put forth some suggestions, which included doing a portrait of Mao Tse-tung; another of Pope John XXIII; a look at Rimini on the order of his essay, *My Rimini*; a tour through an American factory (Fellini style); and a visit to a Tibetan monastery.

Fellini had enjoyed doing *A Director's Notebook*, his first experience with television, and though he had strong doubts about its being a proper medium for a film artist, he was attracted by the size and the immediacy of the audience. *A Director's Notebook* had been shown twice and had been seen by many millions.

He agreed to make two of the specials during 1970 for NBC—one would be on Mao and the other on the Tibetan monastery. NBC, he said, reacted with enthusiasm, although the executives who came to see him kept changing. It was agreed that NBC would pay expenses for his travel and research into the subjects, but only after the trips would he decide whether or not to make the films. All was agreeable until Fellini came upon a clause in the contract that gave NBC the right to broadcast the films or to shelve them. At this, Fellini balked.

RAI, the Italian national television and radio monopoly, had embarked on a program of encouraging and funding its more important film artists and, hearing about Fellini's impasse with the American network, its executives approached him about doing a special for Italian television. They wanted, however, an Italian subject.

The always fertile Fellini quickly came up with one. "Let's make a film about clowns," he said. "One Sunday afternoon," he related, "I chatted about it with Bernardino Zapponi at his house at

Zagarolo. We made a trip to Paris looking for something—I didn't know what—and when we got back, after a few days, the screenplay was done." In this seemingly haphazard manner, things began moving. His feeling for clowns and the circus was well known, and soon enough, with word out, international negotiations were underway. RAI became the principal partner in the production arrangements, with French, German, and Italian interests also involved because of the expected theatrical releases. First, however, Fellini embarked for America and the openings there of *Fellini Satyricon*.

His party included Giulietta and his producer, Grimaldi. Their first stop was in Los Angeles, in January. They were put up at the Beverly Hills Hotel, and the presence of Fellini drew substantial space in the Los Angeles newspapers and the Hollywood "trades." He was invited by George Stevens, Jr., founder of the American Film Institute, to participate in a symposium at its Los Angeles headquarters, Greystone, the former Doheny estate. The institute's students were outnumbered by members of the film colony. Anthony Quinn sat on the dais with Fellini and Giulietta, and among the listeners and questioners were Sidney Poitier, Ray Bradbury, Billy Wilder, George Plimpton, Samuel Fuller, Jack Lemmon, and Haskell Wexler.

The young film-makers present were especially interested in his methods of "improvisation," and particularly in how he got his actors to come up with their lines. The young generation was making its inroads at the time, with successes such as *Easy Rider*, and the students regarded script work as a somewhat unnecessary adjunct to the making of films. (Ironically, Fellini almost never gave his actors lines to say, but usually asked them to recite numbers, dubbing in the dialogue during the editing process.)

George Stevens, Jr. remembered the shocked silence in the conference room when Fellini gave his reply. "He all but stood them on their heads," Stevens said with some satisfaction.

"That is stupid gossip," Fellini said, scathingly. "It's absolutely impossible to improvise. Making a movie is a mathematical operation. Art is a scientific operation. What we usually call improvisation is, in my case, just having an eye and an ear to available happenings during the trip of the picture. To be strictly faithful to what you've written four or five months before is a little bit silly. But that is not improvisation."

The questions followed fast and furious. A student asked about the locations for *Fellini Satyricon*. Another surprise: "The picture was completely shot in the studio."

"Even the ocean scenes?"

Fellini said his producers refused to put an ocean in the studio, so for those scenes he went to a real one. But "I think an inventor must invent in an undisturbing atmosphere," and so all the settings, except for the ocean, were created at Cinecittà.

Did he watch rushes? "No, that is a great preoccupation for the producers."

(During the making of *8½* a laboratory strike had occurred, and he was unable to see rushes. He found that he enjoyed making the film in the dark, so to speak, and from then on delegated checking the daily results to his cameraman—in the case of *Fellini Satyricon*, Giuseppe Rotunno.)

Ray Bradbury was struck by the answer, and saw that—contrary to normal studio practice—Fellini was able to free himself each day from the work done the day before. Fellini was well aware of Bradbury as a writer and asked him if he reread a book during the writing process. Bradbury said he did not, and was gratified by an affinity between himself and Fellini.

The session, which was recorded, was a remarkable and freewheeling exchange between an internationally renowned film artist and an intensely interested sampling of the Los Angeles film community. The American Film Institute subsequently made the transcript available as a pamphlet, the first, as it turned out, in a long and continuing series called *Dialogue on Film*.

United Artists, with a major investment in *Fellini Satyricon*, saw to it that Fellini received a maximum of exposure during his American tour. When he arrived in Los Angeles, he was asked what he wanted to do first. He wanted to see *Hair*, he said. It happened to be playing at a theater on Sunset Boulevard, and off he went.

United Artists' executives sensed that *Fellini Satyricon*

would appeal to young people, who were now the dominant audience for films, and concentrated its promotion efforts in their direction, but not before putting on a more typical Hollywood première party on a studio sound stage following the first showing. The stage was covered with plastic grass. The bartenders wore Roman togas and sandals, and dispensed drinks from bottles in the shape of bunches of grapes. Waiters in more plebeian Roman costumes fed the guests from huge platters of roast pig.

From Los Angeles, Fellini headed east, making one- and two-day stops for press and television interviews—although he was once mistaken for an authority on Italian cuisine—and good-humoredly cooperating with his publicity attendants. In New York he was besieged by columnists and critics, but the highlight of his visit was a midnight showing of the film following a rock concert at Madison Square Garden.

"There were about 10,000 kids there," he said later, "with hashish and heroin all over the place. It was an army of hippies. Outside it was snowing, and the skyscrapers were lighted. The showing was thrilling. There was applause, some were asleep, some were making love. On that huge screen, in that atmosphere, *Satyricon* seemed to have found its rightful place."

The New York critics saw the film in a more prosaic atmosphere, and a good many of them were unable to appreciate the kind of parallel between ancient Rome and contemporary New York that the Madison Square Garden showing afforded.

Vincent Canby of the *New York Times* came through with an appreciative review, calling it "the quintessential Fellini film, a travelogue through an unknown galaxy, a magnificently realized movie of his and our wildest dreams," but others were waiting with sharpened knives. Pauline Kael in the *New Yorker,* titled her review "Mondo Trasho," and made little attempt at critical analysis, simply calling it "a really bad, a terrible movie." John Simon, still waiting for Fellini's return to *Vitelloni* and *La Strada,* obtusely compared him to Petronius and voted in favor of the latter. Richard Corliss granted Fellini his artistry, but saw him as an artist in decline. Writer Parker Tyler declared *Satyricon* "the most profoundly homosexual movie in all history," while Moira Walsh in *America* was unable to gather any sort of meaning from it. Each to his own viewing, it seemed.

Fellini, having done his publicity chores for United Artists, returned to Italy, saying he had had an exciting trip. He had liked the young people he came across. "I think they have changed America completely," he said. "Maybe these young people, with their communal living, their clothing, their beads, their bizarre make-up, their gentle smiles, have changed the scene."

He went immediately to work on *The Clowns*, immersing himself in clown lore before setting up an eight-week shooting schedule at Cinecittà. From the outset he announced he was not doing an all-encompassing documentary on clowns, but would limit himself to "a personal excursion into my childhood in Rimini, and to the circus world of Paris and Italy."

He journeyed to Paris with a crew of forty in time to film scenes at the Cirque d'Hiver. "Paris," he announced, "gave to clowns a dimension of art." Most of what he shot at the circus, however, he later scrapped, preferring a circus of his own invention.

One early morning while in Paris, he awoke to let some air into his hotel room. The window refused to give, and somehow the pane broke in his hand, a shard of glass nearly severing half a finger. The concierge sent up a doorman, who called a doctor, who gave him the address of a clinic. The taxi driver went first to the wrong address; then, at the clinic, payment was demanded before treatment. Fellini, however, was still in his bathrobe, and had brought no money. By the time he was treated and bandaged, he had lost all patience with the French, and Paris became one of his least favorite cities.

The filming that began in mid-March 1970 lasted well into July, but was interspersed with on-the-scene interviews with aged and retired clowns, and circus specialists. While these appeared to be spontaneous, done by a small and sometimes inept crew, they were actually shot by a large and skilled crew Fellini had brought with him. This allowed him the opportunity to gently parody the documentary form while still providing an adequate amount of information. He didn't like interviewing, he later admitted. If he asked a question, he found himself not really interested in the answer. "In the middle of the making," he said. "I realized I was doing less of a documentary than what was inside my mind. I made a joke of me, my crew, and the documentary itself."

The film, one of Fellini's most winning, turned out to be less a documentary than a personal film essay in three main parts. The first dealt with his reminiscences of circuses and clowns he had seen as a child; the second with a search for the clowns of old, their routines, and the meaning of their clownish acts; the third, as might have been expected, was his own clown fantasia, an apotheosis of clowndom.

In England, John Russell Taylor saw the result as a Fellini form that had its beginnings in *A Director's Notebook*. It was "the Fellini essay film. They are personal, seemingly casual, shaped with precision and consciously created."

Fellini boldly put himself on camera, playing the role of a documentary inquirer at the head of a small film crew. In the very first scene he creates an episode similar to an anecdote he had told about himself as a child. A small boy awakes to the sound of noises outside his room. Leaving his bed, he peers through a window and sees a circus tent being erected. Later on, he is taken to the circus. The boy is presumably Fellini himself. Then the mature Fellini introduces his audiences to real-life "clowns" from his town: a midget nun, tramps and semi-idiots, a comically pompous stationmaster, a fussy Fascist official.

But caricature blends with evocative nostalgia during a scene in a poolroom bar. A prosperous couple drive up in a vintage 1930s sports car, and enter the room in search of champagne. (There is none.) The man is elegantly overdressed in a camel's hair driving coat, gloves, and goggles, while his blonde companion seems to be imitating the prevailing fashion in Hollywood films. The Nino Rota score has "Fascination" playing in the background. Among the pool players is a tall young man—the dandy of the town—who seems to regard himself as the epitome of masculine appeal, suddenly confronted with his dream woman. He gives her a soulful look, to which she appears to respond slightly. The moment is shattered when one of the pool players makes an obscene gesture. The scene, which lasts only a few minutes, is like a gem of a visualized short story, and it is pure Fellini. The face, the eyes, the expressions of the provincial dreamer tell volumes.

During the "documentary" sections, Fellini develops the concept of two basic types of clown; the so-called "white clowns," who, in white make-up, are elegant, dignified, and more or less in charge of what goes on in the circus tent; and the white clown's partner, the *"augusto,"* or *"auguste,"* who is clumsy in his baggy pants and overlarge shoes, but invariably good-natured.

Fellini's view, stated in the film and in interviews, has the white clown as the symbol of authority—the mother, father, the teacher, and even the state and the church—who is always right. "The *augusto* is yourself, doing all the things you'd like to do, making faces, shouting, rolling on the ground, throwing water at people."

During the film, the careers of two such clowns, Dario and Bario, are evoked. In typical Fellini fashion, he eschewed the use of genuine clowns, and employed instead an extra who looked like a shepherd, and a Swiss deaf-mute who had once worked as a mime. Attempting to train them for their roles, he shoved them, cursed and raged at them, and threw foul insults at them for their lack of ability. Somehow he bewildered them enough to achieve what he was after, and Dario and Bario came vividly alive.

One thesis of the film is that the clown is dying, or already dead, because, according to Fellini, "the clown was always the caricature of a well-established, ordered, peaceful society. But today all is temporary, disordered, grotesque. Who can still laugh at clowns? . . . All the world plays a clown now."

So, Fellini and his crew go on, seeking the spirit of the clown. During the interviews, faded snippets of film record the old clown routines; others are re-created. Then, in the brilliant final sequence. Fellini expands his vision of the death of the clown spirit. A mock clown funeral is held, but a funeral like no other. The coffin collapses as soon as the nails are hammered in. There is no body inside. The clown has died at the age of 200 while trying to swallow an ostrich egg; but he is reborn when he is shot out of a huge champagne bottle. During the merrymaking an interviewer asks:

"Signor Fellini, what message are you trying to give us here?" Before he can answer, a bucket falls over Fellini's head, then another over the interviewer's. The answer is clear and sufficient.

The loveliest of all the sequences closes the film. The arena is now deserted, except that high up on the seats are seen, on one side, the white clown, and on the other the *augusto*. Each in turn plays his trumpet as they descend the steps toward the center of the arena. They stand side by side in the spotlight and disappear, leaving only the spotlight. It is not only nostalgia for the clown, but Fellini nostalgia, bringing back memories of Gelsomina and her trumpet, and the old clown in *La Dolce Vita*.

The film was shown first on Italian television. Fellini was angry because the showing was in black and white, and even though the film was made possible by RAI financing, he felt the ritual of television viewing was not suitable for the film artist. In an interview with the editors of France's intellectual *Cahiers du Cinéma*, he took a lofty tone, saying that "film is a way of expressing something with light, while on TV all the expressive components of the picture—the arrangement, contrasts of light and shade—are lacking."

He later modified this view. In an essay accompanying a large and handsome volume on clowns that was published in conjunction with the theatrical releases of the film, he wrote that television was a medium in which he could work easily and casually, that he found it favorable to the imagination. "The imaginary audience is narrowed down to a single person watching the set. For this reason you find yourself being more open and more available."

He did not, however, take advantage of further offers by RAI to make more specials but concentrated, rather, on bringing new film projects into being. To producer, Alberto Grimaldi, he offered suggestions for three films. One was a fantasy documentary, *Roma*, which, he said, would be the impressions of a young man arriving in the city in the late 1930s, poor and jobless. (Shades again of Moraldo.) Another would be the resurrection of *City of Women*, expanded from the screenplay that had met disfavor with Universal Pictures in the ill-fated Bergman collaboration. The third was called *The Unknown Woman*, and would deal with a man "who can no longer stay with a woman because he has projected on her everything." After the breakup of the relationship, the man becomes obsessed and looks for her everywhere. "He locks himself in the villa where they lived, becomes a fetishist, begins to change into her. . . . In the grip of a delirious love, he becomes her."

The idea seems out of tune for Fellini, and more characteristic of Zapponi's mordant imagination. On the other hand, it also contained Felliniesque features. He told Grimaldi that he wanted to film it in a northern town, "amid the fogs on the motorway . . . the lights, the silence, the colors, the unseizable images." The film (to be called *The Unknown Woman*) would be set in 1928, and would deal with Italy's deep cultural isolation during the "imbecilic" Fascist years.

Grimaldi did not take to the idea, but, as was habitual with Fellini, elements from it would turn up in a later and different film. A temporary break in relations occurred, and Fellini went on yet another search for producers. It has been estimated that at around this time he was making at least 200 telephone calls a day. An early riser—he was unable to sleep more than four or five hours a night—he would go over his list to see whom he might wake as early as seven in the morning. The real situation was that he was looking less for a producer than for a financier.

XVIII

GRIMALDI, in this period, was, like other Italian producers, interested in establishing firm financial contacts in America. *Satyricon* had done reasonably well at home, but not abroad. The vogue for "spaghetti westerns," which had flourished during the 1960s and which had boosted Grimaldi into prominence, was dying. The Hollywood money that had flowed into Cinecittà and other Italian studios for cheap westerns was drying up as youthful tastes changed. Westward-looking, too, was De Laurentiis, who was busy planning large-budget "blockbusters" for American studios. Italy's film industry was in crisis yet again. The situation could not help but affect Fellini, with his knotty attitude toward producers. Financing became his major problem.

The Italian social scene was also undergoing profound change, and Fellini was sensitive to it. After the student riots of 1968, violence and terrorism flourished in Italy. Amidst general unrest, increasing inflation, and an economic downturn, the cinema suffered, too. State-supported and independent television had made inroads into the theater-going habit. Many cinemas closed and production declined. Film artists began to look for help from RAI and other quasi-governmental organizations.

Financing for *Roma* was arranged through three such companies: Cinecittà, and government-controlled laboratory and distribution entities. As the project expanded from its original $2-million budget, United Artists helped with an additional infusion of cash.

The idea, Fellini told Thomas Quinn Curtiss of the *International Herald-Tribune* in January 1971, was to do ten or twelve sequences evoking the city, two at a time, with no specified date for completion. He was making the film in stages because the production was so difficult that he was "obliged to stop from time to time." Or was the arrangement necessary because the length of the film would depend on how the budget was utilized? Fellini's reputation for staying on budget and finishing in time was not good. And certainly *The Clowns* had taken longer and cost more than any other film made, presumably, for Italian television.

Curtiss's lunch with Fellini took place at Gigi Fazzi, which Fellini declared to be the most Roman of Roman restaurants. With him was Giulietta, who had entered a new phase of her own. She was writing a syndicated advice column for women—the Dorothea Dix of Italy, Fellini said. Her acting career stalled, Giulietta was making more of a name for herself as an on-the-scene personality. She was a woman of remarkable strength and energy, an accomplished homemaker, a fine cook, and invariably diplomatic in handling inquiries about her famous husband.

Both husband and wife were spending more of their time in Rome. The small apartment on Via Margutta that Fellini had purchased some years before as a *pied-à-terre* was expanding, as space around it became available. Eventually it became large enough to contain a living room for each—necessary, Fellini said, because Giulietta smoked and he didn't. His own living room became his "thinking room." After a time, when his financial affairs became complicated, the house in Fregene was sold (1973), and both Fellini and Masina became permanent Rome residents.

Fellini told Curtiss that the start of production was two weeks away, that large sets were being built at Cinecittà, particularly 400 yards of highway meant to look like the recently built Raccordo Anulare, the expressway that encircles Rome. He planned to deal with the church's might and power in the past, with the brothels of Rome as they once existed; and he would contrast them with today's erotic behavior. He wanted to deal with the generation gap, symbolized by the hippies who thronged the Spanish Steps, with Rome's daily life, its celebrities, and those foreign writers and artists who came to live and work there.

One of the foreign writers he had in mind was Gore Vidal, who had come to Rome some ten years before and established himself in a large flat atop an ancient building, where he did most of his writing. "I'd known him casually," Vidal said in 1983, "and I ran into him at the bar of the Grand Hotel. 'I use you in my film, *Roma*, Gorino,' he said, and I answered, 'Well, I'm sitting by the phone, Freddy.' "

Roma would have no story in a literal sense, nor would it follow a linear progression. "Rome *created* me insofar as I am an artist," Fellini said in one of his statements about the film, "and I— I re-create Rome." It would be *his* Rome. It would be as much the city of his memory and imagination as the contemporary city he saw around him, and that he viewed with a mixture of affection and fear for its future.

Not unlike *The Clowns*, the film began with boyhood memories, when the young Fellini (presumably) learns about Rome through school and the movies. His arrival in the city echoes that of Moraldo in the early screenplay; the actor playing the young man is an American, Peter Gonzales—tall, thin, as was Fellini at that time in his life. But he seems to be there mainly as a viewpoint (a provincial's) from which to see the flowing life of the city: the station, a boarding house filled with bizarre types, and a crowded open-air restaurant, where the mood is happy, the food plentiful, the air filled with raucous good humor—Rome at its earthy best.

Then Fellini returns to the present, appearing as himself in the film and giving orders to his crew. The audience is given a wild, moody ride on the Raccordo Anulare during the rush hour, with its modern-day congestion, accidents, even a near flood from a rainstorm. The ride ends at the Colosseum—symbol of the dead past and of a myriad of contrasts to come.

The contrasts are unending. Back to Fellini's past and a vaudeville show in the fascist World War II years. The acts are poor, the spectators unfriendly, and the scene ends with an air-raid warning. But now it is today's Rome again, and there is a fine new subway being built. Fellini takes a journey through time by accompanying engineers through the strata of centuries, until an archeological discovery is made—an ancient Roman house with frescoes on its walls. Unfortunately, the air let into the excavation chamber disintegrates the paintings, and the faces slowly fade into a monotone of muddy gray. Rome is also the city of the unrevivable dead. Even its phantoms disappear. Fellini attributed the birth of this sequence to a dream he had had while making *Satyricon*. He was in a prison in the bowels of the earth. He heard voices from beyond the wall that faced him. A voice said: "On the other side there are Romans." The wall and the voices faded as the dream ended. Fellini treasured his dreams, and he had no hesitation about using them in his films. For those inclined to be critical, this was seen as one more instance of autobiographical intrusion into his work.

The audience, emerging from the subway, finds itself at the Spanish Steps, observing an army of hippies lying about, embracing and kissing. This out-in-the-open sex is a trigger for Fellini's return to the past and to the city's brothels. Sex was considered dirty and sinful then (not that Fellini altogether approves of the hippie movement, as it turns out); there was class distinction in whorehouses. We visit two, one for poorer customers, another, more elegant, for the wealthy. At the latter, the young and still romantically inclined "Fellini" asks an attractive member of the establishment for a date. There is no indication that he gets one.

The fullest Fellinian treatment is given to an ecclesiastical fashion show in a segment that evokes the power of the priestly class. While it is true that shops around the city featured fashions for members of the church, this visionary segment was entirely imagined (Zapponi claimed to have come up with the notion) and is not only the set piece of the film, but central to it. High fashion designs for nuns and vestments for priests are modeled for an audience of church dignitaries. The show turns surreal. Nuns float by, priests swirl along on skates. Highlighted by Rota's score, the scene is hilarious and awesome by turns. Bridal gowns are worn by skeletons, a black hearse glides by, and the procession ends with the set dissolving into a huge platform bearing a plastic pope with a halo of light around its head. The overawed audience falls to its knees.

"Fellini's city," writes Peter Bondanella, "is a city of illusions and myths—it is the center of Italian cinema, the headquarters of the Roman Catholic Church, as well as of the Italian government, and Fellini seems to view religion, politics, and cinema as human institutions all relying on the manipulation of images and myths."

For Fellini, there is no single Rome, "but a number of images, all of which interpenetrate and enrich the connotations of the others." Clearly, Fellini was bent on deflating many of those myths and, particularly with regard to the church, employing the weapon of ridicule.

While making *Roma*, Fellini gave fewer interviews than in the past. Only four or five journalists managed to see him, according to Liliana Betti, who was still his loyal assistant. She ran the press office for *Roma* and, finding it difficult to make clear to those who inquired just what the film was about, she settled for a list of the various sequences.

"The key to a Fellini interview," she wrote, "is indisputably Fellini himself. The answers he gives, the opinions he formulates, the stories he tells, preserve their meaning and authenticity only if they can survive in their original context . . . made up of a tireless penchant for deforming and expanding everything, an aggressive and provocative sense of humor, an only seeming availability, . . . a misleading game of mirrors that protects an inner reserve."

One of those favored to interview Fellini was a professor and critic, (the late) Charles Thomas Samuels, who had a federal grant to interview noted European film directors, Fellini among them. In Rome, in late April 1971, he managed, through the offices of Fellini's public relations representative Mario Longardi, to get an invitation to lunch with Fellini at the Grand Hotel. He arrived early and enjoyed "the spectacle of Fellini barreling up to the Grand parking lot in a long green Mercedes." When inside, Fellini said, "Ah, you're the journalist I'm supposed to meet." Samuels insisted that he was a professor, not a journalist—the distinction being important to him. Prepared for a long and exhaustive interview, he had brought along a tape recorder and a list of probing questions.

Fellini had a group of three with him: one, he said, for correcting
his English, for his errors, and the third for his lies. If that wasn't
enough, he volunteered to bring others from the studio.

Samuels was in a serious mood, but no sooner did he produce his tape recorder than lunch was announced. His scholarly
purpose was of less importance to Fellini than enjoying his food,
extending greetings to acquaintances around the room, and taking
telephone calls. But Samuels was in luck, said Longardi; usually
there were at least eight phone calls during lunch. Fellini would be
unable to exist without telephones, and he would gladly, if possible,
keep one in his pocket.

Samuels gritted his teeth and began his questions by bringing up Fellini's first film, *Variety Lights*. Samuels's needling aca-
demic questions began to irk Fellini. Why had he done so and so
in the film?

"I could invent ten answers," said Fellini, "but if you want
something sincere . . ."

"Perhaps," Samuels interrupted, "the answer is . . ."

"If you know, why do you ask me?"

"There's a wonderful scene in *Variety Lights* . . ." Samuels
began.

"More *Variety Lights*!"

"I'm sorry," Samuels said, "but . . ."

"We're making this a long lunch," Fellini protested. He
finally gave Samuels an answer to a question, then said, "Are you
happy now? Okay, eat your lunch."

Samuels plodded on, stubborn scholar that he was. And he
was honest enough, too, to include Fellini's put-downs when he
published the transcript. However, most of the tape remained still-
unwound by the conclusion of the lunch. "Today," he told Fellini,
"you have perhaps discovered that I am not a cretin. Tomorrow we
can have the interview."

His persistence was rewarded. Fellini saw him twice more,
and Samuels managed to squeeze out a few details that hundreds of
others had failed to get, and a great deal that they already had.

Fellini's captious way with him was undoubtedly due to his
immediately seeing the pedant in Samuels; yet he managed to find

time for him during a busy schedule that included the making of
Roma—about which he was willing to say little.

With Gore Vidal, whose creative energies he regarded with
obvious respect, he was much more open. Midway in the filming of
Roma Fellini visited Vidal at his apartment, chatted about the film,
and invited him to see what he had done so far. He ran off sections, which included interview scenes with Mastroianni and Alberto
Sordi—his way of acquainting Vidal with the method he would employ with him. (Because of the length of the film, the Mastroianni
and Sordi sections were drastically cut in the versions released in
England and America.) Vidal knew that Fellini dubbed in voices
after the filming. "I made a deal with him," he said. "I want to dub
myself." Fellini agreed.

"I wanted to be in *Roma*, because I was genuinely curious
to watch him work, and the best way to do that was to be his actor.
Well, the day—the evening—came when I was asked to come to a
piazza, which he had hired for the night in order to keep it empty.
There were about six tables, and two other long ones with food on
them—rather disgusting piles of food, some real, some plastic, and
I could tell from where he was positioned what the scene might look
like. Realistic, but slightly off, with a little more food than you'd ordinarily have there, and the fish a little too big and too raw. He
would ask me questions, and I would improvise my bit. He had me
doing it over and over. I was in the middle of take five when all hell
seemed to break loose behind us.

"I looked around. And there were four of the most beautiful white horses drawing an empty cart. 'Freddie,' I said, 'what the
hell is that?'

" 'I don't know, Gorino. It looks nice. Don't you think it
looks nice?'

"I said, 'It's very hard to be heard over that clattering, but
I suppose you know what you're doing.'

" 'Yes, it's nice,' he said. 'I think it's nice.'

"He kept adding things to the scene, then he would take
them away, and finally the horses were gone. I suddenly realized

that it didn't matter what I said, that I could be saying any nonsensible thing in my supposed interview, and that it wouldn't matter because I was part of his composition. What was in his head was the screen, and what happened in the square was happening to fill it up."

Later that year, Vidal performed his dubbing tasks at a studio in the Titanus complex. It was a numbingly cold day, he remembered, and he had a difficult time doing his speeches in Italian. "There were long sentences, with complicated structures that I'm not used to speaking in the language. I just couldn't get them out in time for the synchronization. The film on the screen would stop and I'd still be going. [Dubbing is done on little loops of film.] Finally, I said, 'Fred, you're supposed to be a great director—help me say the line so I get it out on time.'

" 'Before you say a line, Gorino, take a deep breath,' he told me. I took a deep breath and it came out exactly right. 'See,' he said. 'I am a great director.' "

Vidal was kept at the dubbing studio well into the early hours of the morning. Fellini would cut out lines, after which Vidal would have to try to make sense out of what followed an ellipse. He noticed that there was a line Fellini made sure to keep in. "I had said, 'Let's drink to the end of the world. What better place to watch the end of the world than in a city that calls itself eternal?' I realized why later. The line not only had to do with his theme [Rome declining in the sense of losing its spirit and identity], but these foreigners Dolce Vita-ing it while his own world collapses."

"We had amiable rows over his not using direct sound," Vidal remembered. " 'You make silent films,' I told him. 'This is the last country that makes silent films. It's never right when you divorce the actor from his voice—which is all an actor's got.'

" 'I don't like actors,' Fellini replied to me. I went on to say that all the great stars had voices, that they were what the audiences heard. 'You can paint up anyone to look like Hepburn, but you can't sound like her. And without the voice there is no presence of the actor.'

" 'Anglo-Saxons are demented on that subject,' Fellini said. 'Absolutely crazy.' I realized he didn't give a damn about whether or not images and sound went together in realistic terms."

*   *   *

The final and most haunting scene in *Roma* occurs late at night. The city has grown silent, almost ominously so. There is a sudden roar of motorcycles and a horde of cyclists erupts out of the darkness. They wear black helmets and leather jackets, and to one Italian critic they seemed "barbarians of a mechanical and brutalizing civilization, angels of the apocalypse come to announce the end of everything." The cyclists, the angry beams of their headlights piercing the darkness, roar through the fabled piazzas, around the Colosseum, and across the bridges of the Tiber, until the sound of their passage fades away, and Rome is silent once more.

Alain Resnais, the French director, was overwhelmed by the sequence. "Nothing like it," he said, "has ever been seen in the cinema."

Once more the critics, especially in the United States, seemed confused. The *New York Times* split, with Roger Greenspun describing the film as exuberant and beautiful, and "the most enjoyable Fellini film" he had seen in years, while Vincent Canby accused the director of recycling familiar themes. For *Playboy*, it was "a cinematic pearl"; for Pauline Kael an embarrassment for Fellini. Even those who praised the film were seldom able to see much purpose or structure in it.

All the more valuable then was an essay by Aldo Tassone, "From Romagna to Rome," that appeared in the French *La Revue du Cinéma*; it clarified, more than anything else written on the subject, Fellini's purposes and meanings. Tassone took up the attacks on Fellini for his "autobiographical presumptions" and his supposed narcissism. After all, the work of great artists was neccessarily autobiographical, he said. But Fellini was not merely telling the story of his own life. "His biography is a filter, a spyglass which he uses the better to capture life as it is."

Roma, then, was the evocation of a complex relationship between a dreamer and the universe that most stimulated his artistic imagination. Rome was a city, and also a state of mind, and it presented itself to Fellini in three different aspects: as the incarnation of the eternally feminine; as the personal theater of a director; as a mysterious cemetery abounding in vitality. By perceiving the film in these aspects, said Tassone, one could appreciate the richness of its allusions.

Certainly in *Roma*, as in many of his other films, Fellini provided enough examples of the feminine aspect. "It cannot be doubted," Tassone wrote, "that Fellini loves to celebrate the opulent forms of the Latin women." From the huge matron of the boarding house in the early scenes, to the types on display in the brothels, Fellini's surrogate keeps his fascinated young eyes on Rome's women. Robert Hatch in the *Nation* was oddly bothered by Fellini's obsession "with repugnant human flesh." Fellini, he thought, was developing too much of a taste for overeaters.

Another essayist who took the trouble to assess Fellini's work with more depth than the usual was William J. Free. Writing in the *Journal of Modern Literature*, he saw the director as widening the dimensions of the grotesque vision in contemporary art, while rebelling against "the darkness which is so pervasive that it is the established view of life for the modern artist." For Free, it was Fellini's critics who were metaphors of cultural failure, because of "their 'rigidity,' their 'seriousness,' their inability to laugh at themselves." Critics were not themselves creative artists (those who were, like Penelope Gilliatt of the *New Yorker*, were almost always sympathetic toward Fellini, and admirers of his work; directors such as Mike Nichols and Stanley Kubrick held him in highest regard, but their opinions seldom found their way into print) and, being too involved with the processes by which films were manufactured, were unable to see what Fellini was about, or were unwilling to allow him his creative vision.

Yet, commercial success for Fellini's films was dependent to at least some degree on critical support. In Italy there was a wide audience for *Roma*, but the high (for Italy) costs of Fellini's films could be recouped only by success in the international market— most importantly the United States. Neither *Satyricon* nor *Roma* were American box-office successes, and in fact no Fellini film since *8½* had brought much of a return for its producers.

For Fellini, this made the battle with producers—the battle for creative freedom—all the harder. Producers thought in terms of subjects with box-office appeal and star-studded casts. "But, if I don't amuse myself," he said, "making movies is an awful job. It's difficult for me to see my dreams in terms of a financial vision."

Tom Shales, then of the *Los Angeles Times*, wondered how he reacted to the often adverse criticism of *Satyricon* and *Roma*. "I'm very vulnerable on that point," Fellini replied. "To realize that what you say is liked by people—it's good, nourishing, stimulating. But with the critics that are bad, against, I am very weak; I think that maybe they're right. For a creative person to be criticized can be very dangerous. A creative person needs an atmosphere of approval. Like a fighter. You need to be drunk, you need to be exalted, to believe in what you are doing."

He was self-protective, too, in his daily associations. "Fellini tends to see only persons who get along with him. He doesn't care for people who argue with him, and after a time he won't see them. He'll see only those he likes," said Zapponi, who also found himself out in the cold for a time. After *Roma*, Fellini decided on some further filmic exploration of his memories. "I didn't really care much for his early memories," said Zapponi, and so it was to another screenwriter that Fellini turned for assistance.

XIX

I STARTED to make a picture many years ago," Fellini re-marked in his fifty-third year, "and I am still making that picture." He was not referring to a specific film, of course, but by the time he began work on *Amarcord*, in 1972, a distinct, continuing story could be found within a group of his films, although not in chronological order. The first of the group was *I Vitelloni*, in which the character of Moraldo emerged and was carried to the point where he left for Rome. The unmade *Moraldo in the City* would have continued the story, but young Moraldo did not show up again until *Roma*, in the person of the Fellini-like young man of the early scenes who, pre-sumably, will become the journalist of *La Dolce Vita* and, eventu-ally, the film director of *8½*. And episodes in what might arbitrarily be named "The Moraldo Story" are also to be found in *The Clowns*, as when the boy in its first scene wakes up to the sound of the circus tent being raised outside his window.

While admitting the autobiographical content of the films, Fellini preferred to use the term anecdotal—memory enhanced and heightened by imagination and invention, and even suggestions that came while making another film. For instance, he told Tom Shales that images from his past films stayed in his mind, mingled, and re-volved. Characters underwent resurrection and transformation.

A key to much of the work he did after his serious illness of 1966 is to be found in *My Rimini*, the essay he wrote during his convalescence. In it, he recalls being in a café in Rimini when "the door opened and three foreigners appeared. It was as if, say, Hans Albers had turned up with Anita Ekberg and Marilyn Monroe. We all gazed ecstatically at the sight." The man, who was wearing a fur coat, ordered an exotic liqueur, while the more "astonishing" of the women stared into space. The three then left in their "fantastic" car and vanished into the night. Obviously, this memory, or anecdote, found its way into *The Clowns,* as did his memory, recounted in the same essay, of his first encounter with the circus.

When beginning a film, Fellini was characteristically vague about it. But there was no hiding the origins of *Amarcord*; it had been all but outlined in *My Rimini.* The same essay also had an influence on the outline for *The Unknown Woman,* which Grimaldi had rejected. Somewhere along the line *The Unknown Woman* was metamorphosed into the film that became *Amarcord.*

Eventually, in explaining how he came to make *Amarcord,* Fellini told Stuart Byron and Charles Choset of the *Real Paper* that "in my last two pictures, in *The Clowns* and in *Roma,* I began to put in little cartoonlike vignettes of my home town, of Rimini. This point of view, this looking back from a distance—I liked it, and I said to myself, 'Probably one day I'll make an entire picture in this cartoon style, just to say good-by forever to all those ghosts. I'll make an entire picture for them, and after that they won't bother me anymore.' "

Aldo Tassone thinks of *Amarcord* as the first chapter of Fellini's re-creation of his past. "Before *I Vitelloni* there was a kind of *lacuna*; the director had to fill the gap sooner or later." *My Rimini* is important because it is the first draft of his future work; after his bout with illness, and the long dry spell between *Juliet* and "Toby Dammit," "he was able to return to his infancy with the wisdom of a second maturity."

For Fellini, *I Vitelloni* and *Amarcord* were different pictures, in that their points of view were different—"sentimental, romantic" in the former and in the latter "much more detached." The author, according to Tassone, has become older chronologically and his point of view is "uglier. It's a judgment, a sad judgment, a melancholic judgment."

Fellini's first title for the new film was *L'uomo Invaso*—sometimes reported as *Profaned Man*. Then, as the project took shape, the title became *Borgo*, meaning suburb or small community. Another thought was to call it *Viva Italia!* For his collaborator on the screenplay he chose Tonino Guerra, a poet who had worked on the screenplays of several of Antonioni's films. Guerra was also a Romagnolo; he had been born only five miles from Rimini, in the hill town of San Arcangelo. "The same dialect ties us to each other," said Fellini, "a childhood spent in the same countryside, the same snow and sea."

Fellini found a new producer in Franco Cristaldi, noted for several successes including *Divorce, Italian Style*, and also as the husband of Claudia Cardinale. While Fellini was nominally the co-producer, all financial dealings were left to Cristaldi. "I get bored with the whole process of organization," Fellini said. Cristaldi was able to bring in Warner Brothers to the tune of $2 million, allowing for a total budget of $3.5 million. Donati and Rotunno were again engaged as designer and photographer, respectively and, remarkably, there was no seeking after or insistence on star names for the cast. Fellini was name enough for Warner Brothers, although the company did ask for a title that might look better on the marquee.

Fellini didn't object. Titles for him were always a problem. "One day," he said, "I was lunching with a friend, and I idly wrote the word 'hammarcord' on a napkin. It was an invented word, but I later realized I was thinking of a phrase in my native Romagnola dialect, *amarcor*, which means 'I remember.' "

When he announced the new film project late in December of 1972, the title was *Hammarcord—L'uomo Invaso*, but, by the time of release, it had been shortened simply to *Amarcord*, leading to much discussion of the meaning of the word.

His intention, Fellini said of the new film, was to suggest the isolation from reality that Italians experienced under Mussolini and he hoped that, though "not an optimistic film, it might stimulate reflection on the gradual extinction of so many simple and less simple pleasures." Other than that, he gave the inevitably inquiring reporters little clue to the film's content. As with previous films, he spent several months in preparation—much of that time devoted to finding the faces and types he wanted. The advertisement went out—and two weeks were spent in Rome seeing the crowds of people who showed up. He then went on his travels, took hundreds of photographs, and eventually summoned the most likely prospects to Rome for interviews. Some were actors in amateur or provincial companies. One was a newspaperman who, for years, had wanted to be in one of his films. Fellini dressed him as a tramp and gave him an accordion—not exactly what the man had had in mind. A lissome young actress he convinced to play a hunchback.

From his store of envelopes he found a face he liked; it belonged to a sailor. An assistant, asked to locate him, managed to find the sailor's father who confessed, rather embarrassed, that his son had had a sex-change operation. "Wait!" Fellini told his assistant. "I have another character." The former sailor showed up, and was given a small female part.

A key role was that of Gradisca, the voluptuous young woman Fellini had described in *My Rimini*. Walking outside the Café Commercio, "dressed in black satin that flashed in a steely, glittery way, she was one of the first to wear false eyelashes." She was also the first in Rimini to have a permanent wave. Her name, Gradisca, came to her, he said, when she was asked to entertain a "prince of the blood royal" who was stopping over in Rimini at the Grand Hotel. "When she was naked before the prince, careful of what she had been told, she offered herself with the word, '*Gradisca!*'" meaning, "May it please you." When, later on, the real-life "Gradisca" was located by journalists, she stoutly denied the encounter had ever occurred. Fact or fiction, the incident was used in *Amarcord*. Two versions were shot: in one, Gradisca bares her impressive breasts to the prince; in the other, which was kept, the scene is shot more impressionistically. For Fellini, no one would do for Gradisca but Sandra Milo, who had retired from films. He convinced her to test for the part, although she did so secretly, her new young husband being vehemently opposed to her going back to acting.

Fellini, she told Maria Pia Fusco, tried to convince her that cinema was her true world. When she arrived for her test at Cinecittà, he said, "Don't you feel as if you've come back home, that your true family is this one?"

"For him," she said to Fusco, "the movies were really his family, but for me, no."

Fellini explained that Gradisca was to have something of a carnal quality, that she was spirited, fun, somewhat childish. Milo hated the make-up given her, the long black curls, with bangs. She asked that it be done over with very short hair. Trial shots were taken and Fellini expressed his satisfaction.

They said goodnight to each other on the studio steps. Milo was in a hurry because her husband did not know her whereabouts. "Suddenly," she told Fusco, "I felt a touch of melancholy."

Fellini said to her: "I have something of a feeling we won't see each other any more."

"No, no," Milo said.

At home she told her husband about the test. "He blew up and absolutely forbade me to be in the film." Despite Fellini's pleadings, Milo refused to sign a contract. Finally, she said, "He sent me one hundred red roses with a beautiful, sadly desperate card." The roses and the message failed to sway her.

Fellini, who had already had his memory town re-created on the Cinecittà stages and lot, and was due to begin filming in a week, hastily replaced Milo with an equally satisfactory choice, Magali Noël, the only "name" of stature in the entire cast. Although he denied that the impressive sets at Cinecittà specifically represented Rimini, there were enough resemblances for journalists to be forgiven for making the identification. There was a piazza with the facade of a cathedral on one side, even a cinema named the Fulgor, with posters of Gary Cooper and Fred Astaire in front.

Fellini once more ignored linear narrative conventions. The form of his film is circular, in that it begins with the onset of spring and ends a year later with spring arriving again, the herald on each occasion being the puffballs blown into the town by the wind. There is no real hero, and if any character can be said to be its center, it is the adolescent Titta—presumably suggested by Fellini's boyhood friend. Titta is seen at home, at school, confessing to a priest, and in an amusing scene taken whole from *My Rimini*: Fellini's boyhood encounter with Gradisca in the Fulgor Cinema.

Titta must deal with his sexual frustrations, Gradisca with

her fears of remaining a spinster. Titta's father is secretly a socialist, rebelling against the prevailing Fascist powers. A pedantic lawyer appears from time to time, narrating some of the town's history.
There are aunts and uncles, one of whom is insane and, taken for an
outing, isolates himself in a tree, yelling that he must have a woman.
A midget nun eventually gets him down. Rather than a plot, there is
a cavalcade of incidents: a Fascist rally and parade, the annual road
race, the arrival of a prince at the Grand Hotel. Change comes with
the seasons: Titta and his friends (sans females) dance in the autumn mist outside the Grand Hotel. In winter the boys pelt Gradisca's rear with snowballs. The pent-up sexual energy in the town
manifests itself in different ways. The fat tobacconist pushes her
huge breasts into the terrified Titta's mouth. In a car outside the
town, a group of boys masturbate in unison, their combined energy
making the headlights glow.

Fellini's earthiness flirts with scatalogy. The Fascists punish
Titta's father for a political transgression by filling him with castor
oil, with predictable and humiliating results. The tone of the film is
often humorous, but Fellini professed to have a serious sociological
motivation behind his making of it. The people of this town lived in
terms of symbols and myths, and he wanted to break those myths,
some of which he believed were still prevalent.

In an interview with Valerio Riva, a journalist, he talked of
the "psychological, emotional manner of being a fascist." It was a
sort of "blockage, an arrested development during the phase of adolescence . . . living with the comforting sensation that there is
someone who thinks for you (one time it's mother, then father, then
the mayor, another time Il Duce, the Madonna, the bishop) and in
the meantime you have this limited, time-wasting freedom which
permits you to cultivate only absurd dreams. . . ."

Ironically, what came through in the film for many viewers
was a sense of nostalgia for the simplicity and earthiness of a vanished time. And this was strongest of all in the scenes of the passing
of a great ocean liner, the *Rex*. In a flotilla of small boats, the people
of the town stay up most of the night watching for it. At a magic
moment, the ship looms up huge and dreamlike, its decks and masts
ablaze with lights. The sight reduces Gradisca to tears—for her it

represents an escape to a world of ease and adventure. Then the ship disappears into the fog. The marvel and eeriness of the scene is enhanced by Fellini's deliberately constructing the ship on a stage out of papier-mâché. David Lean was a visitor to the set at the time of the shooting, and was amazed that Fellini was able to get what he wanted in a matter of two takes.

Another marvelous moment comes when a peacock suddenly flies into the piazza in mid-winter, awing the townsfolk with the sight of its magnificent tail feathers. "The peacock's beauty," cautioned Peter Bondanella, "should not cause the viewer to overlook its symbolic connotations of vanity and, in Italy, of death."

These moments, and others that come like apparitions out of night and fog, give the film a visionary quality, at times even a visual poetry, but there is also sharp characterization, vitality, and teeming life. The people shout, and spit, and urinate. And they have dreams, and share their patriotic and romantic illusions. At the end, Gradisca marries a local member of the military. In a toast, the people shout, "Viva Italia!" The puffballs float in again. . . .

Amarcord was a year in the making, and the results exceeded all expectations. A popular and critical success in Italy, the film was chosen to open the 1974 Cannes Film Festival in May—with special lifetime achievement honors paid to Fellini and René Clair. Following Cannes, fall openings were scheduled for Paris, London, and New York. Meanwhile, Fellini was at work again. For years he had talked about the possibility of basing a film on the memoirs of Casanova, the eighteenth-century Venetian adventurer. Now, Dino De Laurentiis took him at his word and offered him a contract, with one stipulation—that the film be made in English. The budget was large, as indeed it would have to be to re-create an entire historical epoch.

Giovanni Giacomo Casanova, born in 1725, had recorded his life in twelve volumes. He was a traveler, a society figure, a dabbler in the occult, a gambler, a spy for the Venetian inquisition, and, most prominently for his subsequent reputation, an unscrupulous seducer of women. The problems began for Fellini when he read the *Memoirs,* all twelve volumes, not only once, but twice. He was not amused by this scoundrel who would bilk an old woman by prom-

ising to make her young. Instead he found him "positively obnox-
ious," his writings "a species of telephone directory. He roamed the
whole world, and it is as if he never moved from his bed." Either he
must come to some understanding with this "vacuum" of a Casanova, or find a filmic approach, a style, that would express "a life
that has been lived under ice."

For the screenplay, he returned to Bernardino Zapponi,
whose mind was more open than Tonino Guerra's to the symbolic
and fantastic style he had in mind. He opened a new office near the
Termini Station for the customary interviews, and a work room for
the design experiments of Danilo Donati. The more elaborate these
grew, the more arguments developed with De Laurentiis and his
budget-conscious associates. The script Fellini developed with Zapponi was visually exciting but had about as much human warmth as
a polar icecap. Nevertheless, De Laurentiis was enthusiastic. He saw
Robert Redford as Casanova, a bevy of enchanting females and,
more important, American distributors lining up for the package.
There was an impediment: Fellini did not want Redford. He was not
the Casanova the director had begun to envisage. Jack Nicholson
and Michael Caine were suggested. Fellini ruled them out, too.

Eventually, they agreed to disagree. De Laurentiis bowed
out. He sent word to the press in July 1974 that his heavy production schedule would not allow him to give the Casanova project
the attention it deserved. "Rather than do a poor job, we have
dropped it."

But not Fellini. In spite of his dislike of the character, he
had committed himself, and his preparations were well advanced,
except for the vital casting of the main role. It took very little time
for the Rizzoli empire to come to his rescue, as it had before. Angelo, the father, signed the contract; the picture would be produced
by his son, Andrea. Fellini transferred his offices to Cinecittà. There
his assistant, Liliana Betti, began a documentary for television on
the preparations for filming. "Fellini," she wrote, "sank deeper and
deeper into a tempestuous intimacy with Casanova."

He went, she said, to see Gustavo Rol, the magician and medium, at his home in Turin, where contact was made with the eighteenth-century philanderer in person. "Whether this was imaginary

or entirely true was an inane distinction in Fellini's strongly meta-
morphized world."

Rol is now in his seventies, bald, imposing, with a severe,
sharply featured face. He lives in an old house stuffed with books,
not far from the river Po. Of Scandinavian stock, he has been described as an impassioned doctor of the soul, a seer, a visionary, and
a psychic. To an interviewer, Rol said, "I have foreknowledge of
misfortunes that befall others. I act. At times I am successful. What
I do astonishes me, and I am frequently amazed." Tullio Pinelli was
once treated, with some friends, to a demonstration of Rol's magic.
The manifestation that occurred before Pinelli's eyes could have
been a trick, but, if so, he could not imagine how it was done.

In the séance that Rol arranged to contact Casanova for Fellini, the libertine somehow appeared, and a dialogue ensued in
which Casanova addressed Fellini as Signor Goldoni, a comedic
playwright of his own time. Fellini asked him if he was pleased that
he was making a film of his life. Casanova stiffly enjoined him to
"please use the polite form with me" (the formal *voi* instead of the
familiar *tu*). Rol thereupon materialized several pages of crabbed
script presumably written by Casanova. The meeting between the
seducer and the director did not go well. On leaving Rol's house,
Fellini came upon a card in his pocket. It was Casanova's calling
card, and it contained some sexual advice for Fellini: "Never on
your feet. Never after eating." Fellini could only feel that they were
truly worlds apart.

That summer, Fellini, a lover of automobiles, gave up driving. While driving through a suburb of Rome in his prized metallic
green Mercedes, with its sun roof and automatic transmission, he
was crashed into by a boy in a Topolino who had gone through a
light on a one-way street. Fellini attracted a crowd of nearby café
sitters as well as the police. He insisted he'd had the right of way,
but the onlookers—and the police, too—irrationally maintained the
opposite. He decided then and there to rid himself of the car. He
had assistants, such as Ettore Bevilacqua, to drive him.

A German tourist, a witness to the car accident, heard Fel-

lini give his name to the police and offered to buy the car as a gift
for his wife in Hamburg—the car of the famous director of *La
Dolce Vita*! The arrangement was made then and there, with the
crowd looking on and clapping hands.

"Perhaps I'd gotten tired of owning cars," Fellini recalled
later. "Too many tickets, too many places with no parking, taxes
and fees. The garage was too far, and too many criminals and mad
people were around in other cars. Assassins! There are taxis. I like to
sit and talk, to sit up front and talk to the driver."

He discovered there was always someone around to drive
him, and if caught in the rain, he would plant himself in the middle
of the street, staring at passing cars and waving as though he knew
the person driving, then pretending he'd made a mistake. "Someone
always stops to offer me a ride," he said, modestly.

In August 1974 he was in London, staying at Claridge's and
interviewing actors for *Casanova* in his suite. At lunch with Sidney
Edwards of the *Evening Standard* he explained why he was thinking
of an English actor for Casanova. "I want to make a psychological
portrait of the Italian prototype. I don't know really why I want an
Englishman, but I need a *real* actor, a stage actor, because of the
stylized nature of the film." Who, he wanted to know, was Ian Richardson? He had seen his face in the papers that morning. He left
London, his search for an actor still unrewarded, and before the
opening of *Amarcord*. But London was well prepared for it; the
news of its success at Cannes had been reported by the British critics.

His next overseas stop was New York, during the last week
of September, to aid the publicity campaign for *Amarcord*, which
had already opened to a torrent of critical praise and was doing well
at the box office. His entourage included Giulietta, Franco Cristaldi,
and Tonino Guerra, his writer, who like the others had traveled in
first class.

A *New Yorker* "Talk of the Town" reporter was waiting at
the airport, and rode into town in Fellini's limousine. He hadn't
wanted to come, Fellini said, and take a week out from his work in
Rome. But friends had insisted. "I came just like a suitcase. I am

the author of the picture, not a salesman. But I am asked to help, so I try to help." The help included interviews with film reviewers on the NBC and CBS morning news shows, and with reporters from several newspapers.

To those who couldn't understand his method of getting a peacock to spread its tail feathers in the midst of a snow fall, he first said that "you have to know the peacock's language and whisper to it in a very convincing way," but then he admitted that it was an electronic peacock, the manufacture of which was not really of interest to the audience.

With such powerful media as *Time, Newsweek,* and the *New York Times* hurling praise, *Amarcord* restored Fellini to the pantheon of international hit-makers and, as the *New Yorker* commented, Fellini, "after a decade or so of being 'out,' is 'in' again," and more than ever before.

The film, *Newsweek* said, was "the fully realized incarnation of Fellini's quest for a form flexible and capacious enough to contain his teeming imagination." Jay Cocks of *Time* called it "some of the finest work Fellini has ever done—which also means it stands with the best that anyone in film has ever achieved." And so it went, with a few holdouts including, as one might expect, John Simon, who was then trumpeting his opinions from the columns of *Esquire.*

Simon was never one to understate, and he did not disappoint. Fellini was now making, he said, some of the world's worst films, his "last clinker" being *Amarcord,* a title that "should have gone on: 'I Remember, I Reuse, I Rereuse, Until I Don't Even Remember What it is I am Rereusing.'" Simon's invective was familiar, too.

At almost the same moment, the *New York Times* allowed Simon a full page and more in its Sunday drama section to respond to the highly favorable review by Vincent Canby. This time Simon went after Fellini like Jack the Ripper at one of his London prostitutes. He titled his piece, "The Tragic Deterioration of Fellini's Genius," attempting to prove his point with a rundown of the filmmaker's entire output. The tone, in general, was that of a prosecuting attorney making a charge to the jury.

Fellini was apparently nettled by attacks such as these,

because, in interviews, he would profess not to understand why some critics thought he loaded his films with ugly or grotesque characters. "Anybody," he said, "would think that the world was full only of beautiful people. Look around you in the street. How many people are beautiful in the accepted sense of the word? I remember parties in London and New York where people accused me of filling my films with freaks. Then I looked around me and felt my characters were normal by comparison. So I like fat women. Must I apologize for it?"

Back in Rome, with the role of Casanova still uncast, preparations went forward for the start of filming in February 1975. Fellini began thinking of an Italian actor for the principal role, notably Gian Maria Volonte, who had recently emerged as a star of some magnitude. With the budget still rising day by day, spurred on by Italy's mounting inflation, Fellini was put off by Volonte's asking price, and turned again to the idea of an English-speaking actor. The name of Donald Sutherland was put forward. Fellini vaguely remembered him from the scene he had done for Paul Mazursky's film, *Alex in Wonderland*.

Andrea Rizzoli was meanwhile casting about unsuccessfully for some American financial participation. Fellini was enjoined to chop a budget that had reached $8 million. Suddenly, just before Christmas 1974, Rizzoli abandoned the project. Fellini claimed that he had worked for four months attempting to get costs down to $6.5 million. "It meant tearing whole chunks out of the script," he said, "reducing the number of characters, and sets and costumes. But it was impossible to get it any lower, and I haven't heard from Rizzoli since." He called in lawyers to begin a suit for breach of contract.

Rescue came in the person of Alberto Grimaldi, who called from Hollywood to say he would take over the production of *Casanova*. Grimaldi had made a major world-wide success with Bernardo Bertolucci's *Last Tango in Paris*, and was producing the same director's *1900*, in which Donald Sutherland was playing a leading role. Learning that he might be considered as Casanova, Sutherland sent Fellini flowers with a flowery note expressing respect and love. Grimaldi was able to secure a commitment of $3 million from Universal on the basis of Sutherland's participation, but with the condition that he would speak the part in his own voice. There was another condition: that the script be rewritten by a writer approved by the studio. Fellini brought up the name of Gore Vidal, who was still living in Rome. Word came back that Vidal was acceptable.

"He came to see me," Vidal remembered, "and said, 'Gorino, I am doing this Casanova. We need more money, which Universal is willing to give us if . . .' He took about an hour to get around to it, but finally said I was the approved writer he needed. 'That's you, Gorino,' he said. 'They love you at Universal.' I said, 'Sure, I'll do it.'

"He sent me the script Zapponi had written, and I thought it was pretty good. We had a meeting, and I asked him if he would mind if I made it better. There were scenes with Voltaire that bothered me—I thought you owed something to the memory of a great man that he say something intelligent. Fellini was agreeable, but he then told me, 'Don't make Casanova sharp in any way. He's an idiot. I detest him.' That led to some interesting conversations between us."

The main matter of discussion was the unsympathetic portrayal of Casanova. Vidal, of a more literary bent, was bothered by Fellini's attitude toward his subject. "I said to him, 'You know one of the first rules of art, even as practiced by your extraordinary self, is that you cannot make a work of art about a figure that you detest. You can't do it. It's an old rule, but one that you break at your risk.

"He said, 'Well, it isn't that I hate him . . .'

"I said, 'No, no, you do.' "

Fellini described how he wanted the character to look—tall, straight, like a walking erection. Who would play him, Vidal wanted to know? "He asked me what I thought of Donald Sutherland, and I told him I thought he was a good actor. 'Plainly, you don't want a handsome Casanova,' I said. And I thought that was correct, because the original wasn't.

" 'I like Sutherland,' Fellini told me, 'because he has a wonderfully stupid look. He looks unborn. I want a character who is unborn, still in the placenta.'

"I wrote the script," Vidal said, "and Fellini showed it to Universal. They okayed it, and the money he needed came through.

Then, Freddie delicately lets me know that he will not be using my script version, that he will not work in direct sound, as had been specified, that he would work in English when he felt like it, and in Italian when the actor was Italian. I don't think he used any of the script I wrote. He did use some of what was in the Zapponi script I saw, but to my mind, Fellini is essentially a painter rather than a narrative artist, and with *Casanova* the painter took over again."

Zapponi commented: "Fellini didn't really like the changes he made in the story, and he didn't like having arguments with him. So he stopped seeing Vidal." Later Fellini brought in the novelist Anthony Burgess to brush up the English dialogue. And, unknown to Zapponi at the time, Tonino Guerra did some additional work on the script.

"To work with Fellini," Zapponi said, "one must understand that it is necessary for him to transform, that he is unable to do it another way. He never invents simple personages; he has to transform everything with his imagination. If he wants to portray a Roman politician, he takes someone with a nasty face. I felt he hated Casanova, because he was his own opposite. Casanova was a man of the world, very active. Fellini is not. He's really something of a coward when it comes to real life, and his courage is in what he makes. He won't accept compromise. Even if he starved, he would continue on his own way."

Soon after hearing that he could resume preparations for *Casanova,* Fellini also received word of new honors for his *Amarcord.* Already showered in Italy with the David de Donatella and the Grolla de Ora of St. Vincent awards, along with five Nastri d'Argento, he received the New York Film Critics Circle award and the Oscar for Best Foreign Film.

For Fellini, *Amarcord* had been an imaginative journey into his past; now he was making a journey into another time, with a character who seemed entirely alien to him. Did he see in Casanova not so much a man as a side of himself that he detested? Or, more than that, the characteristics of what he regarded as a typical modern Italian male. "He's all shop front," Fellini fumed to a reporter for *Time*. "A public figure, striking attitudes . . . in short, a braggart Fascist."

The tall Canadian actor Donald Sutherland arrived to play this "typical Italian" in July 1975. Already commissioned of Danilo Donati, again Fellini's designer, were fifty-four sets, pruned down from the original seventy-two. Fellini had ordered 500 wigs (at $350 each) for the extras who would populate the film and, strangely, in view of the fact that everything would take place in the artificial environment of the Cinecittà studios and visual fantasy would prevail over a realistic account of Casanova's life and times, he insisted that all the costumes be colored with the same vegetable dyes used in Casanova's day.

While Sutherland was kept waiting for Fellini to make his final decision, he had prepared himself for the role by reading all twelve volumes of the *Memoirs*, and he had found them much more fascinating than did Fellini (who, in his rage, had ripped pages out of a treasured early edition owned by Zapponi). More than that, Sutherland read books about Casanova and his period, and he came to Cinecittà ready to discuss his character authoritatively. But Fellini steadfastly refused to discuss with the actor how he was to play the role. "I want you to *say* something," Sutherland prodded him.

"Let's talk about him when the filming is over," Fellini replied.

"Perhaps," Fellini said later, "Donald saw himself as a John Barrymore or a John Gielgud in the part of a Casanova who would be much like Don Giovanni. Instead he found out that he had to play a Casanova who resembled a Pinocchio."

Sutherland was surprisingly uncomplaining. "I didn't come to make *Casanova*," he said. "I came to make Fellini's *Casanova*." He saw his job as understanding what Fellini wanted of him and "to embody it as clearly as I could."

This understanding was not easy to achieve, since Fellini offered few definitions of the role. "Poor Sutherland," he told one reporter among the increasing number who came to visit the set, "the only thing you need to remember about Casanova, I said to him, is that he is a *stronzo* (a turd). I think I bewilder him. He thinks I am not serious. Why did I choose him? He has a face that's hard to remember. The story is about someone who didn't exist as an individual. He is dim, he moves in a fog—Donald is completely alien to the conventional notion of an Italian male—dark-eyed, dark hair, magnetic, the classic Latin lover." For Fellini, Casanova's sexual athleticism was a denial of life, the seeking for a return to the warm darkness of the womb. Erotic activity would be at the heart of the film, but it would be mechanical, heartless sex. In his travels over the length and breadth of Europe, too, Casanova would find only emptiness.

"In the film," Zapponi said, "Fellini had the sex scenes played in a closetlike room, almost like a coffin, suggesting a funeral."

He wasted little time before imposing his physical notion of the character on Sutherland. "I presented a character," Sutherland said, "and he changed every single aspect of it." His hair was cut off to nearly half way up along his scalp. His eyebrows were shaved, and he was given a false nose and chin. He had to be at the studio at five in the morning for the make-up application, which took four hours. While filming, he was told where and how to move, with Fellini behind the camera miming every action and expression. Sutherland found the first few weeks difficult in that "you were trying to understand not what the language in terms of words was, but what the language in terms of the extraordinary artistic sensibility of the man was, what the keys were to be able to understand and satisfy him." On the other hand, he said, "He caressed and coddled me and treated me more gently and lovingly than ever before in my life—like a permanent self-perpetuating seduction." This included furnishing (at Sutherland's own request) his dressing room in eighteenth-century antiques, and having on order for him a supply of hot, rich cocoa—this after Fellini discovered that cocoa was Casanova's favorite drink.

The opening scenes were a Fellini extravaganza—Venice at carnival time, Venice fallen from its glory days of elegance and prosperity, a city of corruption, spies, and the Inquisition—"the last spasms," wrote Zapponi in a narrative version of his screenplay, "of a decadent civilization."

The theme would be that of "Casanova as prisoner, Casanova in a music box, Casanova in the womb. . . . Venice, a maritime city, becomes a great mother whose waters have long since burst and who is now in the act of giving birth."

Amid the carnival hilarity a ceremony is taking place. "A gigantic statue, the symbol of Venice, is being fished from the sea. Not a whole statue, only a bust." This head, of a strange Venus, is being pulled up out of the waters of the Grand Canal by ropes. A crowned head appears briefly, its eyes appearing to stare in wonder at a bizarre world.

The filming of this moment, though it occurs early in the film, was done near the end of many months of production. Fellini explained to Antonio Chemasi, a writer and editor for *American Film* magazine, that the scene was the result of a dream he'd once had. In the dream, he found himself standing by the sea at Rimini. "His mother," Chemasi wrote, "stood nearby, looking stern. A group of fishermen silently approached, but they would not speak, he understood, as long as his mother remained. He ordered her away by clapping his hands. Then the fishermen turned toward the sea and started hauling on a rope. Slowly the giant head of a woman rose up from the water." Chemasi did not attempt to analyze the implications.

Chemasi described the night shooting of the carnival of Venice and the raising of the Venus head:

The acres of sprawling set had been brilliantly lit; the Rialto Bridge was decorated with oil lamps and mannequins in bright costumes; the gondolas festooned with roses; and the extras—all five hundred—were in full dress. . . . They waited for shooting to start—strong-featured, large-boned Romans; meanwhile they ate, drank wine, and listened to transistor radios. Sprawled on the grass or sitting on chairs, women in elaborate make-up and formidable gowns looked like ladies of quality down on their luck. They had the Fellini features: chunky, an assemblage of large curves, self-consciously sensual. Unlike the men, who smoked and seemed bored, the women, in mounds of hair, like to parade in their outfits. Bearing themselves erectly, they would glide with cool elegance past teasing crewmen.

When Fellini appeared on the set in mid-evening, he was with his wife, Giulietta Masina. She greeted a few guests with a firmly set smile as if she were a candidate's wife dutifully stumping. Her small face was almost hidden behind huge sunglasses; her reddish hair in a frozen seizure of waves. She took a chair and continued to smile brightly at no one in particular.

On the set, Fellini was facing problems. The giant head, now submerged in the water [of the studio-built canal], refused to rise with a crane's help. The extras, herded about by assistant directors, were not where Fellini wanted them. He would call into his megaphone, and assistants—who seemed to have been chosen for their speed as much as for their talent— would rush to him.

Maurizio Mein [an assistant director] would take his instructions and dash off like Mercury on an errand, shouting into his walkie-talkie as he ran. Fellini called often on Mein, and even with the megaphone his tone sounded less like a command than a plea. Fellini has the typical Roman speech habit of dropping his voice on the last syllable of a word, giving words a melodic, almost wistful, quality. Soon the call, "Maureee-zio" began to sound like the voice of one crying in the wilderness.

"Fellini," one young assistant confided, "does everything himself. It can be limiting."

As shooting neared, Fellini moved among the extras arranging them as though choreographing a ballet. Between excursions he retreated to the camera, climbing a scaffold to peer through the lens, jumping up and down on a stool in frustration.

It was after midnight before he shouted into a megaphone, "Places!" A band of crewmen rushed over the grounds, ordering back onlookers. The set in stillness, Fellini left the camera for a slow inspection tour, walking along the shore like a general before the dawn attack. He returned whistling—he does an enormous amount of whistling and humming, all of it sounding as if it had been scored by Nino Rota. Then he stopped. He had spotted a lantern in a sea of lanterns that was dimmer than the rest. Workmen scampered for a replacement.

At close to one A.M., the cameras rolled. At a signal a din of noise rose over the acres of set; lanterns and hands shook in the air; cheers rose from the church steps. In less than a minute, the cameras stopped. Fellini had got his take.

Chemasi was present during much of that week, when filming went on until four or five in the morning.

But the next day, somehow, Fellini would appear at Cinecittà, seemingly inexhaustible, in the same clothes he wore all week—a blue velvet sports jacket, wine-red vest, gray slacks, and, of course, the black hat. He found time for a picnic in the countryside with his staff. He spent hours in the warm afternoons loitering on the set, open to small talk. And at night, in the glare of lights and the din of extras and crew, he seemed revitalized. He restlessly roamed the set, calling on his assistants, pacing arm-in-arm with Donati, embracing visitors. After each shot Fellini would jump out of his chair and greet yet another old friend.

One night, several dozen Italian journalists, at Fellini's invitation, descended upon the set. During a break in shooting, they were driven off to La Caschina, a restaurant tucked in a grove of trees a short distance away. Roaring down the darkened studio roads, the cars might have been from *La Dolce Vita*.

At the restaurant the journalists attacked a staggering array of buffet plates spread out along one wall. But after the food disappeared and the wine glasses started clinking, they slipped into a torpor. At one table, a well-fed woman, finding a strange face across from her, said: "We see the same old faces all the time. You're new."

When the cappuccino came around, a weary-looking Fellini finally arrived. He moved past tables with small waves, settled at one, and, ignoring his cappuccino, huddled in a quiet conversation, his hat still on. Something of a palpable envy soon spread to other tables, and like magnet filings, the writers silently, unobtrusively, moved toward Fellini in a slow-motion stampede. Cameras quickly appeared, and the questions started.

When will *Casanova* be ready? Fellini's answers were virtual murmurs. He wasn't sure, and shrugged his shoulders. "Are you happy?" someone asked. No one seemed to think this question peculiar, least of all Fellini, who murmured an indistinct answer and waved his hands in compromise. The question of Fellini's happiness seems to be of extraordinary significance to the Roman press.

Fellini did not entirely desert Casanova's own account of his amorous adventures: In the midst of the carnival episode, he has a youthful Casanova—much of what occurs is seen through a haze of recollection—appear for an assignation with a lively nun, who already has a lover with a taste for voyeurism. This leads to Casanova's imprisonment, and a daring escape over the roofs of Venice, after which the adventures are taken up again in Paris, in the abode of the elderly and fabulously rich Marchesa d'Urfé, whom, according to the *Memoirs*, Casanova, over a period of years, tricked out of a considerable portion of her fortune. The marquise was a firm believer in and amateur practitioner of the occult. She believed she could be made young again, and Casanova gave her a convincing demonstration of his own "magical" power by transforming an old crone (in disguise) into a beautiful young woman.

Fellini's version, however, made the marquise's transformation dependent (at her insistence) on copulation with Casanova, who makes sure—in order to achieve the proper degree of potency—that he has an enticing young woman furtively revealing herself, from behind a curtain, in inflammatory postures.

Casanova, in Fellini's hands, finds little satisfaction in his pursuit of the erotic, but rather, when the occasion calls for it, seems to perform like a sexual engine. True love invariably escapes him, as when he meets the beautiful Isabella in Berne, at the home of Doctor Moebius. She agrees to rendezvous with him at an inn in Dresden, and when she fails to appear he finds himself participating in an orgy that includes a humpbacked girl and involves activity so furious that the bed scampers about the room.

At the court of the Duke of Württemberg, he goes to the rescue of a pretty girl who turns out to be a cleverly contrived

mannequin. Overcome with desire for her, he makes love to the
doll; and in a final scene, recalling his life and loves while employed
as an archivist in Bohemia, he dreams of a return to Venice, the
waters now turned to ice. There the mannequin is seen spinning on
the ice, and Casanova fades into emptiness as he dances with her.

After five months of filming at Cinecittà, during which several reels of rushes were stolen (and eventually returned), Grimaldi
went into a panic over the pace at which the budget was being used
up and suspended production. Almost all the money was gone, he
said publicly, and only half the film had been shot. "Next to Fellini,"
he charged, "Attila the Hun looks pale." Fellini decided he had
been slandered and went to court, but eventually the dispute was
settled, Grimaldi and Fellini both calmed down, Universal dredged
up some additional money and, after a three-month delay, production resumed and filming was concluded in May 1976.

Sutherland had retreated to Canada during the fracas.
"Poor Donald," Fellini said, "he calls me every week from Canada
to ask me, 'What's happening?' "

Fellini felt that Sutherland had not been treated well by the
Fates during the making of the film. "He had a series of accidents,"
Fellini told journalist Oreste del Buono. "He hurt his foot, he hurt
his hand, as if the real Casanova were persecuting him for having
portrayed the great lover as I had asked him to. He was put through
trials that certainly would have discouraged anyone else. Even until
the last day of work."

The last scene shot was that in which Casanova disappears
into a frozen image of Venice. Sutherland was to film in the morning and leave at one thirty in the afternoon. It was a brief scene and
there would be time for a little party that Fellini had planned for
him. The director knew that Sutherland collected antique pocket
watches, and he had found one for him as a parting gift.

But a rainstorm suddenly came up, and Fellini realized that
there would not be time to finish the shooting and also have the
party. He found Sutherland in his trailer.

"Well," Fellini said, "we've come to the end."

"What?" Sutherland asked.

Fellini saw that he was crying, and was bothered by it, mainly because it was affecting the make-up that had been so laboriously applied. He took out the watch and put it into Sutherland's hand.

"He squeezed it and my hand," Fellini said. " 'I love you,' he said. And when we realized it had stopped raining we got up; we banged our heads against the trailer ceiling. He hugged me, still holding the pocket watch. But not too close. It's difficult to hug and kiss someone with a false nose and chin."

Sutherland's final scene was shot as soon as the sky cleared. At the finish, there was a genuine round of applause for him from the film crew. "Don," said Fellini, "took off his false nose and chin, took off his huge Casanova overcoat and walked away over a field, waving the overcoat like a flag in a final salute to us. Suddenly he disappeared. The coat was so heavy that it dragged him down on the field. He got up, waved again, and fell again. Accidents till the end."

For Fellini there remained the dubbing, and the problem of finding a voice for Sutherland in the Italian version. He wanted him to *sound* dubbed, "like a Pinocchio." During July the dubbing was completed, and shortly before Christmas 1976 the film was ready for release. A feeble effort was made by a citizens' group to have it banned in Italy, but a magistrate found the film "erotic but not obscene." This sort of publicity naturally helped to attract audiences when *Casanova* opened in Rome and other major cities early in 1977. The lines were longer than for *King Kong*, to which De Laurentiis had devoted himself after withdrawing his support from *Casanova*.

XX

BY the time of its completion the cost of *Casanova* was estimated in the neighborhood of $10 million—a cost that would be impossible to recoup without a strong box office in the United States. The laudatory Italian reviews, and the enthusiastic early-audience response, proved to be no barometer of the film's reception elsewhere. (Except in Japan, where it played for three years.) Vincent Canby, usually a supporter of Fellini in the *New York Times*, struck one of many sour notes. "Spectacular," he wrote of the film, "but singularly joyless." The effect was "of celebrating the absolute end of romance and eroticism." There appeared to be some substance in Gore Vidal's prediction that a film about a figure treated with dislike, even disgust, was doomed to failure.

Canby was kind compared to other critics. Frank Rich, in the *New York Post*, racked the film as "mean-spirited, egomaniacal, flatulent, mindless, and gross." For Andrew Sarris of the *Village Voice* it was "a joyless, sexless, often pointless caricature." Pauline Kael's cut was the unkindest of all. She said she had to walk out after only one hour; therefore her review had to remain undefinitive.

Under a barrage of this caliber, the film soon disappeared from view. Yet, later assessments found more value in it, particularly when seen in the context of Fellini's work as a whole. The British writer Roger T. Witcombe, in his book *The New Italian Cinema*

(1982), was judicious in his assessment of *Casanova*: "Although Fellini is obliged to be interested in the sexuality of his hero, he is actually more conscious of his charlatanism, an important aspect of the Venetian inheritance." Witcombe wonders if Fellini's "provinciality confronted with his 'enemy's cosmopolitanism'" finally becomes an impediment. "He was able to participate fully in the project only by introducing a tension between the historical figure and his own disgust for him."

And, for Peter Bondanella, *Casanova* was "an extravagant and visually impressive work, the sets and costumes of which alone reward study." In this new phase of his work, Bondanella said, Fellini was continuing to attack, as he had in *Amarcord*, "the infantile mentality of his countrymen" and "blending his uniquely personal vision of the cinema with contemporary social issues." Even so, a coolness can be discerned in these sympathetic assessments. Fellini's Casanova was much too icy a portrait to attract admirers.

The financial failure of the film was a stark example of the risk involved in backing heavily a film artist who persists in placing his uncompromised personal vision above and beyond the dictates of the box office. Fellini would complain more and more publicly about his difficulties with producers. They still wanted to make a film with Fellini, he would say, not necessarily a Fellini film, but one made by Fellini. De Laurentiis apparently kept up his hopes that Fellini would see the commercial light of day, and the advantages of working in the United States; he even attempted to intrigue Fellini into making a sequel to De Laurentiis's *King Kong*. A new potential backer appeared in the person of *Penthouse* publisher Robert Guccione, who was in Rome producing an expensive and highly erotic version of the emperor Caligula's revels. Fellini once more dredged up *The Voyage of G. Mastorna* and also *City of Women*, the script he, with Zapponi, had written for the abandoned project with Ingmar Bergman.

Which to make? Ramakrishna Sarathy, an astrologer and palm reader from New Delhi, claimed that in 1976 Fellini had shown him the scripts for both these films, and asked his advice on which to do. Sarathy, who said he often advised film-makers, chose

Mastorna. Fellini had been most kind to him; invited to lunch with him at the studio, Sarathy was touched by Fellini's sensitivity in preparing a delicious vegetarian meal for him.

Fellini was angered by the gossip that sprang up about him in the Roman press at this time concerning his being seen frequently with the young and beautiful Olimpia Carlisi, who had appeared as Isabella in *Casanova.* He immediately instituted a suit for libel. Another name sprang up: Capucine, who had been seen in his *Fellini Satyricon.* Fellini was the victim, this time, of the paparazzi. A picture was printed showing him bestowing a warm kiss on Capucine. Rumors were revived, too, of a romance with Sandra Milo.

He and Giulietta appeared together for a joint interview to scotch the stories. "Obviously," he said, "that kind of thing has always been said about actresses with whom I have worked very closely, and it's easy to get pictures of us together." But there was nothing to the gossip, he insisted.

"Olimpia Carlisi is part of our group," Giulietta said. So were others mentioned. But the amorous linkages were silly. "About a week ago, I, Federico, and a group of friends, including Capucine, were at a restaurant together—the Appiceo on Via Amadeo—and, as you know, among us in the theater it's a custom every time we see each other to exchange exclamations and kisses, hugs, pats on the backsides, and Fedi doesn't deny himself this. That's how the picture with him kissing Capucine happened to be made."

Zapponi didn't doubt that Fellini had problems with other women, but if any relationship threatened to go too far, it would be cut off. "I would think he would say, 'How can I leave Giulietta?' My feeling is that Masina, along with the life they share, is a protection for him."

In April 1977 Fellini came to an agreement with Guccione's Penthouse Productions to make *The Voyage of G. Mastorna.* But once again, Mastorna refused to come to life. The reasons are unclear, although Fellini kept referring to the film like a much beloved and lost son who would one day reappear. Later in the year, Guccione was again involved, this time in an arrangement to make *City*

of Women—which the producer said he had preferred from the beginning—with the understanding that it would be shot in English
and with an American or British star. Franco Rossellini, the son of
Roberto, arranged the financing, with Goffredo Lombardo participating as the distributor. Fellini brought in his former collaborator,
Brunello Rondi, to rework and lengthen the originally hour-long
script.

During this period Piera Fogliani, a reporter, obtained Fellini's reluctant agreement to do an interview in his Via Margutta
apartment. She described the room in which they talked as "not
terribly large, with two four-seater couches covered in a bright
fabric with field flowers on a white background." The walls were
white, with lacquered bookshelves. Lamps had blue shades; there
were only two paintings on the walls, and these were still lifes.
There was a round table in blond wood, surrounded by light wood
chairs. To her the room seemed "absolutely simple, with nothing in
it of real importance or of value."

Fellini yawned, stretched, whistled. At fifty-seven, his hair
was streaked with gray, but he still had a young, fresh appearance,
"typical of the robust Romagnolas."

He was unhappy, he claimed, because of taxes. "I'm a victim of persecution and I'll take advantage of this opportunity to say
it openly." He was sure that the taxes he paid were excessive, that
the recently introduced new tax structure did not take into account
the fact that his work was not continuous. "One year I make a film,
for three I don't do anything." It was to pay his taxes, he said, that
he had sold the villa in Fregene.

Since he was not now working at the studio, what did he do
for amusement—the theater, or movies? Fellini claimed almost
never to go to movies, or the theater, or even to watch television. If
he did go to the theater, the only magic for him was the moment
when the curtain went up. "By the end of the first act I don't understand what the relationship between the characters is, who the wife
is, who the lovers might be, nothing. But everything else interests
me—the foyer during intermission, the bar. I like to walk around
the hallways while the show goes on, to see the coatroom girls count-
ing their tips among themselves."

It was the same way with religion. He didn't go to church, normally, "but I might go in, perhaps, when I'm in a state of moral crisis, or because of some mystic call. But I usually go in more out of scenographic curiosity, because of an open door. It's dark inside, and to me that seems irresistible."

He was lazy about keeping himself physically in shape, he admitted, but he did walk about a lot, less for health than out of curiosity. "Sports don't interest me; the Olympics depress me."

The interviewer asked about his sleeping habits. Since he was a child he hadn't been able to sleep more than three hours at a time. After waking, he would go to sleep again, but not more than another two hours. "I'm up at six in the morning. I walk around the house, open windows, poke around in boxes, move books from here to there. For years I've been trying to make myself a decent cup of coffee, but it's not one of my specialties. I go downstairs, outside as soon as possible. By seven I'm on the telephone. I'm scrupulous about choosing who it's safe to wake at seven in the morning without their getting insulted. For some I perform a real service, a wake-up service; they become used to my waking them at seven or so."

Giulietta, he said, was the one who kept his home life organized. "I can come in without warning at any hour with three or four friends, and there will be enough for everyone to eat." It was because of her housekeeper, Irma, Giulietta told another writer, that she was able to provide this hospitality. "She is always smiling, always gracious, even if at the last minute I tell her to set the table for eight." Irma could even recognize voices on the telephone, particularly those of movie people, because her previous employer had been actor Rossano Brazzi.

Fellini set up shop again at Cinecittà in late October of 1977 and began the process of casting and production design for *City of Women*, whose story had gained new relevance with the rise of feminism in Italy and other countries.

It would deal with the surreal adventures of a gentleman of fifty who finds himself at a grand hotel in the midst of a feminist convention. Mistaken for a prying journalist and attacked by the angry women, he flees, and in succeeding episodes, confused and uncertain of his place in a world of changed and embattled woman-hood, travels through strange landscapes, while encountering in fantasies and dreams (one a wild ride on a roller coaster) the women he has known, loved, hated, and idealized during his life-time. Eventually, he is put on trial before a tribunal of women, and after being groomed like a circus animal, is given his liberty to con-tinue seeking his ideal woman, who is seen in the shape of an enor-mous balloon floating above him.

Fellini was two and a half months into his preparations for filming when, in January 1978, they were suddenly halted. As was becoming more and more often the case, one problem was the budget, which was expanding. This led to Lombardo's dropping out of the arrangement. As the Italian distributor, he had good reason. More theaters were closing, and the proliferation of private televi-sion companies now competing with the state-run network was siphoning off audiences even more. They could see dozens of films on TV. The more serious directors were having the hardest time. There was political turmoil, too. Aldo Moro, the prime minister, had been kidnapped, and, some days after, his bullet-riddled body was found in a section of central Rome, profoundly shocking the nation.

Guccione was having his own problems with *Caligula*, its costs having risen to more than $15 million. In addition, he was entangled in a censorship battle over the film and a legal suit with its director. Following a six-week suspension, and new financing from the French firm, Gaumont, Fellini was once more ready to proceed—after securing agreement from Rossellini and Guccione that the film would be shot in Italian. Then, another halt. "Guc-cione," said Fellini, "now insisted the film be done in English with American actors." There were rancorous arguments, which, unre-solved, effectively postponed the film indefinitely.

Fellini did not stay idle for long. He had another idea, one that fitted in with the somber mood of the country in the wake of Moro's murder. Not that Fellini claimed to have been influenced by the event. He had no intention of making a political film, he said; it was an idea "that came to fruition during my disputes with Guccione."

In *Casanova*, the mad Duke of Württemberg has furnished his great hall with six monstrous pipe organs, and enjoys having them played simultaneously by six organists, each without regard to the others. Fellini, however, said the idea for what was titled *Orchestra Rehearsal* had come to him long before, during recording sessions for previous films.

He told Michel Ciment a French critic: "I was always struck by a feeling of surprise and incredulity to see the miracle happen each time. Very different individuals arrived in the recording studio with their various instruments, but also with their personal problems, their bad humor, their illnesses, their portable radios with which to hear sports scores. I was amazed that this heterogeneous mass could be melted down into a unique, abstract form—music. Strong feelings were stirred up in me by this making of order out of disorder. It struck me that this situation could apply, emblematically, to a society where group and individual expression were compatible. So, for a long time I wanted to do a little documentary which would give the spectator the comforting suspicion that it's possible to do something together and still stay one's self."

His "little documentary," written with Brunello Rondi, would take place in a rehearsal hall, formerly a chapel, and would describe a session led by a conductor of Germanic appearance. The rehearsal begins peacefully enough, but rivalries soon erupt among the seventy musicians; there are childish disputes among union members, shouts of revolutionary slogans, graffiti, obscenities both spoken and physical (as when excrement is hurled at portraits of Mozart and Beethoven). Suddenly the squabbling and horseplay stop. A wrecker's ball smashes one of the walls. The musicians pick themselves out of rubble and take up their instruments. Order and harmony are restored, with the conductor in dictatorial command.

Fellini was in London in April, still looking for additional money to salvage *City of Women*; then, on his return to Rome, he went directly to RAI with a proposal to do *Orchestra Rehearsal* as a modestly budgeted television film. RAI, in line with its policy of supporting serious Italian film artists who were having difficulty obtaining traditional financing, eagerly accepted the proposal, but called in an outside producer, Leo Pascarola, to arrange for a share of the financing—the total of which would be well under a million.

Collaboration with Nino Rota was more vital than ever, for Fellini wanted the music played during the rehearsal to be original compositions. Fellini's own relationship with music was ambiguous. He described it as "a defensive one. I have to protect myself from music. I'm not someone who goes to concerts or the opera. I'm afraid of being invaded, conditioned, and I close myself off from it." If entering a restaurant or an apartment where music was playing, he would ask to have it turned off. How, he wondered, could people eat, talk, drink, drive, or read to music? He had been astonished once, while in New York, when De Laurentiis had tried to reach him through a secretary, and he had then been put on hold, to hear music through the earpiece!

But when working with Rota he could involve himself fully. Together they would read the score note by note, and he would have it played on the set during filming, or, if the score was not yet composed, music of a similar nature. Rota wrote, in all, five original pieces for the film.

Fellini wanted to show not only the internal battle between members of the orchestra—each attached and devoted to his own instrument—but to further indicate the divisiveness among them by having each speak in his native dialect. "There is no such thing," Fellini told Ciment, "as pure Italian. So I dubbed the characters in all possible Italian dialects." (When the film was shown, Italians assumed political meanings in the voices used. For a trade union leader Fellini had chosen a Sardinian dialect. As it happened, Italy's trade union leader at the time was a Sardinian by birth, and an identification was made immediately. Fellini quickly dubbed in another voice for the actor.)

He had hoped to use musicians—well-known soloists among them—from major orchestras, but discovered this would be far too costly. Instead, he went to Naples and looked around not particularly for instrumentalists but for the kind of expressive faces he wanted. Of those chosen, only fifteen could actually play an instrument. The remaining cast members were taught how to hold their instruments, and to look as though they actually played them.

He found his conductor's face—that of a little-known Dutch actor named Baldwin Bass—in his file of 20,000 photographs, and tracked him down in Stockholm. Bass had no musical knowledge to speak of, and after training him to look like a conductor, Fellini had a genuine conductor, Carlo Savina, stand behind him and lead the "orchestra"—that is, those among them who could actually play.

"I must say," Fellini said about Bass, "that at the last moment he identified very mysteriously with his character, and played it with a sort of rage, violence, and a great power of suggestion." Complicating the situation was the fact that Bass could speak only Dutch and German, while Fellini spoke neither one. "I communicated my feelings through an interpreter, including rage and insults."

Fellini belied the judgment of those who regarded him as a spendthrift director by shooting the film in sixteen days and editing it in two weeks. The dubbing of voices and music took another month.

During that summer, while crossing a piazza, he met Alessandro Pertini, who was soon to become the republic's president. Pertini, an admirer of Fellini's films, extracted the director's promise to show him his next film when it was finished, and followed the request a few months later with a phone call. Thus the completed film had its first showing at the presidential palace, where Pertini declared it "neither reactionary nor progressive; it's only true. It concerns much more than Italy."

Prime Minister Giulio Andreotti, also at the screening, found moral values in the film, although for his taste, he said, "fewer strong words wouldn't hurt it. But it could be I'm a little behind on current language usage." The president of the Chamber of Deputies, however, a Communist, found no moral at all. "It doesn't go to the heart of the question," he stated.

Soon enough, what looked like a controversy had been stirred up, and all of this prior to its showing on television (though several "private screenings" were held). Whether this caused RAI to delay its showing, or to allow some steam to develop for its sale outside Italy, *Orchestra Rehearsal* languished on a shelf from November, when it was first scheduled by the network, to the following February (1979). Surprised and angry over the delay, Fellini goaded RAI into action. By this time, results had been achieved. Gaumont, a large French company active in production, distribution, and exhibition, took the film on for worldwide sale.

Amidst the discussions, Fellini remained above it all. "I'm a director, not a politician," he told a *New York Times* reporter. "I just wanted people seeing my film to feel a little ashamed, as of an illness." Yet the impression created was that Fellini had, as one writer put it, "finally descended from his autobiographical tower . . . to assess the almost hopeless social tangle with black humor and formidable shockwaves." And Fellini's protestations aside, the general assessment was that he had indeed made his comment, couched in the form of a semiserious cultural allegory. The film's oblique ending—with the conductor assuming a harsher than ever command of the orchestra—was taken as Fellini's message that political anarchy and violence could only lead to authoritarian rule.

Fellini, however, maintained his artistic distance. "If you go to see the film with ideologically tinted glasses," he said, "you don't see it."

Outside Italy, the film caused little or no stir. Harsh and pessimistic, uninvolving to most audiences, it was not a popular success. The variety of dialects that had given it more meaning in its native country were missing in the subtitled or dubbed foreign versions. What did come through was its mordant humor, some of it scatological, as when a trumpet player inflates and bursts a contraceptive on the bell of his horn. The cellists battle over who owns a music stand. A pretty pianist chews on a hamburger under her piano while being pawed over by a militant who wants a new social (and presumably sexual) order. The demolition ball, which has been creating an ever louder thud, finally breaks through. The conductor restores order, saying, "We are artists. We must continue." Fellini was extending the satire to himself.

* * *

His association with Gaumont proved fruitful. The company was expanding and becoming more multinational in scope. In early 1979, it resolved the impasse over the dormant *City of Women* by assuming the major share of its financing, and by not placing a final figure on its cost. Franco Rossellini, producing for Gaumont and his own company, said: "We do not want to limit Fellini in his work. He is an economical film-maker who will keep costs in hand." His optimism was aided by the fact that Gaumont controlled 600 theaters in France, and was acquiring more in North and South America.

By the first of April, Fellini was established once more at Cinecittà, almost literally the king of the studio. He took over all the sound stages and the back lot, along with several administrative offices. With Guccione no longer involved, he had gotten his way with casting, too. The film would be made in Italian, and his muddled, woman-haunted hero would be played by Marcello Mastroianni.

But not a frame had been shot before the next shock. On April 10, Fellini while working on the film, was called to the telephone. "Oh, my God, no!" he was heard to say. Shaken, he told the others that Nino Rota, his most cherished collaborator, had died of a heart attack.

The 68-year-old composer had been preparing to conduct a concert oratorio at the Teatro dell'Opera on May 9, as the official commemoration of the anniversary of Aldo Moro's death a year earlier. As it was, the occasion also served as his own commemoration, and the attendance included not only Alessandro Pertini and other political figures, but prominent people from the arts and the movie world as well.

Rota's greatest fame was for his long association with Fellini, but the genial, likable little man's greatest popular success had come not from Fellini's films but from the scores he had composed for Renato Castellani's *Romeo and Juliet* and Francis Ford Coppola's *Godfather* films, for one of which he had won an Academy Award. He was a prolific serious composer as well, and would have preferred above all to be a composer for the opera.

Curiously, as Rota's output was analysed by critics and musicologists in the wake of his death, more prestige was shed on Fellini's films, particularly in the case of the undervalued *Casanova*. Kristine McKenna wrote in the *Los Angeles Times*, "There's a scene in which Casanova recalls his first arrival as a young man at the eighteenth-century salon of Paris. In memory he sees himself seated at an enchanted table, immersed in a dazzling panoply of color, surrounded by human peacocks magnificent in their outlandishness. As if in a dance, these dazzling creatures move with impeccable balance in slow motion. It's a moment of perfect grace. . . .

"The music accompanying this scene tiptoes by like a striking clock, suggesting both the transience of the moment and the way that time stands still for perfection. An evanescent melody with an edge of dread floats over the chiming rhythm. The two wisps of sound swell together for a second, then evaporate with the image.

"This is a beautiful bit of movie-making and the music is the cherry on the sunset."

It was Rota's very humility, his subservience to the needs of the story and images, that aided and enhanced Fellini's art to such an important degree. "His creativity was a joy," Fellini said about him after his death. "I would sit down with him by his piano, explain the film, what I wanted to suggest, this with this image, or that with that sequence. He would get bored, or would nod, yes. In reality he was setting up a kind of contact with his own themes, with whatever celestial sphere he was in tune with. Then he wouldn't listen to me anymore. He would place his hands on the keys and take off like an artist. I would say, that's beautiful, and he would say, I don't remember it anymore."

Between Fellini and Franco Rossellini there was a relationship stronger than was usual between the director and his producers. Franco was, after all, the son of Fellini's first important mentor. Also, Franco had been made the general director of Gaumont's interests in Italy, and was therefore in a position to protect him. Even closer were Fellini and Mastroianni, the two veterans united for the third time. Fellini's nickname for Mastroianni, Snaporaz, given him during the filming of *La Dolce Vita*, became the name of his character in *City of Women*.

"With Fellini I feel like a friend, not an actor," Mastroianni would say in answer to the perennial question of what it was like to work with the director. And, indeed, he was a friend, as close as, or closer than, many others. Fellini's friends seemed to equate with different aspects of his personality—Gustavo Rol, the mystical; Balthus, the painter; Mazursky, the director colleague. Mastroianni, Fellini said, represented for him the "vague character of an intellectual, sensitive man, still childish, also skeptical, yet full of dreams." And both men appreciated and were fascinated by women in all their variety.

"On the set," Mastroianni said, "I always have the impression of being there to amuse myself, or making a joke. When he wants to realize a scene, it's not work. We just dream together."

When Andrew Sarris attempted to interview the two of them during a visit they made to New York, he got the impression that they were always sharing some inside joke. This came through when, during the same visit, the two were interviewed on public television by Dick Cavett. Along with their sly put-downs, what also came through was the immense respect each had for the other.

The only other actor cast by the time shooting began was Ettore Manni, who had been popular with the Italian public in the 1950s and who later was reduced to acting in "spaghetti" westerns. He would play the opposite of Mastroianni, a philanderer given the unsubtle name, Dr. Sante Katzone (the last translating as "large cock"); for audiences outside Italy, the name was changed to Dr. Xavier Züberkock. Then, in England, Fellini found the voluptuous Bernice Stegers and cast her as a woman who, during Snaporaz's dream, lures him from his train journey. Then, during a performance in Rome, he convinced the Polish-French singer Anna Prucnal to play Elena, the constantly complaining wife of Snaporaz who, to the surprise of the producers, was suddenly turned into a professor of Greek mythology—with, naturally enough, a professional interest in the mythical aspects of femininity. Anouk Aimée had been considered for the part of Elena, and Glenda Jackson had been offered the role and refused because of her commitment to a season at the Old Vic.

When Anna Prucnal came to the set during negotiations on her contract, Fellini asked Mastroianni: "Would you be happy with this kind of wife?"

"If you pay her enough," Marcello answered diplomatically, "it could be that a husband like me could go well with her."

It was Fellini's habit to keep his screenplays away from both his actors and the stream of visitors to his sets. Reporters, therefore, had difficulty figuring out the precise nature of the story. That it dealt with feminist agitation was clear enough, although Fellini claimed the subject was, by this time, old news. Old or new news, it brought to the set such prominent representatives of aroused womanhood as Germaine Greer and Susan Sontag. Geraldine Chaplin came. Paul Mazursky paid a visit. So did Danny Kaye, Ingrid Bergman, and Paul Newman. There was a new saying in Rome: Everyone who visited the city wanted to meet or see only three people—Fellini, Pertini, and the Pope.

It turned out that the feminist revolt was hardly more than a pretext for another of Fellini's self-examinations that had begun with *8½*. In that film, his Jungian interests had led him into the exploration of his own creativity. This time he would look into the masculine and feminine components in the male nature, making use once more of his own dreams and memories, and he would avoid the ambiguity (between what was real and what was dream and fantasy) of *8½*. This time all would be a dream.

"Since the film is a dream," he said later, "everything in it is the dreamer. In the end Snaporaz consciously accepts the fact that he is dreaming. The film is about a man who invents women. She is his metaphor, the part of himself he doesn't know and about which he feels a fatal necessity to create ever-new hypotheses. He seeks the part of himself which is woman. But it is clear he knows nothing about women; he isn't able to create in his imagination a single real person."

But in pursuing this reasonably serious purpose, Fellini larded his story with humor, satire, and also menace. The "dream" was a nightmare, really, of a man feeling threatened by the clamor of women for an equal place in society, by his fear of loss of potency and of total dominance by womanhood. It was a comic answer to the question: what would happen to men if women replaced them as rulers of society?

The gates of Cinecittà were besieged by applicants for the 170 female roles, and the 1,000 more needed for an arena scene in which all the spectators and participants (except Snaporaz, who is put on trial for his virility or lack of it) are women. This arena was designed by Fellini's scene designer Dante Ferretti to include a beauty parlor, a large, well-furnished restroom, a restaurant, and a huge bed suspended in midair.

Another of Ferretti's fanciful designs was the luxurious abode of Dr. Katzone, the woman fancier. It included gardens (which would be besieged by a feminist police force), an immense living room with huge sofas, many guest rooms, and a huge gallery in which were displayed his collection of erotica and pictures of some 2,000 of his female conquests over the years. How Snaporaz would reach this macho refuge did not require explaining or motivation, since it was all part of his dream. At the end of one episode Snaporaz would merely find himself somewhere else, in a new situation.

If Mastroianni was easy for Fellini to work with, Manni was not. The less he felt he satisfied his director, the more he drank. This hardly sat well with Fellini. Neither did Manni's habit of spiriting girls into his dressing room, nor the fact that he always carried a gun. Fellini's constant stream of invectives, calling him a bad actor, a receptacle for alcohol, hardly helped ease the tension between them. It was July, and filming was in its fourth month, when word came that Manni had shot himself to death. An accident, it first was claimed. His gun had gone off and the bullet had pierced the main artery in his thigh. A more garish version, circulating on the set, had it that, in self-disgust, he had shot himself in the testicles. Production was summarily shut down while ways were explored of salvaging the film. Not many of Manni's scenes remained to be shot, but he was scheduled for the final one, in which he and Mastroianni would be carried off by a huge balloon in the shape of a woman—and then shot down by a female terrorist. Insurance details had to be worked out, too.

* * *

During the hiatus, which lasted a month, Fellini was asked by the magazine *Espresso* to list his likes and dislikes. What he didn't like, he answered, were parties, celebrations, interviews, round-table discussions, and being asked for autographs. He did not like to travel, to stand in line; nor mountains, boats, music in restaurants, radios playing loudly, ballet, mushrooms, Gorgonzola, or ostriches. Nor did he like hearing about Brecht and Woody Allen, official luncheons with their toasts and speeches, being asked to make appearances, invitations to screenings and theater first nights. Nor did he care for stenographers, tea—in particular camomile—citations, young-people's films, macho men, Pirandello, crêpes suzette, beautiful countrysides, political films, psychological films, historical films. And he did not like windows lacking shades or draperies. Or ketchup.

What he did like were the following: train stations, airports, Matisse, rice, Rossini, roses, the Marx brothers, tigers, waiting for appointments with the hope that the other would not show up (even a gorgeous woman); Toto, not having been there, Piero della Francesca, anything belonging to a beautiful woman that's beautiful, Homer, Joan Blondell, September, girls' rear ends on bicycles, trains, Ariosto, cocker spaniels and dogs in general, the odor of wet earth, cypresses, the sea in winter, people who don't talk much, James Bond, empty places, deserted restaurants, squalor, empty churches, silences, the sound of bells, being alone in Urbino on a Sunday afternoon, Bologna, Venice, all of Italy, Raymond Chandler, Simenon, Kafka, Dickens, London, gates, roasted chestnuts, taking buses, high beds, Vienna (although he had never been there), stationery shops, No. 2 Faber pencils, variety shows, bitter and semisweet chocolate, waking up, going to sleep, secrets, dawn, night, Lana Turner, actresses, and ballerinas.

The lists made for interesting study by psychoanalysts and would-be film directors. His friends said they made for a reasonably accurate self-portrait, but there was some speculation about why he liked ballerinas and not ballet, and why he had singled out Lana Turner (liked) and Pirandello (disliked).

XXI

CITY of Women finished filming at the end of November 1979 and, after its opening in Italy in March 1980, was shown at the Cannes Film Festival in May, where its feminist subject matter caused mild comment. However, it was not liked as much as Bob Fosse's *All That Jazz*. The irony here was that the autobiographical overtones in Fosse's film owed much to Fellini's influence, and both, as it happened, had been photographed by Fellini's long-time collaborator, Giuseppe Rotunno. It was Fosse who had directed the stage and screen musical, *Sweet Charity*, which had been based on *Nights of Cabiria*.

The reviews of *City of Women* in Italy, and almost everywhere else, were respectful for the most part, but lacked the enthusiasm, or the sharp divisions that had greeted so many of Fellini's previous films. There were a few expected sorties by feminists. In Italy, a young teacher declared the film to be the work of a dirty old man (Fellini, now sixty, had reached the age where he could be victimized by the charge) and said that the women in it were the kind a dirty old man would imagine.

Fellini replied, when the comment was brought to his notice, "If I were to be offended, it would be more for the adjective old and not for dirty. Good Catholic that I am, the phrase 'dirty man' seems to be a medal of honor and distinction."

Another critic, perhaps tired of Fellini's memories of the women in his past—as when Snaporaz slides down a half-mile roller coaster and gets side-show views of his mother, a seductive house-maid, movie stars he adored, mistresses, and prostitutes—said that the subject was becoming banal, and accused him of having a bottomless unconscious. Others, however, saw a continuing inventiveness, fertility, and "healthful humor."

The film was slow in making its way abroad, and did not arrive in the United States until April 1981. Gaumont farmed out its distribution to Daniel Talbot of New Yorker Films and, to furnish him with publicity, sent Fellini and Mastroianni over. Before they arrived, Talbot received a telephone call from Mario Longardi, specifying the kind of accommodations Fellini wanted for himself and Giulietta at the Sherry Netherland Hotel. They must have separate bedrooms, Longardi said, because the two did not sleep in the same room. (Giulietta smoked, and Fellini did not.) And there must be a separate living room. Giulietta, who would not participate in interviews, wanted to be able to slip in and out without being recognized.

Talbot found Fellini obliging, "charming, delightful—and narcissistic. One evening, ten of us went to dinner at an East Side restaurant. There he discussed wines with the proprietor, who brought out an expensive bottle of wine, a Brunello. It turned out Fellini knew the owner of the vineyard. It was a fine, lavish evening, with a bill that must have come to $2,000. Luckily for me, Gaumont was taking the tab."

The film, when it opened, garnered reviews that ran from mixed to good, but generated little box-office business. "The picture had no financial justification," Talbot commented. "Here, it played in less than fifty theaters, and of those, six provided 75 percent of the earnings. I don't know what Gaumont or Fellini could have expected with that kind of personal film. He had lost most of his audience here by then. Which isn't to say that I don't think him one of the great film-makers of the world."

As though oblivious to this state of affairs, Fellini had already begun to pursue producers with other ideas, and he was having more than his usual problems. Not only was the financial news on *City of Women* discouraging, but *Casanova* had also taken losses, making it difficult for him to attract backers for his next project.

"He now had the reputation of being expensive," Zapponi said, "and also of his films losing money." For Fellini, though, there was no lack of ideas, or of enthusiasm for work.

The first of his ideas to meet obstacles was a film on the assassination of the Austrian archduke Francis Ferdinand. Fellini had become interested in the origins of World War I after having come across some new theories on it based, he said, on documents found in the Vatican archives by a priest. The first treatment for this story he later claimed to have written over a weekend with Tonino Guerra.

No financing came through, and the entire year of 1980 passed without his setting foot on a sound stage. Early in 1981 he began looking into the Greek myths. His offices at Cinecittà remained available to him, and there he began work on a script that would have *The Iliad* as its starting point, but would tell "stories of men and gods who wonderfully represent the human creature in all of its most secret psychic components." He made contact with Anthony Burgess, and announced that the author would participate in the writing of the screenplay and that some scholars of Greek mythology would be consulted, too.

He appeared to be juggling projects in the hope that one would solidify, for he announced soon after that he was preparing a series of six crime stories for television. They "would attempt to say something about this terrible resignation for the worst. We have had to become used to living with terror, this fear of a young person's face near us." The stories would be shot in different locations—Rome, Naples, Milan, Siena.

But by late March, when he arrived in New York, he had stopped talking about these projects. Instead he told interviewers that the next film he made would be with Mastroianni, who would play the city editor of a newspaper.

"For some time," he confided to critic William Wolf, "I've wanted to examine the myth that a newspaper is the heart of a town, with the duty to report and interpret. But society is so ambiguous and contradictory that what is going on is not interpretable. The film involves reporters who conceive of themselves as reporting the truth in a society that completely bars us from the facts."

That was the last that anything was heard of the idea.

Back in Rome, he was visited by Sherry Lansing, then the head of production for Twentieth Century-Fox. She invited him to spend three months in the United States at the studio's expense, during which time he could pick a subject that appealed to him. He was tempted—he found Ms. Lansing a most appealing personality—but told her there was no way for him to adjust "to the multi-layered social structure of America."

Dino De Laurentiis wanted to rescue Fellini from his enforced idleness, and strongly advised him to come to America, the Italian film industry being in its usual crisis, especially for "arty" directors. "Direct anything you like," he told Fellini, "but shoot it in America and English."

Fellini made his discontent public in June 1981. He told a group of reporters, on receiving a belated award for *City of Women* from a film critics' association, "The truth is, I'm out of work. I have four screenplays ready, but I can't find a backer to put up the money for them." Italy's producers, he said, were interested only in making second-rate commercial movies, and he might have no choice "but to yield to De Laurentiis's flattery and go to the United States."

He expressed his envy for "painters because they can paint every day for all their lives. They go into their studio, cook some soup and stay there and work and live like a tree through different seasons. They have a real identification with their expression." To lose so much time between pictures gave him "bitterness and unhappiness. I would like to do anything between them: publicity, shorts, take photographs, anything to conquer this stagnation."

The television crime series, to which he had given the title *Poliziotto*, was his best prospect at this time. Gaumont showed some interest in producing it in conjunction with RAI, but the network was slow in giving it the go-ahead.

Serge Sevilloni, an administrator at RAI, said: "We never believed for a moment that he would do the crime series. He never returns to something after he has done it once—notice that he never did the sequels producers wanted after his great successes—so we felt that he would do only one and that would be it. We did enter into negotiations and would have gone ahead, if it were certain he would do them all.

"We knew how he worked—that he does his film 90 percent when he sees what he has done. He looks at what the rushes say to him and then he changes it into his film. But we were always proud to be able to make a film with him, even though we sensed a change in the audience away from him. It happened with Antonioni, too. It's not that Fellini isn't aware of this change. Fellini doesn't think of the public. He makes a film only for himself, as a painter would paint a canvas."

Failing to get an answer from RAI, Fellini put the crime series in the hands of a private producer, Giorgio Salvani, who, in February 1982, confidently announced that principal photography would begin in July and would proceed for thirty weeks on a $7-million budget.

Fellini, meanwhile, announced that he was investigating the mechanism of law and order and the crime areas of Rome and other cities. For company, he had a former detective of the crime squad who would be a sort of model for the protagonist of the series. Salvani noted that Fellini was opening the doors of his ivory tower at Cinecittà and entering the real city.

But not yet. That project, too, was put on hold when RAI suddenly came to life after Salvani's announcement and showed renewed interest in another of Fellini's ideas, the World War I story that he had titled *E la Nave Va* (*And the Ship Sails On*).

"We knew about his money and producer problems," Sevilloni said, "and, as an institution of society we thought it was our duty to help Fellini make the film. So, with Gaumont and with [producer] Franco Cristaldi we built the film's financing. We estimated the budget at about $9 million and, of this, we put up three million—for this we got the television rights and a third of any profits."

While Fellini was struggling to bring a new film to life, another struggle was going on in New York to bring to Broadway a musical version of one of his old films. Back in 1963 Maury Yeston, then a high-school senior, saw *8½* at a neighborhood theater in Jersey City. Yeston dreamed of becoming a composer, and Guido Anselmi's creative dilemma seemed to apply to his own young life.

He went to Yale, eventually became an associate professor of musicology there and, in 1973, wrote songs for a musical based on *8½*, giving it the title *Nine*. After much development, vicissitudes, tryouts, and problems in acquiring rights, the musical (with a book by Arthur Kopit) was readied for a Broadway opening on May 9, 1982. Raul Julia was cast as Guido (his last name changed to Contini), and Tommy Tune was engaged as director and choreographer.

The rights problem had to do with their being split among the Rizzoli company, which had produced the film, and the four screenwriters—Fellini, Pinelli, Flaiano, and Rondi. Flaiano was gone. He had succumbed to a heart attack the same year (1979) that Rota died. But the closeness between him and Fellini had long dissipated. After lawyers determined that Rizzoli owned only film and television rights, and that dramatic rights belonged to the authors, the producers of *Nine* began to pursue Fellini. He was hesitant at first, because he wanted to preserve *8½* uniquely as a film. But he was flattered, too, by the persistence of the *Nine* team, and he finally agreed, after specifying that in advertising and posters no mention be made of the musical's source.

The show was about to go into rehearsal in March when the lawyers discovered a snag: the signature of Angelo Rizzoli, who had produced the film, was needed for potential sale of the musical to film and television. His once powerful financial empire had become the subject of scandal and was then in receivership. Rizzoli couldn't be located by the lawyer hurried over to see him.

The lawyer called Fellini who, puzzled, said: "Why are you here? You don't need Rizzoli. I have the rights."

He agreed, however, to get the signature. Two days went by and no word from Fellini. When he called it was to say that he hadn't yet found Rizzoli.

"We're ruined," the lawyer said, "if you don't get that signature. We've committed the rehearsal money."

Three hours later, Fellini produced the signature.

He was no stranger to appeals for various rights to his films. Early in the 1960s a musical based on *La Strada* had a brief run on Broadway. In Italy it had been made into a ballet, and dramatic versions had appeared in France and Germany. At that moment, he was being asked for the rights to make it into an opera, and *Juliet of the Spirits* was also being discussed for a musical. Even his first film, *The White Sheik,* had served as the basis for another film—*The World's Greatest Lover* (1977), starring Gene Wilder, who also directed, wrote, and produced the movie. In a gesture of *noblesse oblige,* Fellini had given Wilder the right to make his own use of the material with no accreditation or remuneration other than a title card in the credits expressing appreciation.

       Fellini's unemployment came to an end in the middle of June 1982, when financial details for the production of *And the Ship Sails On* were finally ironed out. A fourth partner, Aldo Nemni, had been found in Milan. He was an investor and businessman who had met Fellini after long admiring him and decided that his talent should be nurtured in positive ways. This was his first involvement with films, but he found it so intoxicating that he announced that he and Fellini had "decided to walk together. It's a question of personal esteem and friendship."

       Fellini had not been on a sound stage for two and a half years, and it was the force of his personality and the general admiration for him and his works that made the new film possible. Commercial considerations and the nature of the story were secondary. "People who finance him," Zapponi said, "know there is an excellent chance that they will lose." They also knew that the script they were shown might not altogether resemble what would turn up on the screen. In addition, Fellini would not brook interference with his casting choices, with his method of work, or his artistic demands.

       While waiting for his projects to come to fruition, he had thought of making a documentary on his situation. It would be about what happened to a director during a long stretch between projects. In that time, he told Hank Werba of *Variety,* "I had the pivotal role in a game performed by producers, speculators, Arab investors and strange middlemen who wanted to participate in one way or another in four projects.

       "Some talked about taking them to Hollywood, Mexico City, or Zagreb. At one point my inactivity became a national issue and

Cinecittà was pressured to co-produce and restore me to active
status. But if they invested in Fellini, they would also have to invest
in other directors with problems."

While inactive, his crime series bogged down in inconclu-
sive multi-national negotiations, and he asked De Laurentiis to get
him the rights to several Dashiell Hammett short stories. He believed they could be filmed in Italy, in English, and he could use his
memories of the old American gangster movies he had seen at the
Fulgor cinema in Rimini. But his former producer, Grimaldi, was
ahead of him and had already acquired the rights to the stories.

Fellini complained to Werba that his films didn't cost more
than those of his colleagues, but that a kind of ritual happened
every time a budget was determined. "A million dollars disappears
in little pieces." He had never seen a single lire, he said, from his
supposed profit percentages of his films. It has gotten to a sorry state,
he also said, when he walked in the Piazza del Popolo and a woman
pointed out to a companion that he was the husband of Giulietta
Masina. She had gone into television and two of her series became
highly popular.

It made news in Italy when Fellini was finally ready to start
shooting again at Cinecittà on November 15, 1982. Set construction had been going on for several months. Instead of using a real
ocean liner for a story that would take place almost entirely at sea,
he had had one constructed in twenty-one separate sections on nine
studio stages. Nor would he use a real sea. Instead he had one made
out of thick cellophane: to get it to ripple, workmen were stationed
at either end of the giant transparent sheet, and they shook it whenever the camera was turned in their direction. Lighting effects would
change its aspects. The huge forward deck of the ship filled most of
stage five; a mechanism underneath made it sway according to the
mood of the sea.

Cinecittà's effects department had invented a cloud making
machine. It squirted puffs into the "sky" of the sound-stage in such
a way that Fellini could arrange them and control their shapes. It
was as though he had turned Cinecittà into his gigantic cinematic
hobby shop. He had even constructed a section of the port of Naples,
from which his ship, the *Gloria N.* would depart.

Fellini seemed to be ignoring sixty years of development in film technique and starting anew—and, in a sense, he was. In contrast with the computer-generated imagery and electronic gadgets used by such film-makers as Steven Spielberg and George Lucas, his film would be virtually handmade by the Cinecittà artisans he had worked with for so long. It would take place in 1914, in the moments prior to the outbreak of war and, as he said in explanation after it was finished, "The feeling I wanted to create was that of old photographs, the feeling that nothing you see has survived—photographs of unknown people of whom the only thing known is that they are dead."

He held a noon press conference in a screening theater at Cinecittà the Saturday prior to the start of filming. With him were two of his producers, Cristaldi and Nemni. As usual, he kept reporters starved for details of what this new film would be about, saying only that it would take a critical view of mass communications. He was more willing to explain its origination.

He had come across a news item about a Jesuit father, he said, who had developed a new theory about the outbreak of World War I. "He maintained that the conflict was determined by the desire to give it the image of a spectacle. If the war did break out, according to this father, the fault was on the part of the news, its sensationalism." And it was this that had led to his discussing the item with Tonino Guerra and their writing of the screenplay in a matter of days. Another news item had added to their story conception. He had read an article about ships disappearing in the Bermuda triangle, and from this he "got the idea of an ocean voyage toward some sort of revelation, an explanation for some kind of enigma." But after writing the story, he had not expected he would be able to make the film.

He had completed most of his casting, much of it done in London. To speed things up he had occupied an office at the William Morris Agency and had actors come in every ten minutes. After a few words with them, and a searching look at their faces, he would put their pictures in a folder to take back to Italy with him. Norma West, an attractive 39-year-old actress given a prominent role, had seen Fellini in London ten years before on one of his casting expeditions. "He asked me for a photograph, said he had no part for me for the time being, but he would think of me again at the first possible moment. Then, out of the blue, he called me in for this movie."

Fellini wanted predominantly English actors, he said, because they fitted the international nature of the roles, and because he liked their professional way of working. If they were to be English passengers on the ship, the actors worried, would they be able to use their own voices? Fellini told them he had not made up his mind about any version but the Italian.

The English actors he used were not important stars, but several of them had good reputations. The best known among them were Freddie Jones, who would play Orlando, a vaguely besotted journalist, and Barbara Jefford, a distinguished stage actress who would play the role of a great opera singer.

Fellini chose Freddie Jones in one of his characteristic ways. He was uncertain about him until, returning from London and on his way to Rome, from the Ostia airport, he saw "Orlando" printed large on a poster. This convinced him that Jones was the right choice, even though the poster was an advertisement for ice cream.

Norma West, who was delighted with her role as the sexually frustrated and wayward wife of an impresario, talked with me about what she called the exhilarating experience of being directed by Fellini. If she was put off at times by his shouting at the crew and minor members of the cast, she was struck also by his kindness and sensitivity.

As an example, she told of how the English group of actors had been put up in Rome at the Grand Hotel, a favorite of Fellini. The old fashioned and rather forbidding elegance of the hotel, a former palace, was not to their taste, though they did not complain. Early in the production, Ms. West was invited to dinner with Fellini and one of his assistants. On returning her to the hotel, he asked how she liked her quarters. "They're very nice," she said. Fellini apparently detected a note of uncertainty in her voice, for he immediately got out of the car and said, "Let me see your room."

"He glanced around it," West said, "nodded, as though he

sensed our feelings, and said, 'I will move you all tomorrow.' And he did." He put them up at the Hotel de la Ville, a charming hotel with a fine view at the top of the Spanish Steps.

"There was another thing," she said. "Ever since I was one year old I have kept a little teddy bear doll. Wherever I go I take it with me; just a gray, rather tattered little thing. It's sort of my good luck charm. Fellini would usually give us our lines only the night before we were due to film a scene. One evening he handed me my lines for a scene which would take place in my stateroom the next day, and he said, 'Oh, and Norma, bring your little teddy bear with you.' He had noticed it on my bed, and knew that the touch of familiarity might help me do the scene."

Between its conception and the time it went before the cameras, the film evolved far beyond its original concept. "At first," Fellini told a reporter, "Guerra and I wrote a quick scenario about the causes of World War I. I was only trying to get an advance from Gaumont, but they backed out when I couldn't make their changes." The original idea concerned a ship at sea just prior to the outbreak of World War I, and its role in starting the conflict. During the three years it took to get to the screen, the film took on many different colorations.

Music had played an integral part in his films before, but it took a new form in *And the Ship Sails On.* Fellini had belatedly discovered the joys of opera, but only after Nino Rota, shortly before his death, had urged him to attend a performance. "This Verdi!" Fellini exclaimed. "What music!"

From a mixture of intentions, the film evolved into what Fellini called a "choral drama." He had a style in mind as well as a subject—he wanted to make it, he said, "as though it were a first print, black and white, with damp spots, like one found in an antique film collection. But this would be a fake—which it struck me is what real cinema is." Since all would be fake, counterfeit, there would be no need to go to a real ocean, or to have a real sky, and the moon could be literally made out of paper. ("Doesn't it look like a paper moon?" a woman passenger says of it to a companion.) Since the artifice would be apparent to the audience, and integral to the stylization, the whole film could be done in the studio.

In the early scenes of the film, at dockside, Fellini shot in black and white, silent, as an early cinematographer would have shown the departure of a liner—and in fact a cameraman is there, doing just that. Then, with the period evoked by this sequence, the images gradually take on color, and the sound track is heard. On the ship itself, the settings are meticulous in their details, sumptuously designed in styles that suggest the prewar era—but more floridly, like opera.

He was stimulated, Fellini said when he talked about the film afterward, by the very "foreignness" of the actors in his cast— French and German as well as English. Their photographs hung on the walls of his office at Cinecittà. They had been chosen, he said, because he wanted "faces that could . . . resemble those of people who no longer exist, who are lost in time, and who arouse our interest and touch us. A hairdo that is no longer fashionable, a dress from decades ago, a way of smiling, of gazing at us with a look that is lost forever. . . ."

Gazing at the faces on the walls made him want to develop their stories, "to pry into their relationships, to add friends, relatives, and acquaintances, and invent new situations—in short to make the journey with them."

These days there are music cruises, film cruises, wine cruises, to which celebrities or experts in a particular field are invited for a free ride for giving the passengers the privilege of their company. Fellini's was something different—a funeral cruise. And also an opera cruise. A great soprano, Edmea Tetua, has died and left a request that her ashes be scattered at sea off the island of her birth, near Greece. Accompanying her ashes on this mission is a cosmopolitan gathering of mourners that includes many opera singers, an impresario, critics, actors and actresses, and rich devotees. Aboard, too, is a fat little personage, the Grand Duke of Harzock, and with him his blind sister, who appears to be plotting his overthrow. Orlando, the reporter, has booked passage, too, in order to cover this remarkable event. During the film he comments from time to time on the proceedings, usually in an inane manner.

It turns out to be a voyage like no other—certainly more fantastic than anything the people in *Amarcord* could have imag-

ined as the liner, *Rex*, passed them by in the night. The luxuries on
the *Gloria N.* surely would have surpassed those of the *Rex*. The
tablecloths and napkins in the elegant first-class dining salon have
the ship's emblem embroidered in gold letters; the crystal goblets
glisten; waiters and stewards wear white gloves. The grieving but
also fortunate passengers are dressed in the height of (old) fashion,
and they relax and sleep in large, plush staterooms. But something
is wrong; a stink permeates this dreamship. Being carried in the
hold is a rhinoceros suffering from *mal de mer*. (Fellini had the
beast modeled by Cinecittà's remarkable craftsmen, long used to
the master's odd requests.) It is learned that the rhinoceros is on its
way to a zoo in Amsterdam, once the ashes have been deposited in
the sea. The passengers decide it is less the ship's motion that has
caused the beast's malaise than lovesickness for a lost mate. To rid
the ship of the odor, the rhinoceros is hoisted into a lifeboat, and
swung into a position over the side.

When he was asked why a rhinoceros aboard the ship, Fellini replied, "Experts have assured me there is always a rhinoceros
along on such cruises." He added: "An author doesn't need to have
explanations, necessarily, for his characters and situations. All I can
say is that I saw a rhinoceros there, I saw it on that ship. I do not
want to be forced to find logical, romantic, or para-psychological
reasons for it." To be sure, though, a good many reviewers found
them for him.

For those looking for more symbolism, there were still other
oddities. A seagull has flown into the elegant first-class dining room,
and enjoys the atmosphere so much that it refuses to be chased
away. A Russian basso profundo has made a bet that with his singing he can put a live chicken into a state of catatonia. He borrows
one from the ship's galley and makes good his boast. A count turns
his stateroom into a memorial to the departed diva, and a séance is
held at which she seems to materialize. It is a fake, of course, and
Orlando is there to help expose it. A funeral cruise though it is, Fellini was having the time of his life.

The wife of the impotent impresario wanders the ship in
search of sexual satisfaction, and betrays her husband in their own

cabin. The blind sister of the grand duke conspires mysteriously; several of the opera singers visit the huge boiler room of the liner and vie with one another in singing arias for the benefit of the stokers below. One morning the passengers encounter a number of Serbian refugees who have been taken aboard during the night after the assassination at Sarajevo. Their ship has been shelled and they were adrift in lifeboats. The impresario's wife is fascinated and furtively visits them at night.

An Austro-Hungarian warship looms (a strange warship, it is square in shape) and demands that the refugees be turned over. In spite of these threats, the *Gloria N.* proceeds to its destination and the diva's ashes are dispersed into the wind. (Fellini ordered several batches of ashes before he was satisfied that he had the right powdery consistency.) After the funeral, during which the voice of the diva, singing a Verdi aria, is heard via a phonograph for the assembled passengers and crew, the captain gives way and has the Serbians put into boats to be taken to the warship. But then something unforeseen occurs. A young Serb tosses a bomb into a gun turret of the dreadnought, and while explosions begin destroying the warship, it sends salvos at the *Gloria N.*, which sinks, most of the passengers presumably going down with it. But at the end, Orlando is seen adrift in a lifeboat, the rhinoceros his only companion. "A great piece of news," he tells the audience. "Did you know that the rhinoceros gives excellent milk?"

Fellini spent nearly four months filming this remarkable concoction, working furiously, as though to prove he could hold himself to a budget. Impeccable in a dark gray, beautifully tailored silk suit, a white shirt, slightly loosened at the collar, and a dark tie, he moved restlessly about the deck between shots like a General Patton wishing he could do all the fighting himself.

"Forgive me," Fellini said to the author, "but at this stage I can only think about, to concentrate on what I am doing at this moment. If I had to be able to tell you about the whole film, I wouldn't be able to."

It was noticeable that he was more polite with the English actors than with the Italians. He would insult a hapless extra, scream at a laggard crew member. "The Italians who work with him," Norma West said, "say that it's really only his way of joking, but I'm not so sure. They all adore him, anyway."

For New Year's Eve of 1983 he gave a party for his principal actors at his apartment on the Via Margutta, and insisted that all those from outside Italy make calls home. To Norma West, whom he seemed to especially favor, he gave a copy of the script, translated into English, to satisfy her curiosity as to what the film was about. She must tell no one else though, he insisted. The script did not aid her performing to any great degree. "You would come in every morning not knowing what would happen," she said. "It did no good to learn a line. He would talk to you, look at you, and somehow he made you understand what you had to do."

The English actors left Rome hoping that Fellini would call them back to dub the English-speaking version, but this was not to be. Under pressure to have the film edited and dubbed in time for showing at the Venice festival, Fellini in the end had them all speak Italian.

XXII

THE Italian opening of *And the Ship Sails On* was the occasion for Fellini celebrations. At the Venice Festival, when the film was shown out of competition on September 9, 1983, parties were held in his honor. In Venice, too, was Ingmar Bergman, there to show his new film, *Fanny and Alexander*, and to receive an honorary Golden Lion. Bergman apparently had some fear of unruly crowds, or perhaps of a terrorist act, for he traveled by armored car from his hotel to the festival hall to make his appearance. During the showing of his film he went to another room where he saw Fellini's film at a private screening.

Another week-long celebration took place in Rimini late in September when *And the Ship Sails On* was given its "Italian première"—that in Venice having been billed as the "international première." Over the years the Italian press had created the impression that because of *I Vitelloni* and *Amarcord* a feud existed between Fellini and the people of his home town. This was not at all the case. As he pointed out, he visited the town—now grown to a population of a 160,000—three or four times a year to see his mother and sister.

Years before, he had expressed a wish to have a little fisherman's cottage by the sea that was so much a part of his memories—and of his films; so, several of his old friends, including Titta Benzi and Mario Montanari, got together and presented him with a house. A special exhibit of photographs and faces from his films attracted large crowds. More were attracted wherever he appeared, accompanied by almost as large a contingent of reporters who snapped away at him and everything in sight. The facade of the Grand Hotel was ablaze with ribbons of light bulbs, and the illuminated gardens were opened to the public. Overhead, a plane dropped kites bearing the name of the movie and its director. And, after the gala première attended by townspeople attired in their best, Fellini retired with Giulietta to the most luxurious suite of the Grand Hotel, which had so awed him in his youth.

"Federico, do you remember . . . ?" was the question most asked by his old friends, by people whose faces were no longer familiar. For a moment they shared the spotlight, as reporters questioned them for details of Fellini's boyhood.

It was as though Fellini were now more than an important film-maker, more than an honoree for the sum of his work. He was also recognized as one of the most forceful personalities of his time, as a citizen who reflected light on Rimini and his country. At Milan, too, for another "première" in mid-October, the audience, which received the film warmly, was filled with the celebrated.

Not all the critics were so supportive. One was unkind enough to title his review "And the Ship Sinks." But Fellini also had his loyal supporters, among them Tullio Kezich who wrote, "This is a film with so many secret drawers, so full of double bottoms and surprises that the viewer is taken beyond simple story telling and symbolism" until it becomes "an act of faith in cinema for its own sake."

Kezich, having followed his work for several decades, was well aware of what Fellini was about. But now there were new audiences who did not see his film as one more in a progression of remarkable and original works. To many this story of another time, of "unknown people," had little meaning. Not only did Fellini leave it to the viewers to determine his film's meanings, but then he would disclaim any intention to create meaning. Whatever the viewer saw was what the film meant, he said in effect. He could not answer questions on "Why this?" or "Why that?" Viewers were not meant to "find out anything precise about what 'happens' in the story."

The delightful and magical games Fellini played during the course of the more than two-hour movie created uneasiness among critics and audience alike. What did that seagull, that transfixed chicken, that smelly rhinoceros mean? William Murray, in the *New Yorker*, reported from Rome: "Most of the film's denigrators condemned the director for dealing in obvious symbols and then denying allegorical intent by claiming it as cinematic horseplay."

Murray, who admired the film and saw brilliance in it, wrote, "But the symbols seemed there nevertheless: the ship's mysterious destination, the variety of people and creatures on board, the contrasting of rich and poor (the singers and entourages dine in splendor while the Serbs peer in hungrily from outside on deck), the cargo of ashes, the chunks of opera . . ." And the name of the ship, *Gloria N.*, perhaps meant ironically, *Gloria Nationale.* (Norma West had asked him about that, and he had answered, "Just a name.")

Fellini refused to admit to any allegorical implications, but did clarify the meaning of the title. "It doesn't mean," he said, "the moment when the ship leaves, but in colloquial Italian has the symbolic meaning that, despite everything, it sails on—or, life goes on." Other overtones persisted, however. One can decide that perhaps the deceased soprano represents the end of an epoch, when all of Europe was irrevocably changed. The Serb who bravely, rashly, throws the bomb perhaps equates with today's revolutionary terrorists, and the risk they pose.

The film did not succeed commercially, in spite of the widespread attention it received. For Stanley Kauffmann in the *New Republic*, its richness lay less in its meanings than in "an ingenious arrangement of events that gives Fellini ample chance to exercise his film-making virtuosity." But only, wrote Gary Arnold in the *Washington Post*, "if you're fond of sluggish tempos, static staging, inert composition, and arid panoramas of unfilled wall and floor space." The title of Arnold's review was "Fellini's Sinking Ship." Several others, of course, came up with "Fellini's Ship of Fools." For Kenneth Turan in *California* magazine, it was "Bon Voyage." "Artifice," he wrote, "has never looked more ravishing." The gamut of praise to blame had never before run quite so wide.

Fellini had been expected to come to New York to help with the publicity, but suddenly he changed his mind. It was thought a matter of course that Italy would nominate the film for Academy consideration as Best Foreign Film, but this did not happen. It was the reason, Paul Mazursky thought, that Fellini decided not to come to the United States. In Italy the film was said to be a commercial fiasco.

In his first flush of enthusiasm over the reception of *And the Ship Sails On*, Fellini talked again of reviving *The Voyage of G. Mastorna*. "It comes back to me at the end of every film I make," he said. His backer from Milan, Aldo Nemni, was already negotiating with potential distributors. But soon the project was abandoned, again, seemingly for good. "It doesn't want to be alive," he told me in 1984, "it wants to be dead."

In June 1984, it was noted in the Italian press that Fellini was working on something at Cinecittà. The rumors flew that he was making—a commercial! Fellini was questioned, and as the periodical *L'Europeo* put it, "he reacted as if his honor had been attacked."

"I would really like to know who started that story," he said.

A few days later he vaguely admitted "that to say I have made a commercial message isn't quite true." Finally came the confession: "Perhaps I did make it, but I must have been in a trance."

The commercial was made on behalf of the apéritif, Campari. In past years Fellini had refused offers to make commercials, but he had given in this time, he said, "because Campari is part of Italian family life, and I like the product." It took seven drafts before he was satisfied with the script, and even then it took some urging before he put on film a thirty-second and a sixty-second spot. Once begun, he was as meticulous as with a feature film, and he kept a crew working for nine days. Pressed to say how much the two spots had cost, one of the Campari owners said wearily, "The cost is acceptable."

"I felt like giving it a try," Fellini said. "You don't get very tired and it's a lot of fun."

Boy George, among other pop stars, attempted to persuade Fellini to make a video for him. Fellini went so far as to agree to meet him in Cannes, but cancelled the appointment. A new project was developing.

It owed its origin to an anthology series proposed to RAI

that would feature Giulietta Masina in a variety of roles, six in all, each segment to be filmed by a different director. Antonioni, Zeffirelli, and, of course, Fellini, were among those contacted. Fellini agreed to come up with a story for his wife, who was not only intrigued by the acting challenge, but by the chance to "change the image of women in Italian film and television." For his segment, Fellini created a character called Ginger, a former vaudeville dancer who, during the 1940s, had emulated Rogers and Astaire with a stage partner called Fred. Now she is widowed, a grandmother, and the owner of a small business in the north.

He developed the story with his old script-writing partner, Tullio Pinelli, with whom he had not worked in twenty years. Then, when Marcello Mastroianni agreed to play Giulietta's dancing partner, the combination brought a gleam to the eye of a producer, and *Ginger and Fred*, as the story was titled, became a feature film project instead. Tonino Guerra was brought in as co-writer, and Fellini returned, happily, to his favorite workplace, Cinecittà.

The story, as originally conceived for television, was relatively simple, a wistful tale of two aging people brought together for a nostalgic reunion on a Christmas television variety show; even though bewildered by the turmoil of contemporary television, they would achieve their final performance with courage and dignity. In expanding the story, Fellini seized the opportunity to satirize the inanities and idiocies of the medium that, ironically, was making his new film possible. The samples of television fare he wanted to create sent the budget skyrocketing, leading inevitably to arguments about finances. Again he complained, "They don't want a Fellini film. They want Fellini and their idea of a Fellini film."

Rescue came in the person of one of his former producers, Alberto Grimaldi, who, several years before, had transferred his activities to the United States and was living handsomely in Beverly Hills. "A call from a friend in Rome came," he said, "telling me that Fellini's new project was in a crisis." Grimaldi flew to Rome, and after two months of negotiation took over the production. He also acquired the rights to the remaining five television specials, and an assurance of Giulietta's participation.

It was a vastly relieved Fellini I met when I visited him

again late in 1984. He was well aware, he said, that his problems
with producers were not one-sided. In a very real sense he was his
own producer, and the people who called themselves his producers
were the people who brought the financing. For years he had been
engaged in a fruitless search for someone who would stand between
himself and the money people, who would relieve him (protect him,
really) from the tensions caused by his needs and the understandable needs of producers. Was there such a person? he wondered. He
seemed to doubt it.

With this film, he said, he wanted to recapture "the essence
of those old variety shows" he had seen in his youth, and also "the
vitality and enthusiasm of the period in which we discovered the
magic of the American style." The former dancers of his story are
tracked down by television scouts for a show called "We Are Proud
to Present . . ." and for a day they are taken through "this laby-
rinthine, enchanted palace of TV." He intended to have some fun
with the medium, but not in a cruel or unkind way. "Perhaps a little satire," he said, smiling. It would be a "small film." Probably he
meant a minor film, because by the time the film went into production at Cinecittà in March 1985, Grimaldi estimated that it would
be two-hours long, although still a "very simple, straightforward human story."

Fellini, however, devoted a major portion of the shooting
time to the less human aspects of television, and though he continued to say he was just having a "little fun" with the medium, he
appeared to be taking on contemporary society as well—a society
dominated by the omnipresent video tube. He did admit that by
creating a fictional show of which the dance team would be but one
act, he would be presenting an amalgam of the kind of thing that
spilled from the tube every day and night, and more than that, "a
specimen board, a vision of today's humanity." He hoped, he said,
that "through this film I can advise the public on how to watch TV
in another way, to be less dependent and more critical."

At Cinecittà the sets featured lobbies, rooms, and corridors,
even a train station, filled with TV monitors; each flickering with a
segment of a different program, or with commercials. Fellini spent
months shooting 100 sequences of brief duration, merely to fill the

monitors. He was re-creating "the style, the panorama, the fresco of TV images," he said. In addition to the dancers, the story would present "every kind of character—politicians, gangsters, actors, and actresses of today's society."

By the time Giulietta as Amelia (Ginger) arrives at the frenetic train station for her reunion with Pippo (Fred), television is all-pervasive. A huge screen is showing commercials. The luxury hotel she is taken to by her TV hosts is in a barren suburb on the edge of a city dump. Every corridor in the hotel and at the studio has its TV screen displaying a nonsensical mix of commercials and programs—the parody not far from what is being parodied.

While at work on the film, Fellini was invited by the Film Society of Lincoln Center to be the 1985 recipient of their annual award for outstanding cinematic achievement, the first time that someone from outside the United States would receive the honor.

The gala ceremony took place on June 10, 1985. Avery Fisher Hall was filled with patrons who had paid up to $150 for their tickets. The more one paid the more one got, such as a cocktail party or a dinner at which Fellini and Giulietta would appear, not to mention Donald Sutherland, Anouk Aimée, and Marcello Mastroianni, all of whom had come to pay their respects to the maestro. The best moments of the evening came from "A Tribute to Federico Fellini," a one-hour reprise of scenes from several of his films. The nuns skated by in their fashion show, the peacock spread its glorious tail in the snow of Rimini, the little boy gazed out his window and watched a circus tent take shape, Casanova made love to a mannequin, and Guido joined the players of his life and dreams in a circus parade of joy and love.

"When it's over," Vincent Canby wrote about the tribute, "you want to rush out and see the complete films all over again." He wondered whether any other film director of our century had created so enduring and original a body of work.

Critic Richard Corliss gave an answer in his program notes for the evening: "What may once have looked like outrageous cartoons of sensuality and sacrilege have become, in retrospect, pre-

views of a moral system spun wildly off its axis. And because this
film-maker is incapable of a stillborn frame, his pictures celebrate
what they criticize; they amount to a cautionary blueprint for sur-
vival in the Atomic Age."

For Fellini, who gave a nice little speech about the debt he
owed to the American films he had seen during his youth in Rimini,
there were other festivities, including a boring (for the guest of
honor) lunch given by a wealthy couple in Connecticut. He continued celebrating after the tribute and into the early morning hours
by going out on the town and visiting discothèques. "He was rather
appalled by one in Soho we took him to," said Charlotte Chandler,
a friend. His New York visit with Giulietta lasted three days, after
which he hastened back to Rome and to Cinecittà to complete work
on *Ginger and Fred*. "That is the happy place," he told a reporter
before leaving. "In the center of my story is where I feel the center
of my existence. That is the reason for which I exist—doing what is
really the reason of your destiny."

Ginger and Fred had its Rome première in February 1986,
and was greeted favorably by critics, many of whom saw in it less a
story of two people brought out of the past, than an attack on the
television of the 1980s as seen, according to *Variety*'s Rome correspondent, "from an oldster's point of view, as all trashy advertising
and apocalyptic horror, a universe of omnipresent boob tubes broad-
casting nonstop nonsense and vulgarity." But, "hard as it is to parody a TV show, the Fellini touch at least makes it lavishly visual."
The action was fast and fun, yet "a dark hand of melancholy over-
shadows all."

When MGM/UA (the firm that had acquired the American
distribution rights) opened the film in New York on March 28,
1986, the critical response was along the same lines, with here and
there some complaint. *Time* found the performances of Masina and
Mastroianni "lovely, observant, original and infinitely appealing."
For Vincent Canby of the *New York Times*, the film looked and
sounded "like the work of no other director." He noted, however,
the "amalgam of two quite different Fellini movies, one of which—

the perfectly specific, emotionally involving tale of the reunion of Amelia and Pippo—keeps being overwhelmed by a gaudy, impressionistic film that recalls *The Clowns* and *Fellini Roma*."

The reunion of Amelia and Pippo occurs on a comic note. Amelia, attempting to get a night's sleep in her hotel room before the show the next day, is kept awake by stentorian snores from the next room. When she bangs on the wall and then the snorer's door, she faces a haggard, alcoholic Pippo, a broken man who needs the fee for this performance. It is Amelia who is the hardy survivor.

Fellini finds Amelia, for all her bewilderment in this electronic world, a woman of courage, faith, and humanity. She will do her best, and help carry Pippo through the ordeal of the show, which includes a host who wears a gold-sequinned jacket; an audience of 5,000 who applaud every grotesquerie on cue; a priest who has married and is persuaded to kiss his bride in full view of millions; a troupe of midgets dancing a fandango; a transvestite offering to provide sexual services to pent-up prison inmates; and an inventor who demonstrates his vitamin-enriched edible panties by chewing them off the hips of a model.

In the midst of this freak show, Amelia and Pippo maintain their professional stance, even managing a moment of rehearsal in an empty corridor before going on stage in a studio the size of a sports arena. There had once been an affair between them, but Fellini allows them only a final good-by in the train station (still showing commercials). Pippo is still the lonely, shattered alcoholic, and must borrow some money from Amelia for a drink.

Reviewers, without exception, found the dance sequence the high point of the film. "When these two icons of the Italian cinema finally dance," Molly Haskell wrote in *Vogue*, "the effect is magical."

But despite enough praise from reviewers to assure lively attendance for the film, and perhaps commercial success, its appeal was not universal. "He insists," Richard Schickel remarked in *Time*, "on pumping out more of the 'Felliniesque,' his trademark blend of the grotesque and the surreal, than we need to get his point that TV is vulgar and coarsening." Molly Haskell, too, would have wished for fewer "gargoyles" and more "feeling" for his people.

In *New York* magazine, David Denby wrote that "on the

whole I disliked *Ginger and Fred*, but there's no doubt that Fellini has captured this peculiar rite of our civilization better than anyone before him." And he wondered, "Why pick on TV?" To answer that last question would have required his taking a long and detailed look at Fellini's entire career. Reviewers, after all, are concerned with the film of the moment. From *Ginger and Fred* they must hasten to another screening room to view the latest horror show for teen-age audiences. It's not an easy calling. Fellini, as his most recent film illustrates, has always exhibited two distinct and sometimes contradictory impulses in his work. On the one hand there is his bent for caricature; on the other his deep understanding and feeling for the human.

An artist changes and matures. There are periods in his work. In the midst of all the machinery and insanely complicated financial dealings of the film industry, Fellini continues to develop, not as a maker of hits, but as a film artist of remarkable distinction. A thorough assessment may come eventually—he has shown no sign of flagging—but it is already clear that in his later phase he is using his great gifts, his power to fascinate visually, not only for his audience's entertainment, but as a criticism of the values of the society to which he belongs. *Ginger and Fred*, in that sense, is one more panel in the huge "fresco" he continues to create.

"For all of us who attempt to make films honestly," Paul Mazursky said, "he is a great inspiration. His soul is very large."

Fellini visited New York for some dutiful publicity on *Ginger and Fred*. He gave interviews and was trotted around to television studios, probably quite aware that he, too, was being made part of the endless parade. Suddenly there came word that Ginger Rogers was suing him for defaming the artistry of her own dancing.

"Perhaps she has not seen the film," Fellini told Gene Shalit mildly on the *Today Show*, "or has been misinformed." He looked tired. He had injured his leg, and if not for the accident would have made the trip to Los Angeles to help present the Best Picture award at the Academy festivities. Then, on Cable Network News, beamed around the country from Ted Turner's Superstation, a pretty young blonde interviewer informed him that she had heard he was a genius. "Are you a genius?" she demanded. He stared at her in astonishment. "What would you like me to say?" he asked, as though suddenly finding himself in his own movie. She smiled, waiting helplessly. "It would be nice to think so," he told her, tolerantly.

She wasn't finished. "What would you like to be if not a director?" she asked.

He sighed, but did his best. "An actor," he said, "a singer, a painter, a circus performer, a musician, a writer, and a doctor in a mental hospital. I am very fortunate. As a director I can be all of these."

"Remarkably," said Mazursky, "through all his work and struggle, he has retained his humor. Without it, for me, he would not be Fellini."

FILMOGRAPHY

SCREENWRITING

1939–1945

Prior to 1945, Fellini contributed to or collaborated on several screenplays. For the first four films—released in 1939 and 1940—on the list that follows he furnished comic material in the form of gags and small sketches. The others were written with one or more collaborators.

1939 *Lo vedi come sei?*
1940 *Il pirata sono io*
         Imputato alzatevi!
         No me lo dire
1941 *Documento Z–3*
         Bentornato Signor Gai
         Sette poveri in automobile
         I predoni del Sahara
1942 *Quarta pagina*
         Avanti c'è posto
         Campo dei fiori
         L'ultima carrozzella
         Chi l'ha visto?
         Apparizione
         Tutta la città canta
1945 *Roma, città aperta* (*Rome, Open City*); screenplay collaboration with Sergio Amidei and Roberto Rossellini, the director. Also served as assistant to Rossellini.

1946–1950
1946 *Il delitto di Giovanni Episcopo* (*The Crime of Giovanni Episcopo/Flesh Will Surrender*); screenplay collaboration; directed by Alberto Lattuada.

Paisà (Paisan); story and screenplay collaboration with Roberto Rossellini, Sergio Amidei, and others; assistant director to Rossellini.

1947 *Senza pietà (Without Pity)*; collaborated on story and screenplay with Tullio Pinelli; assistant director; Giulietta Masina's first film appearance.

1948 *Il miracolo (The Miracle)*; one of three parts of *L'amore,* only two parts of which were shown in U.S. as *Ways of Love*; wrote story, collaborated on screenplay with Tullio Pinelli, assistant director to Roberto Rossellini; Fellini took the part of the stranger who seduces the peasant girl played by Anna Magnani. *In nome della legge (In the Name of the Law)*; screenplay collaboration; director, Pietro Germi.

1949 *Il mulino del Po (The Mill on the Po)*; screenplay with Tullio Pinelli; directed by Alberto Lattuada.

1950 *Francesco, giullare di dio (Flowers of St. Francis)*; screenplay with Roberto Rossellini; assistant director to Rossellini.

Fellini began his directing career in 1950, but continued writing for others until 1952, usually with Tullio Pinelli. Some years later he collaborated with Pinelli and Ennio Flaiano on the story and screenplay of *Fortunella* (1958), directed by Eduardo de Felippo, starring Giulietta Masina.

1950 *Il cammino della speranza (The Path of Hope)*; collaborated on story and screenplay; director, Pietro Germi.

1951 *Cameriera bella presenza offresi (Attractive Maid Available)*; collaborated on screenplay with Tullio Pinelli; director, Giorgio Pastina.

1951 *La città si difende (Passport to Hell)*; collaborated on story and screenplay; director, Pietro Germi.

1952 *Il brigante di Tacca del Lupo (The Brigand of Tacca del Lupo)*; collaborated on story and screenplay; director, Pietro Germi. *Europa '51*; Fellini's work on this Roberto Rossellini film was on the treatment only.

THE FILMS

1950 LUCI DEL VARIETA *(Variety Lights)*; co-director with Alberto Lattuada; story by Fellini; screenplay, Fellini, Tullio

Pinelli, Ennio Flaiano, Alberto Lattuada; photography, Otello Martelli; set design, Aldo Buzzi; music, Felice Lattuada. Cooperative production, Capitolium Film.

CAST: Checco Dalmonte   Peppino De Filippo
Liliana   Carla Del Poggio
Melina Amour   Giulietta Masina
Johnny   John Kitzmiller
Liliana's lover   Folco Lulli
Comedian   Dante Maggio

1952 LO SCEICCO BIANCO (*The White Sheik*); story by Fellini and Tullio Pinelli, from suggestion by Michelangelo Antonioni; screenplay, Fellini, Pinelli, Ennio Flaiano; photography, Arturo Gallea; music, Nino Rota; set design, Raffaello Tolfo; producer, Luigi Rovere.

CAST: Wanda Cavalli (wife)   Brunella Bovo
Ivan Cavalli (husband)   Leopoldo Trieste
Fernando (the White Sheik)   Alberto Sordi
Cabiria (prostitute)   Giulietta Masina

1953 I VITELLONI (*The Vitelloni*); story by Fellini, Ennio Flaiano, Tullio Pinelli, from a Pinelli idea; screenplay, Fellini, Flaiano; photography, Otello Martelli, Luciano Trasatti, Carlo Carlini; Music, Nino Rota; set design, Mario Chiari; produced by Peg Film (Rome)/Cité Films (Paris).

CAST: Moraldo   Franco Interlenghi
Alberto   Alberto Sordi
Fausto   Franco Fabrizi
Leopoldo   Leopoldo Trieste
Riccardo   Riccardo Fellini
Sandra   Elenora Ruffo
Fausto's father   Jean Brochard
Natali (the actor)   Achille Majeroni

UN'AGENZIA MATRIMONIALE (*A Matrimonial Agency*)—episode IV of L'AMORE IN CITTA; story and screenplay, Fellini, Tullio Pinelli; photography, Gianni Di Venanzo; music, Mario Nascimbene; produced by Cesare Zavattini for Faro Films.

CAST: Antonio Cifariello   Journalist
Livia Venturini   The girl
(and student actors from the Centro Sperimentale di
Cinematografia)

1954 LA STRADA; story and screenplay, Fellini, Tullio Pinelli; collaborator on screenplay, Ennio Flaiano; artistic advisor, Brunello Rondi; music, Nino Rota; photography, Otello Martelli;
art direction, Mario Ravasco; costume design, Margherita
Marinari; produced by Dino De Laurentiis, Carlo Ponti.

CAST: Gelsomina   Giulietta Masina
Zampanò   Anthony Quinn
Il matto (the Fool) Richard Basehart
The widow   Marcella Rovena
The young nun   Lidia Venturini

1955 IL BIDONE; story and screenplay, Fellini, Ennio Flaiano,
Tullio Pinelli; collaborator, Brunello Rondi; music, Nino Rota;
photography, Otello Martelli; set and costume design, Dario
Cecchi; production, Titanus (Rome)/S.G.C. (Paris)

CAST: Augusto   Broderick Crawford
Roberto   Franco Fabrizi
Picasso   Richard Basehart
Iris   Giulietta Masina
Crippled girl   Sue Ellen Blake

1957 LE NOTTI DI CABIRIA (*The Nights of Cabiria*); story and
screenplay, Fellini, Ennio Flaiano, Tullio Pinelli, from a Fellini
idea; script consultant, Brunello Rondi; additional dialogue,
Pier Paolo Pasolini; music, Nino Rota; photography, Aldo
Tonti; sets and costumes, Piero Gherardi; production, Dino De
Laurentiis (Rome)/Les Films Marceau (Paris); distribution,
Paramount.

CAST: Cabiria   Giulietta Masina
Oscar   François Périer
The movie star   Amadeo Nazzari
Wanda, Cabiria's friend   Franca Marzi
Movie star's friend   Dorian Gray

1960 LA DOLCE VITA; story and screenplay, Fellini, Ennio Flaiano,
Tullio Pinelli; script collaborator, Brunello Rondi; music, Nino

Rota; photography, Otello Martelli; sets and costumes, Piero Gherardi; produced by Angelo Rizzoli and Giuseppe Amato; a production of Riama Film (Rome)/Pathé Consortium Cinéma (Paris).

CAST: (major characters in order of appearance)

Marcello Rubini	Marcello Mastroianni
Paparazzo	Walter Santesso
Maddalena	Anouk Aimée
Prostitute	Adriana Moneta
Emma	Yvonne Furneaux
Sylvia	Anita Ekberg
Robert, her fiancé	Lex Barker
Frankie Stout	Alan Dijon
Steiner	Alain Cuny
Priest (at miracle)	Alex Messoyedoff
Children's mother	Rina Franchetti
Children's uncle	Aurelio Nardi
Signora Steiner	Renée Longarini
Poet guest	Iris Tree
Woman writer	Leonida Rapaci
Paola (innocent girl)	Valeria Ciangottini
Marcello's father	Annibale Ninchi
The Clown	Polidor
Fanny (chorus girl)	Magali Noël
Prince Mascalchi	Prince Vadim Wolkonsky
Sonia (English woman)	Audrey MacDonald
Maddalena's lover	Ferdinando Brofferio
Nadia (the divorcée)	Nadia Gray
Laura	Laura Betti
Villa's owner	Riccardo Garrone
Feathered girl	Franca Pasutt
Monster fish	a construction

1962 LE TENTAZIONI DEL DOTTOR ANTONIO (*The Temptations of Doctor Antonio*)—Part II of four-part film, BOCCACCIO '70, conceived by Cesare Zavattini; story and screenplay, Fellini, Ennio Flaiano, Tullio Pinelli, with collaborators Brunello Rondi and Goffredo Parise; photography, Otello Martelli; music, Nino Rota; settings, Piero Zuffi. Producer, Carlo Ponti.

Joint production, Cineriz (Rome)/Francinex-Gray Film (Paris).

CAST:

Dr. Antonio Mazzuolo	Peppino De Felippo
Anita	Anita Ekberg
Commendatore La Pappa	Antonio Acqua
The child	Eleonora Nagy
Antonio's sister	Donatella Della Nora

1963 OTTO E MEZZO (8½); story, Fellini, Ennio Flaiano; screenplay, Fellini, Ennio Flaiano, Tullio Pinelli, Brunello Rondi; music, Nino Rota; photography, Gianni di Venanzo. Sets and costumes, Piero Gherardi; make-up, Otello Fava. Produced by Angelo Rizzoli for Cineriz (Rome)/Francinex (Paris).

CAST:

Guido Anselmi	Marcello Mastroianni
Carla (his mistress)	Sandra Milo
Luisa (his wife)	Anouk Aimée
Claudia	Claudia Cardinale
Mario Mezzabotta	Mario Pisu
Gloria (his girlfriend)	Barbara Steele
The intellectual	Jean Rougeul
Maurice, the magician	Ian Dallas
Maya (his mindreader)	Mary Indovino
French actress	Madeleine Lebeau
Her agent	Neil Robertson
American journalist	Eugene Walter
His journalist wife	Gilda Dahlberg
Hotel manager	Prince Vadim Wolkonsky
Guido as a boy	Marco Gemini
Guido's mother	Guiditta Rissone
Guido's father	Annibale Ninchi
The producer	Guido Alberti
Rossella (Luisa's friend)	Rossella Falk
Luisa's sister	Elisabetta Catalano
Enrico (Luisa's suitor)	Mark Herron
Guido as a small child	Riccardo Guglielmi
His grandmother	Georgia Simmons
Saraghina	Edra Gale
Airline hostess	Nadine Sanders
Jacqueline Bonbon	Yvonne Casadei

Black dancer	Hazel Rogers
The Cardinal	Tito Masini
Cardinal in "test"	Comtesse Elisabetta Cini
Claudia's agent	Mino Doro
Clown	Polidor

1965 GIULIETTA DEGLI SPIRITI (*Juliet of the Spirits*); story, Fellini, Tullio Pinelli, from Fellini's idea; screenplay, Fellini, Ennio Flaiano, Pinelli, Brunello Rondi; photography, Gianni di Venanzo; music, Nino Rota; sets and costumes, Piero Gherardi; make-up, Otello Fava; interior decoration, Vita Anzalone; hairdressers, Renata Magnanti, Marisa Fraticelli. Produced by Angelo Rizzoli. A Federiz Film.

CAST:		
	Giulietta	Giulietta Masina
	Giorgio	Mario Pisu
	The mother	Caterina Boratto
	The grandfather	Lou Gilbert
	Valentina	Valentina Cortesa
	Dolores (Dolly)	Silvana Jachino
	José	José Luis de Villalonga
	Suzy, Iris, the circus girl	Sandra Milo
	Suzy's mother	Alessandra Mannoukine
	Suicidal girl	Dany Paris
	"Arabian Prince"	Fred Williams
	Lynx-Eyes, the Detective	Alberto Plebani
	Psychologist	Federico Valli
	Bhishma	Waleska Gert
	Don Raffaele	Felice Fulchignoni
	Headmaster	Friedrich von Ledebur

1968 TOBY DAMMIT (Episode III in *Tre passi nel delirio*; other episodes, *William Wilson*, directed by Louis Malle, and *Metzengerstein*, directed by Roger Vadim); story and screenplay, Fellini, Bernardino Zapponi, loosely based on Edgar Allan Poe short story, "Never Bet the Devil Your Head"; music, Nino Rota; photography, Giuseppe Rotunno; sets and costumes, Piero Tosi; special effects, Joseph Nathanson. Produced by Alberto Grimaldi for P.E.A. (Rome)/Les Films Marceau and Cocinor (Paris).

CAST: Toby Dammit   Terence Stamp
Father Spagna   Salvo Randone
The actress   Antonia Pietrosi
The devil girl   Marina Yaru

BLOCK-NOTES DI UN REGISTA (*A Director's Notebook*);
script, Fellini, Bernardino Zapponi; photography, Pasquale De
Santis; music, Nino Rota; English dialogue, Eugene Walter;
Producer, Peter Goldfarb, for NBC Productions International.

CAST: Fellini   himself
Marcello Mastroianni   himself
Giulietta Masina   herself
Professor Genius   himself
Script girl   Marina Boratto
Archaeology professor   David Maumsell

1969 FELLINI SATYRICON; story and screenplay, Fellini, Bernar-
dino Zapponi, freely adapted from the *Satyricon* of Petronius
Arbiter; photography, Giuseppe Rotunno; music, Nino Rota
with collaborators Ilhan Mimaroglu, Tod Dockstader, Andrew
Rubin; sets and costumes, Danilo Donati; make-up, Rino Car-
boni, Pierino Tosi; hairdresser, Luciano Vito; special effects,
Adriano Pischiutta. Produced by Alberto Grimaldi for P.E.A.
(Rome)/Les Productions Artistes Associés (Paris).

CAST: Encolpio   Martin Potter
Ascylto   Hiram Keller
Gitone   Max Born
Trimalchio   Mario Romagnuli
Eumolpo   Salvo Randone
Vernacchio   Fanfulla
Fortunata   Magali Noël
Lica   Alain Cuny
Trifena   Capucine
Young emperor   Tanya Lopert
Young Oenothea   Donyale Luna
Old Oeothea   Maria Antonietta Belizi
Patrician   Joseph Wheeler
Patrician's wife   Lucia Bosè
Slave girl   Hylette Adolphe
Nymphomaniac   Sibilla Sedat

Her husband	Lorenzo Piani
Hermaphrodite	Pasquale Baldassare
Widow of Ephesus	Antonia Petrosi
Soldier at tomb	Wolfgang Hillinger

1970 I CLOWNS (*The Clowns*) ; story and screenplay, Fellini, Bernardino Zapponi; music, Nino Rota; photography, Dario di Palma; costumes, Danilo Donati; make-up, Rino Carboni; sets, Renzo Gronchi; producers, Elio Scardamaglia, Ugo Guerra. A co-production: R.A.I. (Rome)/O.R.T. (Paris)/Bavaria Film (Munich)/Compagnia Leone Cinematografica (Rome).

CAST: (*as themselves*)
Liana, Rinaldo, and Nando Orfei, Anita Ekberg, Pierre Etaix, Annie Fratellini, Victor Fratellini, Victoria Chaplin, Jean Baptiste, Tristan Rémy.
(*the Italian clowns*)
Billi, Scotti, Fanfulla, Rizzo, Pistoni, Furia, Sbarra, Carini, Terzo, Vingelli, Fumagalli, Zerbinati, Valentini, the Martanas, Maggio, Janigro, Sorentino, Bevilacqua.
(*the French clowns*)
Alex, Père Loriot, Maiss, Bario, Ludo, Charlie Rivel, Nino.
(*Fellini's troupe*)

The director	Fellini
Script girl	Maya Morin
Cameraman	Gasperino
Soundman	Alvaro Vitali
Woman assistant	Lina Alberti

1972 FELLINI ROMA; story and screenplay, Fellini, Bernardino Zapponi; music, Nino Rota; photography, Giuseppe Rotunno; scenery and costumes, Danilo Donati; interiors, Andrea Fantacci; make-up, Rino Carboni; frescoes and portraits, Rinaldo Antonello, Giuliano Geleng; producers, Danilo Marciani, Lamberto Pippia, for Ultra Film (Rome)/Les Productions Artistes Associés (Paris).

CAST:	
Fellini	Himself
Fellini at 18	Peter Gonzales
Dolores (young prostitute)	Fiora Florence
The Princess	Pia De Doses

Catacomb guide	Marne Maitland
The Cardinal	Renato Giovannoli

(cameo appearances:)
Gore Vidal
John Francis Lane
Anna Magnani
Note: Marcello Mastroianni and Alberto Sordi were cut from version released outside Italy.

1973 AMARCORD; story and screenplay, Fellini, Tonino Guerra; music, Nino Rota; photography, Giuseppe Rotunno; scenery and costumes, Danilo Donati; make-up, Rino Carboni; special effects, Adriano Pischiutta; interiors, Andrea Fantacci; producer, Franco Cristaldi. A co-production of F. C. Productions (Rome)/P.E.C.F. (Paris).

CAST: Titta	Bruno Zanin
Titta's mother	Pupella Maggio
Titta's father	Armando Brancia
Titta's grandfather	Peppino Ianigro
Mad uncle Teo	Ciccio Ingrassia
Gradisca	Magali Noël
The lawyer	Luigi Rossi
Fat tobacconist	Maria Antonietta Beluzzi
Volpina	Josiane Tanzilli
Fascist leader	Ferrucio Brembilla
Headmaster	Franco Magno
The emir	Viscenzo Caldarola
The prince	Marcello di Falco
Gradisca's bridegroom	Bruno Bartocci

1976 IL CASANOVA DI FEDERICO FELLINI (*Casanova*); screenplay, Fellini, Bernardino Zapponi, freely based on Giacomo Casanova's *The Story of My Life*; music, Nino Rota; photography, Giuseppe Rotunno; sets and costumes, Danilo Donati; scenic style conceived by Fellini; frescoes, Mario Fallani; magic lantern designer, Roland Topor; set decorator, Emilio D'Andria; sculptures, Giovanni Gianese; make-up, Rino Carboni, Gianetto de Rossi, Fabrizio Storza; hairstyles, Gabriella Borzelli; choreography, Gino Landi; dialogue consultant, Anthony Burgess. Produced by Alberto Grimaldi for P.E.A. (Rome).

CAST: Giacomo Casanova   Donald Sutherland
      Sister Maddalena   Margareth Clementi
      Annamaria   Clarissa Mary Roll
      Giselda   Daniela Gatti
      Madame D'Urfé   Cicely Browne
      Marcolina   Clara Algranti
      Henriette   Tina Aumont
      Giantess   Sandra Elaine Allen
      Duke of Württemberg   Dudley Sutton
      The Pope   Luigi Zerbinati
      Casanova's mother   Marie Marquet
      The "Doll"   Adele Angela Lojodice
      Madame Charpillon   Carmen Scarpitta
      Entomologist   Mario Cencelli
      Olimpia   Olimpia Carlisi
      Hunchback girl   Angelica Hansen
      Countess of Waldenstein   Marjorie Bell

1979 PROVA D'ORCHESTRA (*Orchestra Rehearsal*); story, Fellini; screenplay, Fellini, with Brunello Rondi; photography, Giuseppe Rotunno; music, Nino Rota; set design, Dante Ferretti; musical consultant, Carlo Savina; produced by RAI-TV (Rome)/ Albatros Produktion G.M.B.H. (Monaco).

CAST: Orchestra conductor   Baldwin Bass
      Harpist   Clara Colosimo
      Pianist   Elizabeth Labi
      Cellist   Ferdinando Villella
      First violinist   David Mauhsell
      The unionist   Claudio Ciocca
      Interviewer's voice   Fellini

1980 LA CITTA DELLE DONNE (*City of Women*); story and screenplay, Fellini, Bernardino Zapponi, with Brunello Rondi; photography, Giuseppe Rotunno; music, Luis Bacalov; set conceptions, Fellini; designed by Dante Ferretti; paintings and frescoes, Rinaldo and Giuliano Geleng; costumes, Gabriella Pescucci; special effects, Adriano Pischiutta; executive producer, Franco Rossellini, for Opera Film Produzione (Rome)/ Gaumont (Paris).

CAST:
Snaporaz	Marcello Mastroianni
His wife	Anna Prucnal
Woman on train	Bernice Stegers
Sante Katzone (Dr. Xavier Zuberköck)	Ettore Manni
Motorcycle girl	Iole Silvani
Donatella	Donatella Damiani
Feminists	Sylvie Wacrenier
	Carla Terlizzi
Aged woman	Mara Ciukleva

1984 E LA NAVE VA (*And the Ship Sails On*); idea and screenplay, Fellini, Tonino Guerra; photography, Giuseppe Rotunno; art director, Dante Ferretti; costume designer, Maurizio Millenotti; music, Gianfranco Plenizio; lyrics, Andrea Zanbotto; produced by Franco Cristaldi for R.A.I./Vides Produzione (Italy)/Gaumont (France).

CAST:
Orlando	Freddie Jones
Ildebranda Cuffari	Barbara Jefford
Aureliano Fuciletto	Victor Poletti
Sir Reginald Dongby	Peter Cellier
Teresa Valegnani	Elisa Mainardi
Lady Dongby	Norma West
Grand Duke of Harzock	Fiorenzo Serra
Princess Lherimia	Pina Bausch
Count of Bassano	Pasquale Zito
Prime Minister	Philip Locke
Ship's captain	Antonio Vezza
Edmea Tetua	Janet Suzman

1986 GINGER AND FRED; story, Fellini, Tonino Guerra; screenplay, Fellini, Guerra, Tullio Pinelli; photography, Tonino Delli Colli, Ennio Guarnieri; music, Nicola Piovani; production designer, Dante Ferretti; costume designer, Danilo Donati; make-up, Rino Carboni; choreography, Tony Ventura; produced by Alberto Grimaldi; a co-production of P.E.A. (Rome)/ Revcom Films, Les Films Arianne, FR3 Films (Paris), with R.A.I. Uno.

CAST:

Amelia (Ginger)	Giulietta Masina
Pippo (Fred)	Marcello Mastroianni
TV host	Franco Fabrizi
Admiral Aulenti	Frederick Ledebur
Assistant director	Martin Maria Blau
Pretty journalist	Barbara Scoppa
Clairvoyant	Ginestra Spinola
Mobster	Francesco Casale
TV hostess	Isabelle La Porte
Panties inventor	Pippo Negri

BIBLIOGRAPHY

BOOKS

Betti, Liliana. *Fellini.* Translated by Joachim Neugroschel. Boston: Little, Brown, 1976.

Bondanella, Peter. *Italian Cinema.* New York: Frederick Ungar, 1983.

————, ed. *Federico Fellini: Essays in Criticism.* New York: Oxford University Press, 1978.

Boyer, Deena. *The Two Hundred Days of 8½.* Translated by Charles Lam Markmann. New York: Macmillan, 1964.

Budgen, Suzanne. *Fellini.* London: British Film Institute, 1966.

Costello, Donald P. *Fellini's Road.* Notre Dame: University of Notre Dame Press, 1983.

Fava, Claudio G., and Aldo Vigano. *I Film di Federico Fellini.* Rome: Gremese Editore, 1981.

Fellini, Federico. *La Dolce Vita.* (The screenplay, taken from the finished film.) New York: Ballantine Books, 1961.

————. *Fellini on Fellini.* Translated by Isabel Quigley. New York: Delacorte Press, 1974.

————. *Fellini's Satyricon.* Edited by Dario Zanelli. Translated by John Matthews and Eugene Walter. New York: Ballantine Books, 1970.

————. *Intervista Sul Cinema.* (A cura di Giovanni Grazzini.) Rome: Giuseppe Laterza & Figli, 1983.

————. *Juliet of the Spirits.* Edited and with introduction and interview by Tullio Kezich. Translated by Howard Greenfield. New York: Ballantine Books, 1966.

————. *Moraldo in the City/A Journey with Anita*. Translated and edited by John C. Stubbs. Urbana and Chicago: University of Illinois Press, 1983.

Hughes, Eileen Lanouette. *On the Set of Fellini Satyricon: A Behind the Scenes Diary*. New York: William Morrow, 1971.

Ketcham, Charles B. *Federico Fellini: The Search for a New Mythology*. New York: Paulist Press, 1976.

Kezich, Tullio, ed. *La Dolce Vita*. (Complete screenplay, with lengthy introduction by Kezich.) Bologna: Capelli, 1959.

Mayer, Arthur. *Merely Colossal*. New York: Simon and Schuster, 1953.

Micciche, Lino. *Il Cinema Italiano Degli Anni '60*. Venice: Marsilio Editori, 1976.

Milo, Sandra. *Caro Federico*. Milan: Rizzoli Editore, 1982.

Murray, Edward. *Fellini the Artist*. New York: Frederick Ungar, 1976.

Ortmayer, Roger. "Fellini's Film Journey." In *Three European Directors*, edited by James M. Wall. Grand Rapids: William B. Eeerdmans, 1973.

Perry, Ted. *Filmguide to 8½*. Bloomington: Indiana University Press, 1975.

Petronius. *The Satyricon*. Translation and introduction by J. P. Sullivan. New York: Penguin Books, 1977.

Price, Barbara Anne, and Theodore Price. *Federico Fellini: An Annotated International Bibliography*. Metuchen, N. J.: Scarecrow Press, 1978.

Rosenthal, Stuart. *The Cinema of Federico Fellini*. South Brunswick, N. J.: A. S. Barnes, 1976.

Salachas, Gilbert. *Federico Fellini*. Grenoble: J. Glenat, 1977.

Samuels, Charles Thomas. *Encountering Directors*. New York: G. P. Putnam's Sons, 1972.

Schoonejans, Sonia. *Fellini*. Rome: Lato Side Editori, 1980.

Solmi, Angelo. *Fellini*. Translated by Elizabeth Greenwood. New York: Humanities Press, 1968.

Stubbs, John C. *Federico Fellini: A Guide to References and Resources*. Boston: G. K. Hall, 1978.

Taylor, John Russell. *Cinema Eye, Cinema Ear.* New York: Hill and Wang, 1964.

Witcombe, R. T. *The New Italian Cinema.* New York: Oxford University Press, 1982.

Zapponi, Bernardo. *Fellini's Casanova.* (Novelization of screenplay.) New York: Dell Publishing Company, 1977.

PERIODICALS

Of the large variety of periodicals and other sources consulted in Rome, London, New York, and Los Angeles, the following were of particular value in the preparation of this book.

Alpert, Hollis. "Fellini at Work." *Saturday Review* (July 12, 1969).

The American Film Institute. "Dialogue on Film: Federico Fellini." Center for Advanced Film Studies, 1972.

Antonucci, Giovanni. "Giulietta: Speranza e Paure." *Il Settimenale* (March 5, 1978).

Biagi, Enzo. "Fellini: 'I miei film esistono per le donne.' " *Corriere Della Sera* (December 23, 1979).

Bluestone, George. "An Interview with Federico Fellini." *Film Culture* (October, 1957).

Brustein, Robert. "La Dolce Spumoni." *New York Review of Books* (December 23, 1965).

Buono, Oreste del. "Arriva Una Nave Carica Di . . ." *Europeo* (September 27, 1982).

Byron, Stuart, and Choset, Charles. "From Rimini to Roma: An Exclusive Interview with Fellini." *The Real Paper* (December 16, 1974).

Caen, Michel. "Tête-a-Tête avec Federico Fellini." *Lui* (August 1969).

Cantwell, Mary. "Fellini on Men, Women, Love, Life, Art and His New Movie." The *New York Times* (April 5, 1981).

Care, Ross. "Nino Rota." *Take One* (May 1979).

Celli, Teodoro. "Innocenti Melodie: E Morto Nino Rota." *Il Messagero* (April 11, 1979).

Chemasi, Antonio. "Fellini's *Casanova*: The Final Nights." *American Film* 1, no. 10 (October 1976).

Ciment, Michel. "Prova D'Orchestra: Interview with Fellini." American Film Institute, Feldman Library Files. (Conducted at Cinecittà, December 21, 1978; first published, *Positif* [April 1979].)

Coletti, Lina. "Vita Mia, Tutta Sesso e Allegria: Sandra Milo Si Confessa." *Europeo* (March 14, 1983).

Constanza, Constantini. "Donald Sutherland: Un Casanova che non fa Mai L'Amore." *Il Mondo* (September 4, 1975).

Cott, Jonathan. "Fellini's Language of Dreams." *Rolling Stone* (May 10, 1965).

Davis, Melton S. "First the Pasta, Then the Play." *New York Times Magazine* (January 2, 1966).

Fellini, Federico. "As Fellini Sees Rome." The *New York Times* (June 3, 1973).

———. "The Bitter Life of Money." *Films and Filming* (January 1961).

———. "Clown Who Punctured a Myth." *Daily Telegraph* (November 31, 1964).

———. "End of the Sweet Parade: Via Veneto." *Esquire* (January 1963).

———. "Fellini's Formula." *Esquire* (August 1970).

———. "How After Three Years I Launched My Ship." *Epoca* (Translated by Antonio Chemasi.) (September 16, 1983).

———. "How I Create." (Interview with G. Mazzocchi, translated from *L'Europa Letteraria*.) *Atlas* (March 1965).

———. "My Dolce Vita." *Oui* (March 1973).

———. "9½: A Self-Portrait of the Movie Director as Artist." *Show* (May 1964).

———. "What Fellini Thinks Mastroianni Thinks About Women." *Vogue* (August 15, 1963).

"Fellini on Films: The Magic Art." *Show Business Illustrated* (October 17, 1961).

"Fellini Remembers." *Time* (October 7, 1974).

"Fellini's Masterpiece." *Newsweek* (June 24, 1963).

Ferre, Giusi. "Tatacord, Federico? Il Grande regista ha fatto il suo ritorno ufficiale a Rimini." *Epoca* (October 3, 1983).

Gorbman, Claudia. "Music as Salvation: Notes on Fellini and Rota." *Film Quarterly* (Winter 1974–1975).

Gruen, John. "Fellini's 9½." *New York Herald Tribune* (August 1, 1965).

Hughes, Eileen Lanouette. "La Dolce Vita of Federico Fellini." *Esquire* (August 1960).

Kast, Pierre. "Giulietta and Federico." *Cahiers du Cinéma* (March 1965).

Kauffmann, Stanley. "Landmarks of Film History—Fellini's 8½." *Horizon* (Spring 1976).

Kezich, Tullio. "Fellinopoli è una Nave Che Va, Ma Non Sa Dove." *La Repubblica* (December 21, 1982).

Knight, Arthur. "The Noblest Roman of them All." *Saturday Review* (November 9, 1957).

Krims, Milton. "Fellini's Rome." *Holiday* (January 1974).

Lane, John Francis. "For Fellini, the Search Goes On: New Film will be called 'Hammarcord.' " *Rome Daily American* (December 24–25, 1972).

Langman, Betsy. "Working With Fellini." *Mademoiselle* (January 1970).

Lee, Laura. "The Dreams and Fears of Fellini." *Philadelphia Sunday Bulletin* (October 17, 1965).

Levine, Irving R. " 'I Was Born for the Cinema,' A Conversation with Federico Fellini." *Film Comment* (Fall 1976).

Lewalski, Barbara K. "Federico Fellini's Purgatorio." *Massachusetts Review* no. 3 (1964).

Livi, Grazia. "Fellini: Interroghiamo Gli Artisti Del Nostro Tempo." *Epoca* (November 11, 1962).

Lusini, Arturo. "Non Sparare Sul Regista: Giulietta difende Federico." *Gente* (March 1976).

McBride, Joseph. "The Director As Superstar." *Sight and Sound* (Spring 1972).

Mado, Lilliana. "Fellini parla del film con Bergman: 'Una confessione sulle nostre donne.' " *La Stampa* (November 4, 1969).

Matthews, Christopher. "Feasting at Casanova's Five Day Banquet." *Rome Daily American* (May 2, 1976).

Meehan, Thomas. "Fantasy, Flesh and Fellini." *Saturday Evening Post* (January 1, 1966).

Moravia, Alberto. "Dreaming Up Petronius." *New York Review of Books* (March 26, 1970).

———. "Federico Fellini: Director as Protagonist." *Atlas* (Translated from *L'Espresso*, Rome) (April 1963).

Neville, Robert. "Poet-Director of the Sweet Life." *New York Times Magazine* (May 14, 1961).

———. "The Soft Life in Italy." *Harper's* (September 1960).

Patellani, Federico. "Il Nuovo Mistero Di Fellini." *Tempo* (April 5, 1975).

Pende, Stella. "Bentornati al Circo Fellini." *Panorama* (October 11, 1982).

"Playboy Interview: Federico Fellini." *Playboy* (February 1966).

Rondi, Gian Luigi. "Federico Fellini: Se Questa Orchestra è l'Italia . . ." *Tempo* (November 5, 1978).

Ross, Lillian. "10½." *The New Yorker* (October 30, 1965).

Sarne, Mike. "Meeting Fellini." *Films and Filming* (April 1978).

Schwartzman, Paul. "Fellini's Unlovable Casanova." *New York Times Magazine* (February 6, 1977).

Simon, John. "The Tragic Deterioration of Fellini's Genius." The *New York Times* (November 24, 1974).

Spagnoli, Luisa. "Io Non Vivo, Sono Un Artista." *Il Mondo* (March 13, 1975).

"A Talk With Federico Fellini." *Cahiers du Cinéma* (Translated by Marjorie Drabkin.) (May–June 1971).

Walter, Eugene. "The Wizardry of Fellini." *Films and Filming* (June 1966).

Wiseman, Carter S. and Edward Behr. "Magician of the Movies." *Newsweek* (August 18, 1975).

INDEX

HOLLIS ALPERT, former film critic for *Saturday Review*, is the author of several novels and theatrical biographies, including *Burton* and *The Barrymores*. He has served on the fiction staff of the *New Yorker* and as a contributing editor on *Women's Day*, and he is a founder of *American Film Magazine*, where he was editor-in-chief for five years before leaving to resume his writing career. His articles have appeared in such magazines as *Esquire, Playboy, Partisan Review,* and the *New York Times Magazine*. He now lives on Shelter Island, New York.